Walking Wet

A Journey
Along England's
Salt Path

Rick Rogers

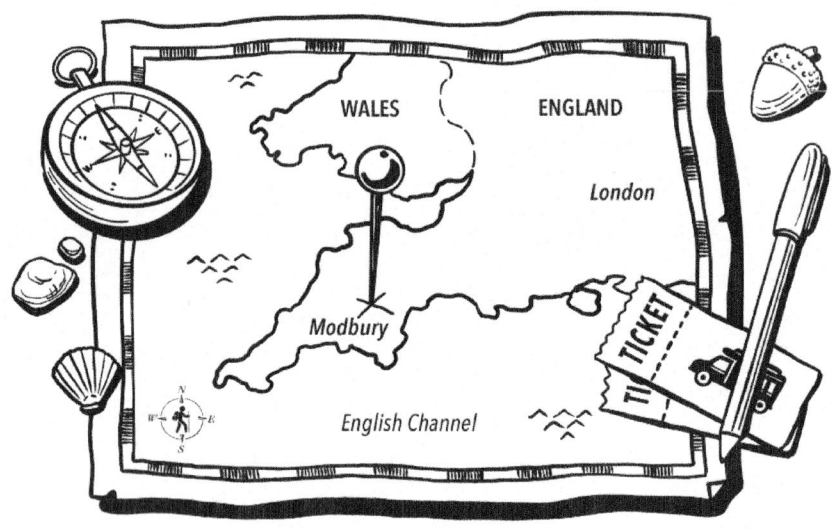

Walking Wet © 2025 by Rick Rogers. All Rights Reserved.
ISBN 9798315896722
Illustrated Maps by Emilija Mihajlov @serpent_scrolls
Edited by Kirsty McQuarrie
Cover by Ken Leeder

    All rights reserved. No part of this book may be reproduced in any form or by any electronic or mechanical means, including information storage and retrieval systems, without permission in writing from the author. The only exception is by a reviewer, who may quote short excerpts in a review.

    The following is a true story told as best I remember it. When I could, I shared the draft manuscript with the folks who appear in these pages and got their input before publishing. In cases where I couldn't track someone down, their names and identifying details have been changed to respect their privacy.

Thank you to...

My wife Monica for letting me write when I could have been doing something productive.

My sister and son for going with me, and then letting me stay.

All the wonderful and memorable people patient enough to chat with me in England.

Scott the story editor, Kirsty the copy editor, Emilija the illustrator, and Ken the artist.

My close circle of supporters, cheerleaders, and sometimes therapists who stuck with me while I got on with this adventure at my keyboard.

You know who you are. What follows is largely your fault.

Maps & Such...

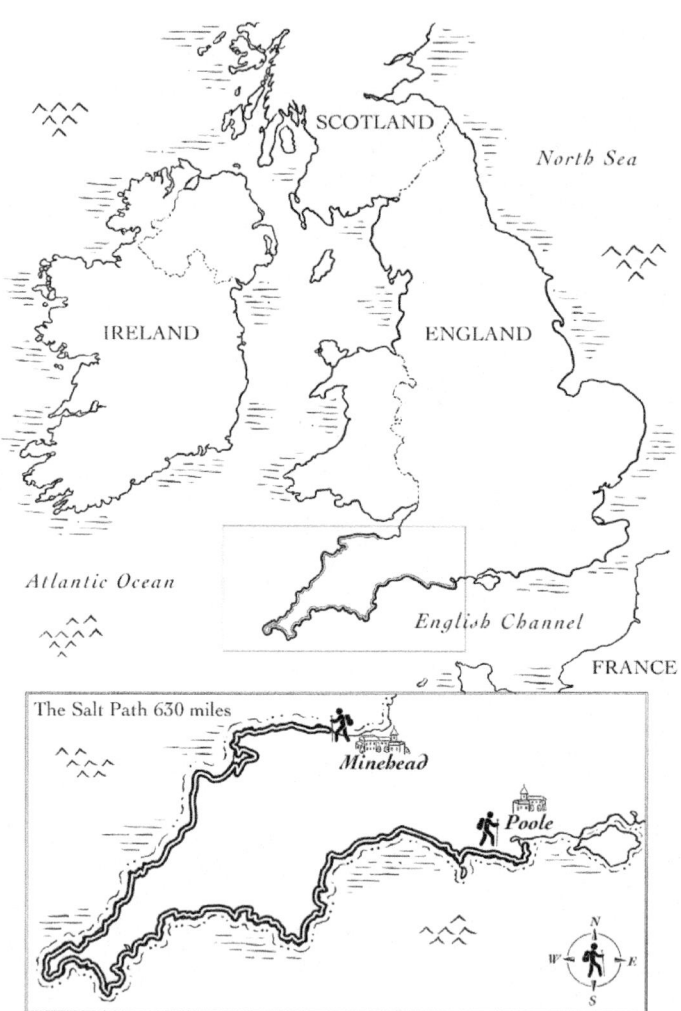

The maps above show where we will be in the following story.

Also, most of the chapters will be accompanied by illustrated maps. These are not drawn exactly to scale but should help to locate ourselves in the story.

Chapter Statistics…

       12 ⋯ DAYS WALKING
       45 ⋯ PATH MILES WALKED
       62 ⋯ TOTAL MILES WALKED
       https://www.southwestcoastpath.org.uk/walksdb/136/

You will also see at the beginning of each chapter a running total of trail statistics for the walk. All the running stats show progress along the path as of the end of that chapter. The running stats are…

    DAYS WALKING …
    Number of days since starting the path.

    PATH MILES WALKED…
    Distance made good along the path.

    TOTAL MILES WALKED…
    Total distance walked, including side trips, walking to or from camps, and those few times I was accidentally walking the wrong way.

I've also included a hyperlink to specific pages of the Southwest Coast Path Organization's website… https://www.southwestcoastpath.org.uk/

For each chapter along the Southwest Coast Path, also known as The Salt Path, you can see beautifully shot photos and videos and find information for the path section in that chapter. In those chapters that include more than one path section, the hyperlink brings you more or less to the first path section visited in that chapter.

Enjoy. Now, let's go for a good long walk.

Table of Contents

Maps & Such…	iv
Why Again?	1
A Jump Over the Pond	5
Short Legs	17
Rhonda	23
I Hate Shakespeare	29
Matthew	36
Trust in God and Keep Your Bowels Clear	45
A Victory Over Smugness	61
Diddly Squat	79
Dyin's Their Favorite Pastime	89
Walker's Brain	99
Cuttlefish Skeletons	109
Red Right Hand	117
A Right Bloody Wanker	127
Aren't We the Eloquent One?	141
Isotopes in the Soil	151
Every Night Booked	159
Feels Like Enough	169
Four Ways to Say Widow	179
Never Die Stupid	191
Epilogue. Stonehenge	199
Appendix	204
About the Author-	212

Why Again?

In those days before cell phones, streaming internet, and social apps, daydreaming was a necessary skill, and for many of us, the only thing that made our teen years survivable. And if you grew up on a farm and went to a small school like I did, keeping yourself sufficiently distracted was difficult. Our cows were half-ton barrels of clumsy that would trample you without a thought, and the feed we harvested for them was done with dubiously maintained machinery apt to snatch at loose clothing and yank limbs away. Time for daydreaming was precious.

And small schools make hiding behind invisibility impossible. Teachers, gangly nerd buddies, and the occasional gauntlet of bullies made daydreaming at my school as difficult as it was at home.

For teenagers, life has always been full of unwelcome intrusions to be endured. Luckily, I had daydreams powerful enough to carry me past these distractions and return me to an agreeably comfortable and hazy absentmindedness.

I'd read the cover story of the June 1971 National Geographic about four guys walking from Mexico to Canada on the newly established Pacific Crest Trail. The idea that you could point your feet and walk, just walk away from where you were and take yourself beyond the visible horizon, was irresistible. I would hike the 2,600-mile trail.

It became the main thing I thought about, and the more I thought about it, the more vividly I saw myself actually doing it. I even began to worry that my daydreams weren't ambitious enough.

How hard could it be? I thought. The Pacific Crest Trail starts at the Mexican border in California and ends up north at Canada, and Canada is an unmistakably large and unmissable target.

Breaking away from my stepfather and the dairy farm, I was indentured to and making my own way in the world brought a load of new distractions. It brought stints of firefighting, ambulance driving, mountain guiding, heavy machine operating, and more dairy farming. As I became busier doing things,

Walking Wet

I had less time for dreaming things, and the core daydreams that had kept me buoyant through my teen years became waterlogged with traces of humility and doubt.

A midlife career change brought college coursework, building permitting, teaching, map-making, and a long stint of wild animal tracking and research. It brought the end of one marriage and the commencement of another, fatherhood, and an assortment of minor personal tragedies and triumphs. It brought a lot of... well, life.

But finally, in late middle age, I really did point my feet towards the horizon and hike that 2,600-mile Pacific Crest Trail. I had been right about Canada being an easy target to find. But getting there wasn't the sure thing I'd imagined as a kid. I took down some of the surprising things I saw and the thoughts I'd had about them as I walked and put them in a book I wrote about the adventure. And that book opened up another career for me, which was fortunate, because not long after finishing the Pacific Crest Trail and returning to my day job, I got fired.

I had been tracking wildlife and counting fish for an Indian Tribe for twenty years, and their administrative slap-fights had always reminded me of the cows and cantankerous machinery I'd grown up with. Best to just do my job and whatever else needed doing, I'd decided, and leave all the drama to folks with more aptitude for it. I remember a coworker asking me once why I never engaged in the theatrics, and telling her, "There always has to be someone around here who just gets the work done."

"And why's that?" she asked, which probably should be a strange question. But it wasn't. I should have known better than to ignore the flywheels that eventually snagged me.

We've all finished the sentence, "If I had it to do over again, I would..." hundreds of times. But our lives aren't games where time-travel exists and do-overs are given for free. All we can do is finish the sentence, take the lesson, and apply it going forward.

Unless, of course, you have offspring. Then you can encapsulate your experience into little pearls of wisdom to drop on their heads.

"Never work for people who don't respect you," I told my son, Matthew.

"Never work. Got it." Having a smartphone meant that Matthew never developed his daydreaming skills to the heights I had reached in my teenage prime, but he has impressively mastered the art of selective hearing. This makes any advice I offer easy for him to accept.

"You'll need to have a job, you know, so you won't be homeless."

"I won't be homeless. I'm going to live in an old school bus."

"Oh, right," I said. "With eight children."

"Seven kids, Dad. Don't you ever listen? Seven. There's got to be room for chickens in the back."

Sometimes, I can't tell if he's serious or not. "Your mother thinks you're joking," I said.

"She's been wrong before." Matt's dreams and ambitions worry me sometimes. On the other hand, if he weaves through life's distractions to his goals as roundaboutly as I did towards mine, he'll be in his late fifties before his residence is a school bus anyway. So why worry about it just yet? And really, that chicken and kid-filled bus idea would die at the feet of his first girlfriend anyway. Or so I thought.

When I met his first girlfriend, I took the opportunity to throw the ridiculous idea out there for her to stomp on.

"Did you know Matt's life ambition is to have seven kids and live in an old school bus?" I asked her. I waited, expecting fear and revulsion. But when she answered, it just wasn't there.

"Huh," she said. "I can see that. I'd set up a tent outside for a kitchen, though. Easier for cleanup."

I couldn't tell if she was serious or not, either.

And what if they are? I don't know. I'd expected to reap the rewards of honest work, but my last stint doing that dealt me a kick in the chops instead. It's possible that a life of bus-dwelling and endless surfing, of barefoot homeschooling and excessive procreation wouldn't yield any worse. Life is, after all, a gamble, and the art to living it well is deciding what balance to strike while you hedge and make your bets. Because you're not going to win them all.

When you're thinking about your next bet, there's value in stepping back and finding a quiet stretch to calculate the odds. We often say we're living in the 'hustle and bustle,' but I think 'inside the chatterbox' is a more accurate description. No doubt, technology has done a lot to raise our standards of living, to make us more productive. But it's also made us exploitable, easier, and more profitable to manipulate by flavoring our very thoughts and emotions. We're unmoored in a chatterbox that transmits desire, insecurity, anxiety, and fear. The conviction that whatever we have or whatever we do, it will never be enough.

Hiking a long trail is the perfect antidote.

There's plenty to keep you busy on long trails. But there is far less noise, and the chatterbox shrinks. If you walk alone or with a partner who's sufficiently quiet or thoughtful, the chatterbox shrinks so that you are no longer immersed within it. A week on the trail and it's shrunk down so that it's only between your ears. Keep walking, and the chatterbox shrinks small enough to quit interfering with your thinking, and your own chain of thoughts can emerge. That's what a long-distance hike can do, and that is its power.

I suspect that before TikTok, Instagram, Facebook, YouTube, or cable news, before there was so much content and programming that more of us

Walking Wet

indulged in contemplation and philosophy. Surely today, where we can barely think or hear our own thoughts, rational thinking or even daydreaming is maddeningly difficult. Online, inside the chatterbox, meaningful thought and originality are scarce. In there, we're more likely to consume and regurgitate vitriol and conspiracy theories, only adding to the cacophony.

For me, a good long trail helps. Admittedly, deep thinking doesn't come to me naturally. My instinct is to latch onto any idea that pops up first and then run into the ground with it. But I've found that sometimes, things happen… like losing a job, for instance, or reacting to offspring that act impulsively, and it's not always best to do the first thing that comes to mind. Sometimes, a little quiet contemplation should be taken first, outside on a trail. And the longer trails, where you're out and away from it longer, give you a chance to practice reacting with thoughtfulness.

After walking the 2,600-mile Pacific Crest Trail, I thought a logical follow-up would be the English Coast Path, a 2,700-mile route that circumnavigates the English coastline. But being away from home for six months just wasn't practicable this time, especially as my son Matthew and my sister Rhonda agreed to go with me. But two months would be enough to do England's pointy bottom-left corner, the 630 miles of shorelines and headlands that make up the Southwest Coast Path.

I'd gone over our southern border once and seemed to insult a majority of the people I'd met. I hadn't worked very hard to learn Spanish, thinking that game attempts at communication with my woeful command of their language would be seen as plucky and cute, but it wasn't. I was handled, shrugged off, or endured as a thoughtless and privileged interloper, which in hindsight is uncomfortably close to the mark. As a consequence, I learned nothing more than the most superficial aspects of their culture. Hopefully, things should go better with the Brits.

So, I'm going over to take a good long walk, see what I can see, learn what I can learn, and possibly hear some stories. I'll show my kid how to contemplate life's mysteries or even daydream while we walk. I might even engage him in philosophical conversations.

Right. That should be easy.

Let's hope the trail is long enough.

A Jump Over the Pond

"There's no way all that's going to fit," I said.

My sister Rhonda was leaving for England with Matthew and me in the morning, and she and her husband Ron were spending the night at our house on the eve of the adventure.

I had her backpack nearly full, but most of the stuff she wanted to bring with her was still spread out on the floor. She also had a fabric shopping bag filled with even more clothing.

"Just get what you can in there, and I'll carry the rest in the shopping bag," Rhonda said. "I carry this thing around with me all the time. I call it my 'granny bag'."

"How's that going to work when you're using hiking sticks?" I asked. "And this isn't the backpack I'd listed on the spreadsheet I sent to you. It's too small."

"Yeah, the one you told me to get was too expensive."

"Well, this one doesn't have a hip belt on it, so all the weight will be on your back. And your stuff won't fit."

"Just cram it tighter and hang some gear off the back of it."

"If it's stuffed too tight, it bulges on your spine. And hanging things makes it swing around and pull you backwards and makes it even worse." I dumped her backpack out onto the floor again and started sorting her things into two piles. Rhonda watched.

"So, what's that pile?" she asked. "And what's that pile?"

"These are the things that you will take, and these," I said, pointing to the bigger pile, "are the things that your hubby will take back home. You can do without those."

"Well, I need those pajamas," she said, plucking them from the pile I'd put them in and dropping them onto the other. "No one's going to see me at night without my pajamas on."

"You'll be in a tent. You won't be walking around when it's time for bed, and when you get out of the tent in the morning, it'll be time to go."

"We're sharing a tent to save weight."

"Yes. So?"

"So, you're not going to see me either in there without my pajamas on."

"Look," I said. "When you're thinking about all this stuff, you've got to ask yourself, 'Is this something I'm willing to carry six hundred miles?' If you answer that question with anything other than 'Absolutely,' then it stays here in this pile."

"Already did that. And the pajamas are an 'Absolutely', definitely," she said.

Ron and my sister Rhonda have been married for forty years, and this wouldn't be the first time Rhonda had gone on a trip without him. But this trip would be the longest and the farthest away.

"My only concern is her health," Ron said. "I don't want her having a heart attack over there trying to do too much, like trying to keep up with you or Matt."

"Well, I won't even be trying to keep up with Matt," I told him. "Plus, it's all civilized over there. If one of us gets tired, we'll just Google for a bus or call a taxi. Should be a piece of cake."

"Okay," he said doubtfully. He pushed his glasses up, frowning. "If you say so."

"I do say so. Nothing to worry about."

"If you say so," he said again.

"Right now, we've got to figure out how to get all this packed. Some of it, we can parcel out into Matt's backpack or mine."

"Put whatever doesn't fit in the granny bag," Rhonda said again. "I'm taking it with me on the plane anyway. We'll just figure out the rest when we get there."

I didn't see how that could work.

"Well, if you say so," I said.

***

The next morning at the train station, my wife Monica shot a silly video of us to post on Facebook. As the train rolled into the station, we said our goodbyes.

I hugged Monica and whispered, "Thanks again for letting me go," into her ear. And as we pulled apart, I said, "Have fun this summer with your gal pals."

"I will, don't worry. Just take care of our boy." She turned to Matthew. "I'm so proud of you. Love you."

Matthew scooped her up for a bear hug, and she fixed me with a look over his shoulder. "Do *not* kill your sister," she mouthed to me.

Then we boarded the train, and it took us north.

The Vancouver airport was cavernous and almost empty, not at all what we would have had to deal with had we gone through Seattle. We had plenty of time to get through customs and find our gate.

Our flight from Vancouver to London took the great circle route. Touchpads were on the backs of the seats in front of us, and one of the screen menus showed a world map and our progress along our flight's path. The little plane icon was crossing north into the Arctic Circle and back again. We flew over Hudson Bay, over some blocky and snow-covered islands, and then over the southern end of Greenland.

I had a good view of it out the window. It was mostly an ice sheet that fringed down into glaciers. These fed serpentine rivers of cracked ice, flowing down light brown rock valleys lined with boulders, like spectators along a parade route.

The ice rivers thinned and ended in long fjords dotted with icebergs. The cliff walls along the fjords were colored in two tones of brown, a weathered, dark roast espresso at their tops and upper reaches, with lighter decaf lower down. There was a lot more decaf than espresso outlining the fjords. Obviously, the ice was getting thinner, melting faster than the rock could weather and turn dark. No one looking down on the scene would need a climate scientist to tell them that.

As we continued over Greenland, there was more exposed rock along the edges of the continent, and I puzzled over the landform's origins. It looked as though God had made a jumbo gingerbread molasses cookie before icing it, and cracks had crisscrossed its crust when He baked it. The cracks left broad, reticulated plateaus sloping off into randomly aligned valleys.

When we made landfall and flew over the part of England we'd be hiking around, we looked down on a similarly reticulated landform, except covered in green. Woods and villages were in the valleys between grain fields and pastures gridded with low stone walls. The villages flashed and sparkled enchantingly. As the plane flew lower into its glide path, the sparkles revealed themselves to be rooftop solar panels. There were a lot of them.

The Gatwick terminals were as sprawling and vast as Vancouver's but crowded with people and languages. We retrieved our luggage and tried walking to our hotel, just a half mile away. Google's walking directions put us on a road devoid of sidewalks that shortly led to the airport roundabout, a triple-ringed swirling maelstrom of lane-changing cars and lorries darting around each other, all while spinning about in the wrong direction. We stood beside the swirling terror, jet lagged and confused, with our backpacks, (one of us additionally loaded with a granny bag) for a long minute. We retreated back to the airport.

While we waited for a shuttle bus outside the terminal, a fellow who looked as though he'd poked his tongue into a light socket while washing his hair in pickle juice clomped a wheeled suitcase down the stairs towards us. He wore greasy corduroys and an open trench coat over a tattered and stained T-shirt. He moved in jerks, like an amped-up marionette under remote control. When he reached the midpoint landing, he mistakenly crossed over and stepped onto the 'up' escalator.

Somehow, he failed to recognize that the stairs he stepped onto were moving. He watched his feet and continued clomping the suitcase down the steps and jerking about in his robot marionette kind of way, but he wasn't going anywhere; just matching the escalator's speed. He looked up after a while, and when he saw that the distance to the bottom of the stairs wasn't getting closer, he put his head back down with determination and piled on more speed. With that extra effort, he made headway.

By the time he came off the bottom of the escalator, his feet were at a dead run, sprawling him face-first out onto the floor. The suitcase landed on top of him, which he took as a malicious act of agency. He wrestled with it on the ground as if fighting a squarish badger off his throat. Eventually, he prevailed and stood up, but the effort and energy expenditure had pushed him into a rage. He banged the suitcase down hard on the floor, tearing off one of the handle's telescoping struts, while a plastic wheel flew off across the slick concrete floor like a hockey puck shot on goal.

He pulled the suitcase roughly behind him for a few steps, but the damage made it stubbornly willful, even on flat ground. So he punished the little miscreant's behavior with MMA-style body slams and knee drops as we looked on, dumbfounded strangers in a strange country.

"Wow," Matthew said.

"Get that little bugger!" Rhonda encouraged him, ever the cheerleader.

I couldn't help but think he was somebody's son, barely a decade older than mine, and wondered where things had gone amiss. This couldn't have been his parents' plan for him. It would be nice to know that the spectacle couldn't be a preview of anything in our futures, but I'd learned that there's nothing that shakes the confidence one has in their ability to be a parent like becoming one. I hoped my kid wouldn't fry his brain and steal unclaimed airport luggage and start beating on it, but it's unnerving to know that, largely, it isn't up to me.

The shuttle bus dropped us outside the hotel, into rain falling from a shabby gray sky. Inside, it wasn't raining, but still gray and shabby.

Remarkably so, I thought. I'm cheap, and no stranger to cheap hotels, but this had more of a YMCA or Lighthouse Mission vibe than the ones I usually book. It appeared that I'd spent less on a hotel room than I probably should have, but we'd been awake and traveling more than twenty-four hours, and there wasn't much I could do in the moment. Our room wouldn't be ready for a couple of hours more, but there was a bar attached where we could charge our phones and sit on stained and threadbare furniture until we could get in.

I was too jet-lagged and rummy to sleep, so I looked at online reviews and did a little research on our hotel. Better late than never, maybe.

As homelessness rates increased during the pandemic, public health concerns added a push to humanitarian efforts to house Britain's homeless, or "rough sleepers" as they call them. When you don't have a place to come home to, or a warm bed to sleep in, or even a place to keep yourself and your things dry, well, it's tough to stay healthy. And if you do get sick, like catching Covid, when you're sleeping rough, it's harder to fight it off or to avoid dying from it. You'll be sicker, more miserable, and more infectious if you're stuck living outside than in.

So, when the British government enacted Covid lockdowns, it also launched the 'All In' initiative to get its rough sleeping population housed quickly, even if temporarily. Where could they go?

Travel restrictions and the international travel bans meant that hotels, especially those near international airports, had no one to rent rooms to. The government booked those rooms, entire hotels sometimes, for those rough sleepers in need.

It was two or three years before the vaccines came online, and Covid was pushed back in England, allowing the lockdowns and travel restrictions to end. But one of the basic factors underlying Britain's homelessness problem is simply a lack of homes. There are more people, more families, than there are homes for them to live in. Nothing happened during the pandemic to make the situation any better, and quite a few things to make it worse.

Now, the British government, having gotten their homeless off the streets and into hotels with their 'All In' initiative faces a predicament. Homes are still expensive and scarce, and competition for them is intense. The government can't really evict people without housing out of the hotels when there's no humane place for them to go. They can't go into full reverse and start an 'All Out' initiative, only to dump them onto the streets.

What they have done is to go partway. Call it the 'Some Out' initiative if you will. After the lockdowns, the folks who could find and get into more permanent living arrangements moved out of the hotels themselves, and some more were able to move out with government assistance. The government no longer needs to rent entire hotels, only some of the rooms. But some hard cases remain, and some of these have even been given jobs by the hotels they can't leave.

Walking Wet

The Gatwick Travelodge, for instance, had some rooms available for booking tourists like us. Our room, when we got into it, smelled of unwashed clothes and needed airing out, but we couldn't. It was on the ground floor and the window was barred to prevent people from climbing in. One of the long-term resident-employees was just outside, whipping the overgrown grass into tufts with a weed whacker. That the endeavor was so inefficient and pointless made the noise all the more irritating. Luckily, we were tired enough to sleep through it. A little anyway, fitfully.

When we left our room, another fellow sporting a fright wig hairdo held the fire door to the lobby open for us. He was leaning on a wheeled walker and wearing khaki Bermuda shorts over white scaly legs. The tops of his lime-green socks were saturated from serous fluid leaking from open sores on his shins.

"Good morning!" he said.

"If you say so," I answered, wondering what kind of hopes our doorman's parents had once held for him.

***

We were to visit some friends who lived near the Southwest Coast Path and were hiking enthusiasts like me. Duncan and Sandy would meet us at the Taunton Train Station and drive us the last thirty miles to Minehead, at the start of the trail. Taunton is a hundred miles west of Gatwick, but to get there, we first had to go north, because in England, all roads lead to London. The rail lines do as well, so to get anywhere in England, you start by going to the hub in London. We took the shuttle bus back to the train station attached to the airport, and onto the train heading north.

Only one train leaves Gatwick for London, so we got onto it without issue. But the London Station was huge, and noisy, and had throngs of hurried people who knew where they were going and how to get there. We didn't. We peered up at the station monitors with our big backpacks on while a disorienting sea of humanity flowed around us, as if we were confused turtles standing up on our hind legs in an unending school of herring.

"You lot look like lost Americans." An older gentleman was tapping me on the shoulder. "Let's have a look at your tickets, eh?" I handed them over. Then, "Follow me. I have some time before my train leaves, enough to set you straight."

He led us down an escalator to a tunnel deeper underground and onto another train. He rode with us on the tube to Paddington Station. "Now, go up that escalator," he pointed, "turn left, and look on the board for the Cardiff train's platform. Go there. I've got to head off now. My train leaves in six minutes." He looked at his watch. "No, four actually. Nice to meet you." He disappeared back into the tubes.

He was a kindly and smartly dressed septuagenarian widower who seemed sharp enough, but Matt and Rhonda hesitated. We weren't going to Cardiff, but to Taunton. When you're lost, it's rarely a good idea to go running off somewhere else to get yourself even more lost. But I took off straightaway. He was my late father-in-law's doppelgänger, so was automatically entitled to complete trust. No one had ever gone wrong doing what Martin had told them to do. And this time, we weren't either.

Duncan and Sandy are perfectly lovely and gracious people. They met us at the platform, took us to their home, and fed us. It was comforting to sit across from people who knew who we were, where we were from, and what we were doing there in England.

After the last few days, it was a welcome bit of normalcy. The three of us were a bit shell-shocked from the strange and unfamiliar things that had been coming at us while jet-lagged and sleep-deprived.

Myself, I felt disoriented. I could find myself on a map but felt lost. My wristwatch told me what time it was, but it felt wrong. I had no gut feeling of where I was, if that makes sense, in either space or time since leaving home. But sitting there across from such nice folks, even though my stomach was asking me why I'd just put roast chicken breast into it for breakfast, I felt like I could finally relax a bit and maybe puzzle things out.

But then Duncan volunteered to take Matt and me to a store to get cooking fuel.

Duncan's 'runabout' car is a thirty-horsepower Aston Martin from 1954 with manual turn signals, a collector's vintage, which excited Matthew to no end. He got up in front next to Duncan, while my knees and I wedged ourselves into the back. He backed out of the driveway and revved us out onto the wrong side of a less-than-two-lane road.

"There are some things you'll need to know if you decide to rent a car here," Duncan said. "Oh, look there." He pointed at a white stuccoed two-storey under a smoldering haystack. "That house caught fire a month ago, and its thatched roof is still not put out." He got back on topic. "Now, rules of the road are all based on intimidation here. See, that guy is intimidated. We can keep right on." The road was three parking spaces wide there, but only the center one was open as a driving lane. Cars were parked in nearly unbroken lines along both curbs. Duncan shaved them, unconcerned.

"I don't think I'll try driving here," I said. "It's a little tighter than I'm used to."

"It's a bit narrow here for those big American cars you lot drive, innit? But here, those big lunks would be but a laugh."

A truck appeared at the corner ahead of us, oncoming and not at all laughable. "Oops, a lorry," Duncan said. "See? He's got me. I'm intimidated."

Walking Wet

He jerked us over between the bumpers of two parked cars. The lorry he had been playing chicken with whistled by, and we shot back out.

To me, Duncan's car looked as if someone had shrink-wrapped a black London taxi body around a Costco shopping cart. An intemperate choice, I'd think, to play chicken with. Still, I could appreciate Duncan's driving skill and technique.

"Are you like a… like an exceptional driver for England?" I asked.

Duncan turned around to answer me, shaving a few more parked cars as he drove past with only his ear facing the windscreen. "Exceptional? No, I wouldn't say so. Here, we all drive like me."

"Then I definitely won't be driving here," I said.

"I would," Matthew said.

We spent our last night as travelers, as opposed to hikers, in a quaint bed and breakfast on Minehead's Tregonwell Street, just a mile from the official starting point of the path. One of my favorite authors from childhood, Arthur C. Clark, was born in Minehead, so I wandered the streets to marinate in the town's essence, but to no effect. It's been a long time since I've read one of his books, and I've become an impermeable and gristly old slab of meat as a result.

We'd never flown over so many time zones before and were still wrestling with jet lag. So, when bedtime came, it was only early afternoon as far as our body clocks were concerned, and we stayed up late, even though our hike would start in the morning. Rhonda had taken up the TV remote and started scrolling through channels. It was after midnight.

"It'll be a show about making hammers!" I guessed.

"Nope," Rhonda said. Then scrolled to another.

"Chamber music in Antarctica!"

We waited for the commercials to end. "Nope, wrong again." She flipped to the next station.

Matt threw out some guesses. "*Top Gear*! *Fast and Furious*! *Goosebumps*!"

Matt's guesses were shows he would like to see, but mine were purposely random and unlikely. When I've had a rough day of unpredictability, I do a silly self-soothing exercise to convince myself that I'm still in control, the 'What's Next?' game.

The idea is to make guesses about what's next: the next plot twist in a book, what's behind a refrigerator door, what clothing item will be fished out of the dryer next, anything. The guesses should be plausible, yet outlandish enough that when the reveal comes, I can comfort myself in knowing that the real world isn't as weird or unsettling as what my imagination might supply. When I've sort of lost a handle on things, playing the 'What's Next?' game helps me feel like the handle is still somewhere within reach.

So, Rhonda flipping past B-grade movies or telemarketing schlock on late-night British television was just fine with me. It was relaxing because the shows at each click were more mundane and commonplace than any of my guesses... until she clicked onto a reality dating show.

It featured a female host and a contestant who would pick one of six contending guys for a first date. Each contender stood on a different colored dais, silhouetted behind a frosted glass shower door. The game started when the shower doors lifted a few inches, revealing the dating hopefuls' bare feet.

The lady contestant and host inspected their feet, commenting on the physical attributes of each. The contestant then chose one of the prospective dates to be eliminated. The next round started when the shower doors went up to reveal five pairs of kneecaps. Again, more inspection and commentary.

The host pointed and asked the contestant, "What do you think of Purple's calves?"

"I don't fancy long hairy gams, but his toe rings are a bit of me," she answered. "I think Yellow's calves are very fit, but his knees are right knobbly, meself."

They carried on a bit with the others. The emcee tried to make the repartee titillating and suggestive, but it only made me uncomfortable. I wondered if they ever aired male contestants making body judgments about women on the show. I doubted that would go over well, even in England.

"They've got to be wearing Speedos," I said, forgetting all about the 'What's Next?' game.

"I think they'll all turn around, and we'll see a bunch of butts," Matthew said.

"Naw, they'll be pixelated," said Rhonda.

Green, who had shaved his legs, was eliminated. The frosted glass doors rose to the remaining fours' navels. We were all wrong.

I gasped. "What the- "

"Welcome to Europe!" Rhonda said.

Matthew howled with laughter.

"You need to change the channel!"

"Your boy's old enough. I want to see who she picks."

Matt, still howling, pointed at the TV screen. "She's gonna pick that big one! I've *got* to text Jaxon, right now!" He grabbed for his phone.

"Great, just great," I said.

"You can blame me. Tell Monica he saw it with his aunt."

The inspections and commentary resumed, this time even more suggestive and gratuitous.

"How do you fancy testicles?" asked the host. The contestant's response was drowned out by the simultaneous answers shouted from inside our room.

"Pan-fried!"

Walking Wet

"Glitter spray!"

I noted with interest the varied definitions of the verb 'fancy' as interpreted by Matthew and his aunt. Matthew supplied a ready-made solution for bedazzling and making testicles 'fancy' with an aerosol can, while my sister advocated for a treatment that would render them edible.

The camera pulled back for a wide shot and panned upwards to show the parts being commented upon. The emcee and her guest were out of frame, depriving the onscreen view of any meaningful sense of scale. Without context, my eyeballs struggled to explain what they were seeing, and for a surreal moment, my brain decided that someone had raised a garage door just as a clowder of semi-hairless cats had been outside trying to climb it. Now, they were suspended, with their lower halves just hanging there.

As the camera zoomed back in for individual close-ups of frontal anatomies, I did what I often do when things get uncomfortable and made close observations and pointless inferences. I deduced that the ambient temperature where the cats were hanging was warm enough and that the ventilation was too soft to flutter anything about.

Matthew had gotten his laughter under control, but was still shaking and snorting, thumbs ablur as he texted his friends back home. As their comments pinged back to his phone screen, he started howling again.

"Don't get any ideas about going on that show," I told him.

"Ha! Me and Quinn are already registered!"

For Pete's sake, I thought. *It's a good thing we start hiking tomorrow. Whatever we see out there on the trail, it won't be as weird as this.*

I hoped so, anyway. Earnestly.

A Jump Over the Pond

Walking Wet

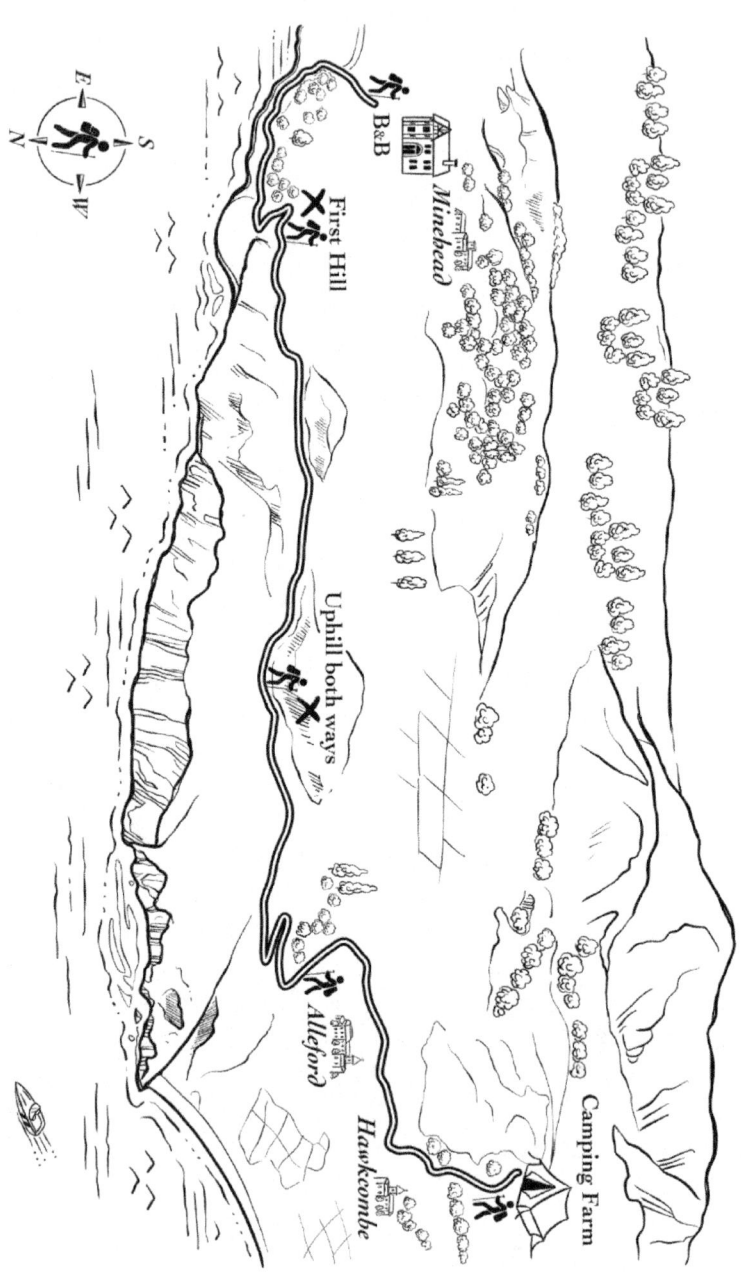

Short Legs

    1 ⋯ DAY WALKING
    5 ⋯ PATH MILES WALKED
  12 ⋯ TOTAL MILES WALKED
  https://www.southwestcoastpath.org.uk/walksdb/136/

"You've lied to me my whole life," Matthew groused. It may have been a lack of sleep making him grouchy, even though the morning's start was later than we'd planned. Rhonda and I were in the dining room when the B&B served breakfast at 9:00, but Matt had gotten back into bed and waited there a half hour longer before coming down.

"He's your father," Rhonda said. "It's his job to lie to you. Get over it."

"No, it's not," I protested. "And I've never lied to him."

"Yes, you did," Matthew said. "'B in B', 'B in B', all this time, you've been saying 'B in B.' You never once said 'B *and* B.' Even when I told you I wanted to stay at a 'B in B' you never called it a 'B and B.' You committed a lie of rendition."

"You mean a 'lie of omission,'" I said.

"I'm with Matt," Rhonda said. "What you did was extreme rendition."

"Well, you'd say that too is my job as a father."

Matt was still talking. "I've always wanted breakfast in bed, and I never got a breakfast in bed. So finally, I get to stay at a B in B and I thought 'Now, I'll get breakfast in bed,' and I didn't. I'd already told all my friends about it, and I was going to livestream it so they could watch me getting served and eating my breakfast in bed."

"That's ridiculous. Who'd want to see that?"

"Everybody. Jeez."

"I'm totally on your side, Matt," Rhonda said. "I think your dad should find us a real B in B to stay in. I want to be served breakfast in bed, too."

"Now, who's committing extreme rendition?" I turned to Matt. "It's B and B, and always has been, okay? You go to one and you get a bed to sleep in and a breakfast when you leave. B and B, see? You only get breakfast in bed if you're in a hospital and your legs are broken."

"I'd say that's a small price to pay to livestream a breakfast in bed. You should go for it, Matt." Rhonda said, laughing.

"You both suck," Matthew said. He started walking faster, leaving us both behind.

"Break a leg!" Rhonda called after him.

"We won't see him now till we get to the camping farm," I said.

"Not my fault you've been lying to him."

Minehead is about midway up the southern shoreline of the Bristol Channel, the sea inlet between the Welsh horn on the north and the long finger of Britain's Devon and Cornwall peninsula on the south. The seawater looked brackish, dull brown with sediment, and the rocky beach on our right was slick with slime and seaweed. With the drizzle from a gray sky, the combination made for an inauspicious start for our quest.

Duncan had warned us that the trail's view past the shoreline had a dull start but assured us that as the trail led on and the channel across to Wales widened, the Gulf Stream would gain dominance over the tides. The water and shoreline would be washed by the warm current, and the slime and mud would give way to clean rock or sandy beaches fronting an azure, pristine ocean.

We walked along the promenade, a wide sidewalk behind a three-foot-high seawall of stonework. The Southwest Coast Path's official start is marked by a metal sculpture of two hands holding a map. From there, the path continued along the cement promenade. We could see Matthew dwindling away in front of us for a couple of miles as he outpaced us.

Between Minehead and Porlock, the next coastal village, is a forested hill, and before long, we were out of town and walking up a graveled road that soon became a lonely driveway. The trail took a sharp left up and away just before the house and became a steep footpath, leading us up into scraggly woods. Brown and crinkly oak leaves littered the trail and forest floor, almost devoid of undergrowth. The trees' trunks were about the size of my upper thigh, not especially impressive to us natives of timber country.

Duncan had told us that England's forests had been shorn off in the late eighteenth century to make masts and hull planks for Admiral Nelson's navy. And since then, Great Britain has been deeply involved in a lot of the world's military and colonial history, so conservation and reforestation just haven't been top of mind until relatively recently. It will take a couple centuries more for the oaks to mature and become again the majestic and ancient forests of Robin Hood's times.

I had time to examine the scraggly oak trees with leisure. And their bark, and the insects crawling around on their trunks, and the spider web filaments strung between them. Because as the trail began ascending the hill, our pace slowed. Agonizingly. Hills weren't something that Rhonda was used to. She had been training for the hike before we left, alright, but only by walking the streets and sidewalks in her hometown. And as her town is situated in a broad valley of fertile farmland, her training routes had been pretty flat. She was having a time of it now.

I'd climbed mountains back in the day, and most of that time was spent carrying heavy packs uphill. And believe it or not, there's an art to schlepping, and techniques you can use to get your stuff up a hill without wrecking yourself doing it. Rhonda may not have been conditioned for walking uphill, but I could see that a lot of what was wearing her down was just a basic lack of technique.

"Okay, there's a couple things you could do to make this easier on yourself," I told her. "First, try taking shorter steps. Taking smaller steps is like shifting to a lower gear. Imagine you are a log truck hauling a load uphill. Gearing down makes things easier on the engine and the transmission, and even the drivetrain. Short steps, big breaths."

"Breathing through my nose," she said. "Don't want to pant. I'll get out of breath."

"You're already out of breath. Don't worry about panting. I breathe through my mouth all the time. When your body is screaming for air, give it all you can. Remember, you want to be like a logging truck. The breather cans on those things are the size of trash bins. Don't restrict yourself."

"Okay."

"Also, concentrate on leaving your heels on the ground. It's natural to try pushing yourself up the hill on the balls of your feet to sort of give yourself a boost. But that takes more energy. You push your body weight up the hill with your quads, but if your heels are off the ground, you're using your calf muscles, too."

Rhonda tried it. "It's stretching my Achilles. I'm afraid to hurt them."

"Take even shorter steps, then. Gear down, don't try to stride up the hill. Relax your calves and let them stretch as much as you can. Leave your heels on the ground and support your body weight with bones as much as possible, not your muscles. If the trail is too steep, I'll do this sometimes, see?" I angled myself towards one side of the trail, then the other, taking short steps and tracing a mini zigzag pattern up the trail. Rhonda followed suit.

"That's easier," she said.

"Alright, now watch me walk. This is called a rest step. See how I'm locking my knee and hesitating at the end of each step? Just here, here," I said, momentarily freezing in place so she could see. "Each time I do that, my quads get a short rest. Freezing for even just a split second that way can make a big difference. Just follow my pace and do what I do. And keep the tips of your hiking sticks behind you. Your sticks should only push you up, never down."

"How much more uphill is there?"

"Not that much more. We'll top out at nine hundred-fifty feet above sea level today, and we've already gone up about five hundred of it."

But we never leveled out that day. Each time the path crested a rise, it would pitch back down to cross a creek, or muddle across some bog or other.

Then it would pitch back up again, forcing us to regain the hard-fought elevation we'd just lost. To me, it was a bit annoying. To Rhonda, it was demoralizing. In one of the bogs, she turned to survey the portion of trail she'd just done.

"This trail is uphill both ways," she observed.

And each uphill, it took Rhonda longer to regain the lost elevation. After she'd mastered the fine arts of pack hauling, keeping her heels on the ground, locking her knees on the back foot, taking short steps, and panting like a steam train, I'd been trying to push her pace back up a bit. When you're going uphill and you need to do it all day, you need to slow down enough to make forward progress sustainable. But there comes a point of diminishing returns where slowing down further does less to aid endurance than it does to prolong the agony. And we'd passed that point.

"Look, Rhonda," I said. "We've got to pick up the pace a li-" I stopped mid-sentence when she looked up at me. Her face was pale, and there were round beads of perspiration across her forehead, on her cheeks, and on her upper arms. She should have been flushed and red-faced, but she wasn't. Her skin looked clammy and pale, and her breathing was ragged and shallow. "Uh, how do you feel?" I asked.

"How do I look?"

"Like shit."

"Well, there you are."

"Okay, let's eat a candy bar and take a look at the map again."

The map showed a public pathway that angled off the Coastal Path, straight down a ravine, and into a village just off the main road.

"It looks like we can do one more sort of short rise, veer left, and take a shortcut downslope to Allerford. From there, we can probably get a bus or a taxi to the farm above Porlock. But the shortcut will be steep."

"But downhill?"

"Downhill."

"Let's do it, then."

I texted Matt and told him our plans. He was already at our farm campsite but would backtrack to Allerford to meet us.

Going down the shortcut was rough, slippery work. It seemed the side trail was mostly used by cows to get between the village and the upland moors.

They'd churned it to mud with their hooves and top dressed it liberally with cow poo, big pies and little pats. I thought Rhonda would slip and fall in some of it, but she didn't.

I checked my phone. There was no cell service down in the ravine. I shouted encouragement up to Rhonda.

"Take your time there, sis. No hurry, and try to stay relaxed. There's no cell service in this ravine, so if you have yourself a heart attack here, I can't call an ambulance, and you'd probably just die."

"Thanks, that's good to know."

"Sure. Monica told me not to kill you."

"That's nice. She never forbade me from killing you, though."

"Thanks. That's good to know, too," I said.

The first paved road we came to in Allerford went under a creek, but there was a stonework walking bridge just downstream of the ford. Rhonda sat on the balustrade and said, "I'm done walking today."

"The bus stop is just another quarter mile," I said.

"I don't think I need to go there."

She was right. The nearest cottage in the village had a plumber's van parked out front, and when the workman came outside to get a pipe fitting, Rhonda struck a deal with him to drive her the rest of the way to the farm campsite we'd reserved up ahead. Nearby was a blacksmith's shop, and I watched craftsmen working a forge until Matt showed up.

The plumber wasn't done yet, so Rhonda waved us away. "Go on. I might even get there before you guys," she said.

I followed Matt back the way he'd come. He took me through Hawkcombe, with old country cottages built along both sides of a creek in a narrow valley. The creek was channeled into a mill race and fed several small irrigation canals of stonework. The mill must have ground barley in the old days, and the canals had probably watered gardens and orchards, but now, the old mill's water wheel isn't connected to any machinery, and turns for charm only, and the canal trickle through flower beds fronting vacation rentals. Still, it was lovely.

"So, what's with Aunt Rhonda?" Matthew asked.

"She was okay for the first couple of hours," I answered, "but when the path went uphill, she had to slow down. She had some challenges."

"Probably because her legs are so short."

"No, I think it's something else." I thought about her lifestyle and the community she lives in. How she is loved by and connected to everyone, and how so many people depend on her, and how sparsely populated and far apart everyone and everything is out there. Doing anything or getting anywhere in such a rural area means spending a lot of time behind a steering wheel.

Walking Wet

Rhonda will drive a hundred miles to a granddaughter's preschool pageant or to visit a friend experiencing a rough patch.

I don't support my friends nearly as well as she does, so I have more time to spend exercising than my sister ever has. I have fewer friends, but it's easier for me to stay fit. Rhonda is generous with her time and has a wealth of friends, but is kind of pudgy. I doubt that either of us are completely satisfied with the tradeoffs that we've made. It's difficult to know which of us is the wisest.

"No, I think it's something else," I repeated. "Her legs have always been kind of short."

Rhonda

Because kindergarten ran half-days my sister had to wait for the bus without her older brothers. But she didn't wait alone. Our mom had brought us kids with her when she remarried and took up with a dairy farmer, and he had a pair of geese on the farm. They were implacable idiots, their heads filled with nothing much more than an irrational hatred of us kids. And every day when my sister went down the long driveway to meet the bus, they'd follow. The hen was about the same height as my little sister, the gander, a little taller, and they took pleasure in terrorizing her every school day morning.

They couldn't waddle fast, but trying to outrun them was generally a bad idea. If she tried, she'd hear a patter of webbed feet behind her accelerating to takeoff speed. Then they'd close the distance fast, with their necks outstretched and their big goose wings flapping just off the ground. The hen, being lighter, would lift off and reach my sister first, patting her head on her way by with a wingtip as if to say, "Trying to outrun us again, dear?" before making an awkward and honky landing some few yards ahead.

But the gander wasn't interested in a landing, honky or otherwise. He'd arrow straight in like a cruise missile, and my sister would be knocked over by a malicious and strangely soft, barn fowl smelly bowling ball. She'd get bitten for trying to flee, and beaten with wings, and become reacquainted with the sharp claws that tipped those ridiculous orange webbed feet.

And stupid as they were, she couldn't sneak past them either. Goose brains are small and mostly useless, but they do have a knack for timekeeping and routine. They knew when the kindergarten bus was coming, and they knew when the little girl they detested would emerge from the house to meet it without her brothers, undefended.

I had been equally terrified of the geese but had recently experienced a double-epiphany. First, I realized that I had somehow grown taller than the geese. And second, that Mr. Gander looked a lot like a bagpipe. Lawrence Welk featured a bagpiper on the show one night, and I'd been smitten by the instrument's wheezy dignity and the pomp and novelty of the bagpiper's traditional dress.

So, when the gander waddled up to terrorize me the next day, my left hand shot out without thinking and seized the goose's throat just under his chin. I scooped him up off the ground and pinned his wings under my free arm, then put his bill between my teeth and blew. I pumped an elbow, squeezing him a few times to 'prime the pipes.' Then I marched, imagining myself dignified and magnificently attired in kilt and tartan, and hummed the classic 'Scotland the Brave' kazoo-style into the gander's bill. He struggled, and his little feet windmilled in futility, while the hen flapped and honked a cacophony behind.

The music we made, as you might expect, was nearly indistinguishable from real bagpiping. With his bill held firmly between my teeth, the gander's protests were reduced to plaintive nasal whimperings, almost perfectly reproducing the undertones so unique to bagpipes. I learned to produce different chords by varying the intensity and duration of my squeezes to the gander's body.

We had regular practice sessions for a while after that first time, and we were becoming passably listenable. But the gander eventually absorbed the notion that to be anywhere within arm's reach of me would get him bagpiped, a humiliation he compensated for by intensifying his attacks on my sister.

Our parents were either too busy on the farm or couldn't be bothered to bodyguard a kindergartner at the bus stop, so Rhonda took an umbrella with her for protection every day. With the umbrella opened, she could shield herself against repeated charges, and sometimes even take offensive action by parrying into the gander's chest with the pokey part. When the bus arrived, she'd make a strategic retreat, backpedaling to the open jib door, where she'd collapse the umbrella and hop onto the bus.

This infuriated the gander further because he couldn't make the jump. He'd push his chest against the bus's first step and lunge at her with his long neck, like a hissing and striking cobra. My sister, with a double-handed grip on the now-closed umbrella, would brain the gander whack-a-mole style from the top of the steps, until she could force a retreat and allow the bus driver to get the door closed.

But the bully my sister is facing now is a different kind of bird and more difficult to face down. Rhonda got Covid before vaccines were available and spent a week in the ICU with it. She also had a vertebral disc that had gone wonky, which made her legs nearly unresponsive and caused pain that made sleeping impossible. But the surgery she needed was delayed because the hospitals were overflowing with pandemic patients. Months later, her back surgery was scheduled, but she caught Covid again. She'd been vaxxed by this time, and a trip to the hospital wasn't needed. But it delayed her back surgery yet again.

Even though this second bout of Covid wasn't as bad as the first, it seemed to linger. At first, she thought she had long Covid, but when she felt pressure on her chest and pain radiating down her left arm, she knew it was something more. A hurried trip to the emergency room led to another stay in the hospital, followed by tests and consultations with a cardiologist. He told her that she would live with new maladies, ventricular hypertrophy and congestive heart failure. He set her up with new medications and tasked her with diet restrictions and exercise regimens. Exercising was especially irksome and grueling with the problematic ruptured disc still in her back. And her heart condition, of course, forced yet another delay for her back surgery.

She fought her way back to tolerably good health, enough to get her spine surgery finally, and the cessation of chronic pain was almost immediate. She was able to sleep, work, and walk again without gritting her teeth. She put a treadmill in her TV room and started walking around town for exercise.

I'd been thinking of a walking trip in England, and it occurred to me that my sister's health could benefit from the trip even more than mine. Rhonda had always dismissed her personal needs as mere whims or fancies, and rarely did anything for herself. Even so, I thought, getting her to leave her family at home for two months to walk with me in England was worth a try. I called to pitch the idea to her.

"You want me to go to England and walk six hundred miles with you? Yeah, right," Rhonda said. "Do I impress you as somebody who walks miles by the hundreds? I can barely make it around the block some days."

"I know it sounds like a lot, but trust me, I think you could do it."

"And why do you think that? I'm on beta-blockers, you know. Not exactly fit for endurance sports right now. It's easy for me to overdo things, and then I get short of breath."

"Well, the Southwest Coast Path isn't like the Pacific Crest Trail. There's no high-altitude mountain terrain or anything like that. It's basically sea level the whole way. Thick air, so it's easy on the lungs. You'd just need to pace yourself."

"Yeah, but that's a long time to be out walking, sea level or not. What if I can't keep up? What if I get halfway through and just collapse in a heap?"

"Anytime you feel tired, just take a bus or taxi to the next town. We wouldn't be in the middle of nowhere. There are villages and towns all along the trail."

"Interesting. It's a long time, though. I'm not sure I could be away that long."

"Sure you could, you'd be just fine. It's all the people who've become dependent on you who would have problems."

"Okay. Consider my reservations duly amended."

"Well, they could get along without you for a while, and they should."

"Ha! I'll tell them you said so."

"Besides," I said, "we won't be out in the wilderness. If one of us gets tired, we'll just Google a bus or call for a taxi."

"Interesting," she said again.

"Look, Rhonda, it's not just about getting some good exercise. It's about the experience. You've been running ragged since before Covid and you deserve a break from everything. Your home treadmill is good for your cardio, but getting out there, really out there... that's good for more than just your heart. It's a chance for adventure."

"I've no doubt about that," she said, "but your adventures seem to come in two types: marginally survivable or barely survivable."

"Funny! I'm expecting less of an epic adventure in England and more of a historic one. A walk through history. Customs officers built the Southwest Coast Path three hundred years ago for smugglers."

"Why would they build a trail for smugglers?"

"No, they built it to catch smugglers. In those days of iffy record-keeping and barter, it was tough to collect taxes, so mostly, they taxed imports."

"And England being an island, everything came in by boat."

"Exactly. Customs officers watched the boats as they were unloaded at the docks. But there are dozens of hidden coves and beaches along the English coastline, places smugglers could land a boat unseen to bring in contraband. The path visits each of those hidden coves and all the towns and fishing villages in between."

"I'm thinking about it."

I gave her a moment. Then, "You should walk with me. I'm telling you, when I did the Pacific Crest Trail, I lost a bunch of weight, and my blood pressure and cholesterol went back to like I was a teenager. And to be honest, most of that happened in the first five hundred miles of the walk. This walk will be just over six. You know, you deserve some self-care time."

"Yeah, yeah." My admonishment prompted her to cut me off, a familiar pattern. "I have my treadmill time."

"Look," I said. "It's not just about the miles, like you can do on your treadmill at home. It's the novelty, the adventure, all the little surprises you get on a long walk; it's all those things. It's being away from home, the noise, and your routine responsibilities that really makes the difference. I'm telling you, I truly think the long walk I did on the Pacific Crest Trail added five years to my life. It turned the clock back that far."

"Hmm."

It felt like home, talking to Rhonda. We'd grown up together and still shared the same dialect, one where people say what they mean.

But that dialect is a rarity. Usually, when I suggest doing something with someone, they won't tell me outright if they don't want to do it. Instead, they give reasons why they can't. When I offer a solution, they move the goalposts and come up with another excuse. And if that problem gets solved, they'll fabricate another. All because they don't want to admit they're not interested. We'll go round and round pointlessly, because my native dialect makes me fall for it every time. I'm dumb that way.

Rhonda had concerns about hiking the trail, and I addressed them. At this point in normal conversations, I'm usually beginning to feel foolish. It was such a relief to know that with my sister Rhonda, I didn't have to.

"You know that donkey you see in old movies," I asked, "that's hooked up to a turnstile and just walking around in a circle day after day in some gristmill? That's you. Let someone else wear the harness for a while. Really, you're not the only ass for the gristmill."

She laughed. "No, but I'm the biggest," she said. "So, how would you get there?"

"I've been looking at that. It's a lot cheaper to fly out of Canada than it is from here. You could come to my house, then we'd take the Amtrak from my place into Vancouver, then fly from there to London."

The phone went quiet as she considered. "I have a doctor's visit coming up, and I should talk to him. If that goes okay, I have my granddaughter's birthday party. I won't miss that for anything. So, you'd have to get the tickets for after that."

"Really? So, you'd go?"

"I'm pretty sure I just said so, didn't I?"

All the people I could meet on the path, all the conversations I might have, any insights I could explore, and all the sights I'd see or the adventures I might have while walking the trail in England; all of them took a step back on the long list of things I was looking forward to. Because being able to hang out with my sister had just taken the top spot.

Two days later, Rhonda sent a text message.

[Creatinine kinase back to normal. Cardiologist says go for a walk.]

I got online right away and bought the airline tickets.

Walking Wet

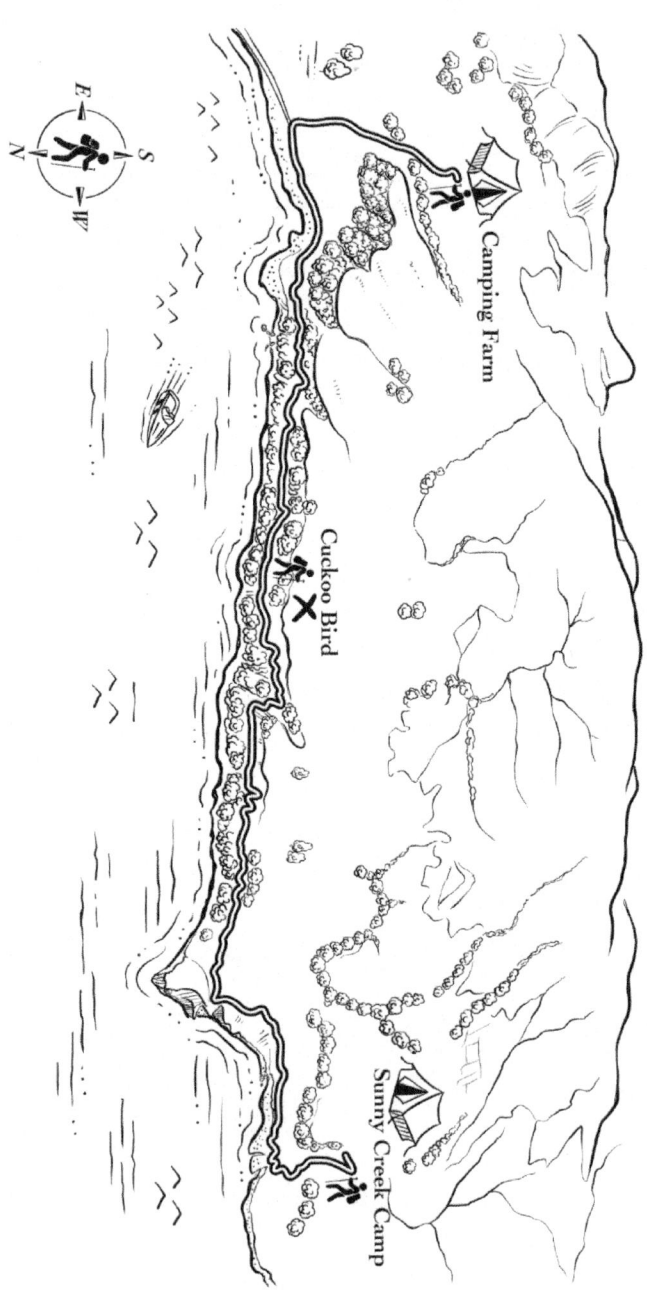

I Hate Shakespeare

3 ⋯ DAYS WALKING
32 ⋯ PATH MILES WALKED
46 ⋯ TOTAL MILES WALKED
https://www.southwestcoastpath.org.uk/walksdb/137/

Rhonda was waiting for us when we got to the farm camp.
"I've got some clarification," she said, "from my cardiologist."
While Rhonda was waiting for Matt and me to walk through Hawkcombe and up the old wagon path to the camping farm, she'd called back home to her doctor's office.

"I told him how much trouble I was having walking uphill, and how my heart wouldn't ramp up. I asked if I should drop the dosage on my BP meds. He said they were already calibrated to where they should be and changing them out here would be a bad idea."

"But the meds won't let your heart ramp up when you need it to," I said. "I thought your creosotinine levels were all back to normal now so you could let 'er rip when you need it to."

"Creatinine, not creosote-neen," she said. "The creatinine tests show how much stress your heart has been under, not how much stress it can take."

"I had a friend on beta-blockers, and his meds wouldn't let him walk uphill either," I said. "They adjusted the dosage or something, and then he could."

"Yeah, I relayed your story to my doc. He said doing that might work for some things, but not congestive heart failure like I have. My heart has some hypertrophy, an area of permanent damage where the heart wall is thicker and less elastic than it's supposed to be. I made improvements with diet and exercise, but that thickened area will always be there. The doctor reminded me that the underlying problem that caused my congestive heart failure in the first place is still here." She touched her chest.

"I thought it was too much salt and calories."

"Well, the salt and calories certainly didn't help the CHF."

"What's a CHF?" Matthew asked.

"Congestive heart failure," Rhonda told him. "It's when your heart can't pump blood out to your body and away from your lungs fast enough, so your lungs get backed up," Rhonda said.

"You have that?"

"Yes, but I have it under control. Until today, anyway."

"So, what do we do now then?" I asked.

"You heard that joke about the guy that goes to the doctor and says, 'Doc, it hurts when I do this, and the doctor says-'"

"-Then don't do that, I know," I said.

"Well, that's pretty much what the cardiologist told me. I need to stop going up hills."

"What if you go up hills anyway?" Matthew asked.

"My heart pumps pretty well, up to a point. But if I work it too hard, it gets all wonky and inefficient. It gets all messed up and starts pumping blood backwards and sideways."

"Then what?"

"Then I'll tip over, you know, and blood spurts out of my eyeballs. And then I'll burst into flames and explode."

"Cool!"

"The doctor thought we'd be touring castles and flower gardens over here. He said he didn't know I'd be carrying heavy stuff straight up hills," she said.

"Sorry about that," I said. "It's a bit lumpier than I'd realized it would be."

"I need a day to recuperate," Rhonda said. "So in the morning, you and Matt take off hiking. I'll find us a campsite in Lynton, the next town, and text you the location. I'll take the bus, do some sightseeing, and meet you there."

***

In the morning, I stuffed Rhonda's pack to overflowing with my things and took it outside to meet Matt, who was already packed and ready to go. I'd hike with hers, and Rhonda would take my backpack with her on the bus to carry the tent we shared. I followed Matthew out of camp, and we ate breakfast bars and brushed our teeth on the move. The miles rolled peacefully out behind us in the early morning dew, and it felt familiar. For the first time since we'd left home, we were doing what I knew how to do. I frowned, though. I'd expected there'd be three of us doing it.

Matthew and I hiked back down the old wagon trail beside the creek and the ancient rock wall, into Hawkcombe, then continued downstream to Porlock and the beach. I had read that the Romans had built saltworks there in pre-medieval times that are still visible and was anxious to see them. I had never seen anything, as far as I know, that human hands had fashioned or touched that long ago.

Even though it was early, some local dogs were already out dragging their humans around by their wrists. Porlock's beach was tough to walk on, being slimy and mostly made of rocks the size and shape of dinosaur eggs. It was low tide on a calm and foggy morning, but the rocks attested to the severity of the storms and waves that come ashore there. It took some energetic hydraulics to move rocks of that size around. The storms had pushed rocky dinosaur eggs up the sloping beach to construct a huge curving berm. Landward of the berm was a protected salt marsh of green springy glasswort growing in iron scum water and mudflats.

A couple of single-car garage-sized rectangles were in the flats, outlined with toppled dinosaur egg rock fences. They may have been the foundations of the old Roman structures, but we couldn't tell. It's hard to imagine that they could have built anything useful with the dino eggs and bowling balls they could get from the berm nearby, instead of quarrying for the squarish flat-sided stones that were available inland.

Whatever they'd built probably wasn't meant to last and wouldn't have either, except that they'd used round rocks that were unlikely to be salvaged and repurposed for anything else. But whatever the ruin was, it was cool to see.

We crossed the mucky water draining the salt marsh, ensuring that our shoes and socks were suitably squishy before getting off the beach and back up onto the road. From there, the Southwest Coast Path led us past a café with umbrellaed picnic tables overlooking a collection of modest fishing boats resting on rocks and mud, and then along some sheep fields before heading back into the trees.

The trail was mostly set back from the tops of the cliffs lining the bay, so there wasn't much to see and not much reason to look at anything other than our squelchy feet on the slimy trail. Drizzle started falling again, perfecting the conditions necessary for thinking profound thoughts and discovering hidden truths through deep introspection.

"Oh, I hate when this happens," Matthew said.

"What?"

"I got a stupid song stuck in my head and can't get rid of it."

"What song's that?"

"'God, I Hate Shakespeare' from that community theatre musical *Something Rotten*. I saw it about eight times, you know. It just keeps going in my head over and over."

"You've got yourself an earworm."

"A what?"

"An earworm. Tunes that get stuck in your head are called earworms. They used to bother me, too. But they don't anymore."

"You know how to get rid of them, then?"

"Nope. I just let 'em spool on out in there," I said, pointing to my temple.

"They don't drive you nuts?"

Walking Wet

"Used to. But then I read this book about the origins of consciousness and how it comes about, and the theory is that our minds are made up of different subsystems. And these subsystems run almost autonomously."

"How's that?"

"Well, it's like one part of your brain is always thinking about how hungry you might be, and another part of your brain is worried about things like how your hair is combed or if you forgot to put your pants on again, and things like that. Another part would be thinking about whatever you're doing with your hands or where you're putting your feet, like now when we're walking. And another part of your brain is thinking about what I'm saying. See? All at the same time. And maybe another part of your brain would be thinking about what you're going to say next."

"I've been thinking about that since you started talking. I've just been waiting for you to quit."

"See? That's what I mean. There are all sorts of sub-systems working in your brain thinking their own thoughts without you directing them, and one of those systems is in charge of playing background music. It decided on 'God, I Hate Shakespeare'."

"Yeah, and I'm tired of it, and I don't want to hear it anymore, but it keeps playing anyway. It's irritating."

"Like I said, I used to get upset with earworms, too. Made me feel like I wasn't in control of my own brain. I'd even start singing something else out loud to drown the earworm out. Sometimes it worked and sometimes it didn't. But after reading that book about all the different compartments of thought that go into making a consciousness, and how they work independently doing their jobs like they're supposed to, I decided to just concentrate on whatever it is that I'm supposed to be doing and let my subsystems go on about their business without interfering. It's not like there's nothing else to focus on. And besides, whatever earworm tune you're stuck with, it could always be worse."

"What do you mean worse? I've had to listen to this same song over and over again for the last six miles." He started singing,

"God, I hate Shakespeare! That's right, I said it! I do!
I hate Shakespeare! I just don't get it!"

"Aargh!" he groaned.

"Know what's been running in my head for the last six miles?" I asked. "That Burger King jingle,

"Whopper, Whopper, eat a Whopper!
Eat a burger, eat a Whopper-" I sang.

I Hate Shakespeare

"Those aren't even the words!"

"At B-K, have it your way. You rule!"

"You've got to be kidding me."
"Nope. True."
"How does that not drive you nuts?"
"I'm just letting that part of my brain do its thing."
"That part of your brain is a zombie. You should fight things like that."
"Naw, don't think so-

"Whopper, hopper, eat a Whopper-...
At BK, have it your way. You rule!" I sang.

"You suck!" He started singing his earworm back at me, louder this time, escalating the conflict in an attempt to infect me with his earworm while I infected him with mine.

"He has no sense about the audience, he makes them feel so dumb.
He doesn't even care that my ass is getting numb-"

The subsystems in charge of our squelching feet kept us moving up the trail while Matthew and I sing-shouted our earworms at each other.

"Cuckoo! Cuckoo! Cuckoo!" An equally loud and aggressive song answered from a tree somewhere nearby.

We stopped. "That sounds like a clock, a big one," Matthew said.

"I think it's a real cuckoo bird," I said. "I didn't know-"

"Cuckoo! Cuckoo! Cuckoo!"

"-that they were even here in England. I always thought they were from Bavaria, you know, where they make cuckoo clocks."

Matthew and I dug candy bars from our backpacks and waited to hear the bird again. A Chesapeake retriever came up the trail from the other direction, pulling a human lady behind him.

"Did you hear the cuckoo?" the human asked. "It's very rare to hear them this late in the season. Most have already flown off to their summer grounds in South Africa. Only the males make that distinctive call, and this late in the season, there must have been some extraordinary trigger to elicit a territorial response like that."

"Whopper, Whopper, eat a Whopper-"

Walking Wet

The earworm part of my brain wanted to speak up and take credit, but my subsystem that handles embarrassment and concerns itself with hair combing and pants wearing overruled.

"Don't know about that," I said. "Haven't heard any triggers."

Matt's subsystem in charge of his pants and other insecurities prodded him to answer as well. "Me neither," he said.

"Cuckoos are fascinating birds," the dog's lady continued. "I've made a study of them. As I said, only the males make that distinctive 'Cuckoo!' call. The female's call is like the chittering of a sparrow hawk. They don't make nests of their own, so they impersonate sparrow hawks to scare other birds off from their nests."

"What? Why?" I asked.

"So they can swoop in and lay their own eggs in them. When the nesting bird comes back, she will care for the cuckoo's egg as if it were one of her own."

"Don't the other birds notice?" Matthew asked.

"Not usually. See, there are only a few species of birds that cuckoos will depend upon to hatch and raise their young. And their eggs' color and designs mimic each of these host species. Very closely."

She's got to be a biologist, I thought. *I could talk with a fellow bio all day.*

"There are four distinct groups of female cuckoos," she continued, "each with their own target species that they seek out. The eggs they lay mimic their target's eggs. They won't change targets."

"You mean there are four species of cuckoo birds then," I said.

"No, just one. The genes for egg shape and color, and their nest targeting instincts are all carried on the female chromosome. That way, females are free to mate with any male cuckoo."

"Free to mate with any male cuckoo," Matthew mused. The subsystem in a teenage boy's brain that never rests was computing the possibilities.

"Right," I said. "They never have a life mate, never raise chicks, and never build nests of their own. It's like these birds are stuck in adolescence their whole lives."

"They do establish winter and summer territories," the woman pointed out, "and shuttle between them."

The Chesapeake offered Matthew the end of a slobbery stick to play tug-of-war with.

"You said cuckoos are usually off to South Africa by now?" I asked.

"Yes, usually," the woman said.

"Then maybe he's not being territorial. Could be this guy is here all alone, and he's just sad and lonely. He never had any family, and maybe now he's too old to make the trip. So, when he heard us coming up the trail, he called out."

The woman looked at me. "What a sad thought," she said.

Matthew was looking for a place to wipe his hands after their tug-of-war match, and the Chesapeake started pulling my new biologist friend back onto the trail.

"It was nice running into you," she said over her shoulder.

We listened for the male cuckoo to call again after they left, but he had given up.

"Hey, my earworm is gone," Matthew observed.

"Really?" I asked.

"Yeah. Maybe I just needed to hear boring talk from someone else besides you."

Sometimes, I think that the development of Matthew's subsystem for being a smartass is outstripping the capacities of his other subsystems, and worry about the consequences it could have on his personality. I started singing-

"God, I hate Shakespeare! That's right, I said it! I do!
I hate Shakespeare! I just don't get it!.."

Matthew

When we were Matthew's age, Monica and I both supposed we would be making children of our own and creating our own families someday, even though it would be a long time before we would meet.

Monica was the fourth of five daughters in her family, and she enjoyed having older siblings blazing the trail and schooling her parents in front of her. By the time Monica came along and started getting into things, her parents were experienced, slow to anger, wise, loving, and patient. She enjoyed being their daughter and always assumed she'd have a couple of her own someday. And maybe even a boy or two for good measure.

Being a child in my family was nowhere near enjoyable. My parents were diametrically opposite to hers, but I wanted to have kids of my own anyway, probably because I'd inherited genes that stubbornly coded for delusional confidence. I had no doubt I would someday be a successful family man. I'd only need to do exactly the opposite of anything I'd seen my parents do.

But as it turned out, neither of us had kids. Character flaws emerged in Monica's first spouse that made him an unsuitable partner, and my first wife and I were just biologically unlucky.

By the time Monica and I found each other, we were at the age some circles refer to as 'reproductively geriatric', and with luck, it could be just possible to muster one pregnancy. Near-hits and false alarms got our hopes up only to be dashed time and again by unresponsive at-home pregnancy tests. For luck, Monica started using martini glasses to dip the test strips into, making our hopeful moments of truth classy affairs. But the strips remained stubbornly unchanged.

Eventually, I scheduled a procedure, we put the date on a calendar, and resolved that if we weren't pregnant by then, we'd never discuss having a child of our own again. When the day came, there were still only the two of us, and we went to the clinic together to memorialize the end of our parental ambitions. I remember being suitably somber and still during the ceremony that was tangibly arranging the finality of it all, but Monica handled our loss differently. She sat at the officiant's shoulder, and they carried on an amiable chat, during which questions like, "Don't those look weird to you?" or "How many of these have you seen?" and "How does this one measure up?" were answered cheerfully with nonchalant honesty.

From then on, we knew that in math for us, one plus one would always equal only two, and so informed, commenced with life together. Until Rhonda called.

Rhonda's nature naturally had made her a confidant and advisor for her students, and her librarian's office in the back became a quiet and safe space for them in times of need. A girl with a volatile family and a growing trouble had come to her, determined not to cut her problem short but to bring it to term. How could she do it, she asked, and how could she find anyone willing to adopt?

"Let me make a phone call," Rhonda told her.

And so, we met Matthew's birth mom and became pregnant, in some ways, and parents forever after, in every other.

We read a lot of child development books when we were new parents, and one of the most surprising assertions was that the earliest communication and nurturing of your child was the most important because a child's personality traits are pretty much set for life by their sixth birthday. Which made Monica and me nervous for a number of reasons, but mainly because even during those early formative years, Matthew was so very often full of crap.

We were lucky to have a preschool at the Lutheran church just down the road from us. The kids learned all their numbers and letters there before kindergarten and performed in musical pageants for parents and grandparents. They learned how to be students and how to interact with teachers and other kids. Some of the friends Matt made in preschool are still among his dearest.

It was a small school with just a handful of students, so the kids got plenty of attention from the teachers and volunteers. Matt loved it and would recount his day to me when I picked him up from daycare after work.

"Pastor Abby let me go up in the steeple and pull the rope that rings the bell today," Matt told me.

"Really?" I asked, impressed. "Is that something she lets anyone do?"

"Yep," he said. "Everybody takes turns doing it, she has a calendar for it. Today was my day."

"So what's it like?" I asked.

"Really loud, like boom-bonga-boom loud. Every time you pull the rope, it's so loud it hurts your ears. Your head goes 'blrrrzzz' inside even when you're done."

That was a little disturbing. But there were about twenty kids in the preschool, so if Pastor Abby had a calendar to rotate them all through for bell

Walking Wet

ringing, that would mean my kid wouldn't be subjected to ear damage more than about once a month. Still, I decided to ask about it.

When I saw her next, I said, "I'll bet it's great fun for the kids to go up in the steeple to ring the bell every day."

Pastor Abby looked at me quizzically. "Our church doesn't have a bell," she said.

Later, I confronted Matthew by telling him what the pastor had told me.

He blinked. "She should probably go look for it, then," he said.

He entertained me with another awkward fabrication not long after. Because his preschool let out at lunch, one of the daycare ladies would drive to the church just past the cornfield to pick up the kids.

"Was it Margaret or was it Mary that got you kids today?" I asked Matthew.

"Neither of them did," he told me. "Today, Tripp took us."

Tripp was one of his classmates. "How does that work?" I asked. "Tripp is four years old. How did he get a driver's license?"

"He doesn't need one. Tripp has a motorcycle."

"So he got eight of you onto a motorcycle?"

"No. He made trips. That's why he's named Tripp."

My parenting books said that experimenting and exercising one's imagination was a natural and healthy part of a child's early development. It was important, though, to listen gently and nonjudgmentally, and to guide your child lest they confound what's real with fantasy. So, when he was a kindergartner and he told me they had a guest teacher that day because "Miss Hummel got her truck impounded," I asked for clarification.

"Is that true," I asked, gently and nonjudgmentally, "or did you just pull that out of your butt?"

Matthew beamed. "Pulled it straight out of my butt," he said.

With Matt in kindergarten, according to my parenting books, time was running short to mold Matthew's personality before it set for life. Whatever becomes of a kid with such a cheerful yet casual relationship to facts and a penchant for embellishment? He becomes a criminal, I worried, or maybe a writer.

But making things up wasn't all Monica and I had to worry about. We suspected that Matthew entertained impulsive behavior more often than his classmates, fears that were confirmed at an open house with a display of second-graders' classwork pinned onto a bulletin board. Apparently, it had been principal appreciation week, (I hadn't known there was such a thing) and the teacher had told her students to draw pictures of the school's principal, and to write a few lines of gratitude by way of a personal message below it.

The texts were penciled block letters that mostly said things like, 'Dear Mrs. Berry, Happy Principal Day! We love you!' or 'You are the best principal ever, Mrs. Berry!' and the drawings were invariably of a stick-figured woman with curly shoulder-length hair, smiling brightly, and holding flowers or waving cheerily.

Like any proud parents would, we scanned the bulletin board for the poster with our kid's name on it.

"Oh, my," Monica said when she found it. It wasn't like the others.

Matthew's stick-woman was seated on a chair in front of a desk, her hands on a keyboard and staring at a computer monitor. The text he'd printed below it read, "Dear Mrs. Berry. I know what you do in the office. I am there a lot."

"Well," I said, "the upside, is uh, that doesn't look like embellishment. That poster looks like the work of a kid with keen observation skills."

"It does," Monica agreed. "That's your upside?"

Even so, Mrs. Berry told us that Matt was one of her favorite students and that his visits to her office usually brightened her day. She recounted one to me when I saw her at a soccer game.

"Matt came to visit me again today," she said.

"Oh, no," I groaned.

"I was busy when he came in, so he went straight to his corner and got himself a book."

"Why was he there?"

"A couple of girls in his class had tied their shoelaces together. When they stood up, Matthew tipped them over onto the grass."

"I'm sorry," I said. "We'll talk to him."

"Oh, I know," Mrs. Berry said. "But it was kind of funny when I talked to him about it."

"Funny how?"

"Well, when I got off the phone," she said, "I asked him why he'd been sent to my office. Without even looking up from his book, he grumbled, 'Olivia and Zoey tied their shoes together. I tipped them over.'

"And I said, 'Yes, Matthew. The playground monitor told me. Why did you push them over?'

"He kept reading. 'Their shoes were tied together,' he said.

"I thought he was being evasive, so I asked again. 'Matthew, I want you to look at me and explain why-' and here I spaced and emphasized my words, 'why you.. pushed them.. over.'

"He put his book down and sighed as if more explanation was tiresome, furrowed his eyebrows at me, and spacing his words similarly said, 'Their shoes.. were tied.. together.'

"Then he picked his book up again, raised his eyebrows, and stared at me.

" 'Oh,' I said. 'Their shoes were tied together.'

" 'Exactly,' he said, and went back to reading his book."

"He 'exactlied' you?" I asked.

"He did, exactly," Mrs. Berry said. "Made my day."

Monica and I often worried that the molding we subjected Matthew to was being outpaced by the acceptance he was imposing on us. Even so, Matt eventually moderated and tamed his impulsiveness on his own, and his personality locked in (if that's what it really did) to make him a relatively pleasant young human.

Matt and I get along reasonably well, especially on hikes or trips together.

We just understand each other somehow. During the pandemic, when our school went to online classes, the two of us took a road trip to explore homelessness. I thought an immersive experience would be educational for him and possibly foster more understanding and empathy. Matt thought it would be a hoot.

"First thing we do is we push shopping carts together and tie plastic bags all over them to make ourselves a shelter," he said, excited about the prospect.

"I was thinking of just parking the truck at a Walmart and sleeping in the canopy," I said.

"Not me. I'm going whole hog on it. I'll get some cardboard too for sleeping on. They'll have a big cardboard squisher thingy in the back. It'll be awesome."

"Hmm," I said.

Five hundred miles south of home, we pulled into a Walmart parking lot, and it wasn't difficult to find the 'homeless section.' We stopped next to a forty-year-old, loose-paneled RV with a spiderwebbed windshield and duct-taped side windows. The store's street sweeper had been detouring around it long enough that a grimy berm had been built up, like a curving property line. Inside the line, a greasy, stubbled guy was sitting on the asphalt and leaning back on one of the RV's flat tires. I noticed that he hadn't thought of, or maybe just wasn't inclined to get himself any cardboard to sit on from the big squisher thingy out back. A dozen or so other people sat or scuffed between questionably drivable vehicles scattered around the section of the lot.

Most of the cars, vans, and RVs had cardboard or trash bags wedged up against their windows, making it impossible to see if anyone was inside them. Except for the driver's side window on a silvery-gray or possibly once-blue Chevy Cutlass. Two drooly pit bull snouts snuffled and slobbered their enthusiasm at us over the barely lowered window. The car bounced and rocked slightly side to side.

"Here's home!" exclaimed Matthew.

I was contemplating the value of deep understanding and empathy and re-evaluating just how immersive this experience needed to be.

"The hell it is," I said. "We're not staying here."

"I am. Look, there's a rack for shopping carts, and there's none in it. That's a great start for my shelter. I'll need to find some string or something to tie the cardboard up to it."

"Whatever. We're camping at the state park."

Matt's enthusiasm was undimmed. "That could be fun for you," he said. "You can leave me here."

"I'm not leaving a sixth grader out- well, out here by himself," I told him. "It doesn't look safe."

"The store is open all night. If you're worried, just leave me a bunch of money and I can, like, put on a mask and go inside and buy something whenever I want."

"I don't think leaving you alone with money out here would make it any safer. Let's go get a hamburger."

While we were waiting in the drive-thru line, his wristwatch alarm went off again. "Beep-beep-beep-beep-beep." It beeped for sixty seconds, stopped, then started up again.

"It does that every day. Why does it keep doing that?" I asked.

"It's 'cause I have two of them." He showed me the two watches he was wearing, stacked on his wrist.

"What? Why?"

"Well, this one," he said, pointing to the lower one, "I set for 4:12, so I could tell if the school bus was late letting me off at home every day. But then I was messing around with it and one of the buttons popped off and now I can't shut it off, so it beeps now for a full minute every day at 4:12."

"But now you have two of them."

"Yeah. So, then I went on Mom's Amazon and got the exact same watch again, and I set this one," pointing to the other watch, "for 4:13 because Nicole the bus driver doesn't like it when my watch goes off on the bus, especially after I couldn't turn it off. So, I set this one for 4:13, when I'm supposed to be off the bus and at the mailbox."

"So, it only goes off on the bus if you're dropped off late."

"Right. But then I was wondering if the first watch was like a lemon or something, so I was fiddling around with the buttons on this new one to see if it was any better, and then a button popped off it just like it did on the old one. Now I can't turn the alarm off on this one either, so it goes off and beeps for a minute every day, too."

"So, why are you wearing both of them?"

"Because. Now this new one has a button missing, and it goes off just like my old one does, which means now the old one is just as good as this new one. So I can't throw the old one away now, can I?"

"It's amazing how much sense that makes," I said.

Matt didn't catch the sarcasm. "Right, see? And because they are equal, I have to wear both of them."

"Huh. Well, that's just some kind of-" I was going to say stupid, but I couldn't. It wasn't not stupid for sure, but it sounded too much like something I would do. Change a few particulars, drop in 'truck' for 'watch' and 'Craigslist' for 'Amazon', and the story would go a long way towards explaining the hulks parked in my driveway.

"-genius," I finished.

"I know, right? Nicole thinks it's stupid, though."

Matthew

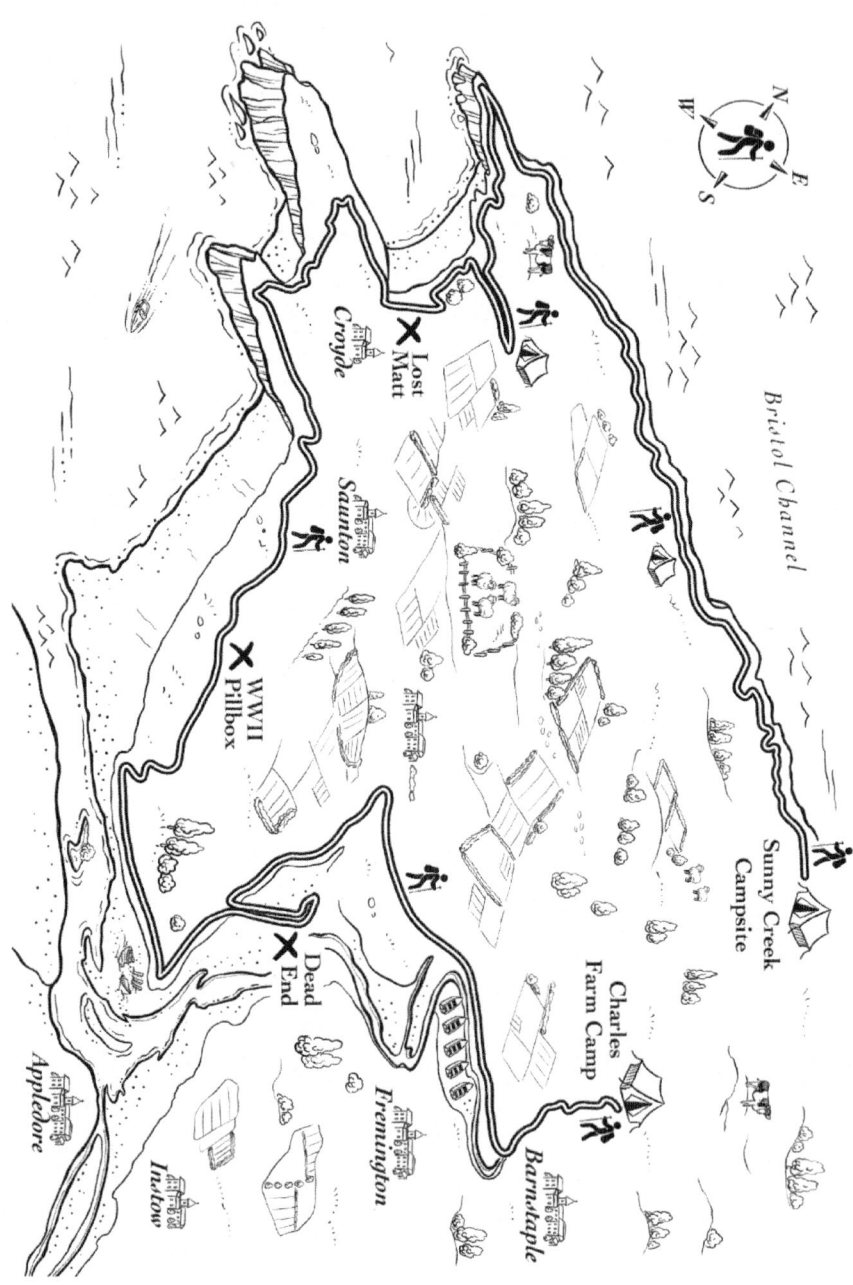

Trust in God and Keep Your Bowels Clear

```
5 ⋯ DAYS WALKING
64 ⋯ PATH MILES WALKED
83 ⋯ TOTAL MILES WALKED
```
https://www.southwestcoastpath.org.uk/walksdb/138/

Rhonda had found us a cheery campsite beside a creek a few miles upstream of town. This was another idiosyncrasy of the trail that I hadn't much considered before: that we would hike the trail, but not sleep beside it.

Camping was very efficient when I'd hiked the Pacific Crest Trail. There, tent sites are free and scattered all along the trail. On the PCT, we'd just walk along, and around late afternoon start looking for a campsite. We rarely camped more than fifty yards or so from the trail. In England, almost all of the Southwest Coast Path is routed on privately owned land, and although the property owners accommodated us walkers tromping through, they wouldn't take to us squatting overnight with a tent. There were dedicated RV sites and campgrounds, and some working farms that allowed camping for the path's hikers, but they usually weren't right on the path. This day, for instance, Matthew and I hiked the twelve miles from Porlock to Lynton. But because the camps we were hiking from and walking to were a few miles off trail, we walked sixteen and a half miles total. Still, it was nice coming into camp and seeing that Rhonda already had my tent set up on a grassy pitch.

She was on the grass, sitting and chatting with Justin and Emma, two hikers who were also out hiking the entire Southwest Coast Path. The other hikers we'd met on the path were doing just a section of it, not just the locals but the foreign travelers as well. I was beginning to wonder if we were weird, so it was nice to meet others like us trying to hike the whole thing.

Rhonda has yet to meet the person who doesn't like talking to her, so it didn't take long to hear their stories. Emma had started in Minehead and, like us, was hiking the path in the usual counter-clockwise direction. Justin had started two months before in Poole, where we were aiming to finish, and had hiked the coast in the opposite direction.

He was a single guy in his forties with a smallish mutt trekking the path with him. They would finish in Minehead the next day. After that, Justin would take a few more days of holiday before going back to work. He was an investment banker from Scotland.

"I'll bet you're looking forward to getting back home and out of that little tent you've been sharing with your dog. I'm sharing a tent with him," Rhonda said, gesturing towards me. "I've only spent one night in the tent, and I already miss my house."

"I don't mind the tent, not really," Justin said. "When we're not hiking, Thatcher and I live in my van. It's nice, but we're used to close quarters."

"Really? It wouldn't work for us. We have horses and too much stuff. And we were always told that making house payments was the best investment we could make, but you probably know better, being an investment banker. So, what should we have been doing?"

"Oh, a house really is a great investment. Tax structures, high demand, and limited supply, you know. I bought a bungalow a while back and lived in it out in the country myself for a bit. And then Covid came, and we went into lockdown. At first, I thought, 'Isn't this lucky? Just as well I got this place in time to work from home.'

"Everyone in banking got used to working remotely, but it ended up boring as hell, just sitting there alone in the house with Thatcher. Thatch loved it. Having me home every day, all day, was fine by him, but it was driving me a wee bit mental. And I started thinking, 'What's the point of being able to work remotely if I'm just sitting on my arse at home all the time?' I wasn't going into the office, but it didn't feel like I was working remotely. I was just stuck in a different room."

"But you didn't have to commute," Rhonda said.

"Yeah, the commute. Well, commuting to work had never really been a problem until I bought the house and moved out of Glasgow. Before that, when I lived in my van, I'd have it close by to transit on weekdays. So it was never an issue getting into the office on time. It was when I bought the house in the countryside that commuting became a bit of a nightmare. Plus, living in the van was a lot cheaper, with less upkeep, and I could move whenever I wanted. It had everything Thatcher and I needed.

"When everyone could go back to the offices, our firm stayed remote. I moved my stuff back into the van and put the bungalow up for sale. Now, I really am remote. I can live and work from anywhere, and I do."

"Did you have trouble selling the house?"

"Not at all, and it went for a decent price. Very decent. Like I said, a house is a great investment. I just don't want to be stuck living in one."

"But what if you had a family?" I asked. "You know, a wife and kids? You couldn't live in a van then, could you?"

"Not easily, though I know families that do," Justin said. "I've nothing against having a family, but I'm happy by myself as it is. When I'm done walking tomorrow, I'll go back to my van in Poole and take the ferry to France. We'll be somewhere in Bordeaux when I get back to work."

"Whoa, not bad," I said.

"Matthew plans to have a bunch of kids and live in a school bus," Rhonda said.

"That does sound pretty spot on," Justin said.

Rhonda turned to Emma. "What about you? Would you live in a school bus?"

"We don't have school buses here, like you have in America," she said, "A double could do the trick, though it wouldn't be nice to park. If I lived here, anyway."

"You don't live here, then? I assumed you were British."

"Oh, I'm British as crumpets and tea. But I've been living abroad since I finished university. I'm based in Guatemala now, but I grew up in a tiny village near Beaminster, just twenty minutes off the Coastal Path."

"How did that happen?" I asked. "You just woke up one day and said, 'I'm going to live in Guatemala?'"

"Not exactly. But even as a kid, I'd always wanted to live in some exotic and faraway place. If that makes sense."

"I think so," Rhonda said.

"So I took a job as a hostess on a cruise ship, along the Pacific coasts of Central America to San Francisco and up to Alaska. My favorite parts were the shore visits. Eventually, I took a different job as a tour guide. I even led a tour in Seattle a couple of times."

"So, how did you like Seattle?" I asked.

She shrugged. "Meh."

"Not exotic enough?" Rhonda asked.

"Not different enough," Emma said. "In Seattle, it was too easy to imagine that the village I grew up in was just up the road. Antigua, where I live now, isn't what I'd call exotic, but it's nothing like Beaminster."

"So, what do you do in Guatemala," I asked, "to make a living?"

Walking Wet

"I put on adventure tours, mostly for women's groups looking for environmental experiences. I'll set up itineraries, lodging, and travel, line up local guides, things like that. Then I go with them, usually hiking up and camping on volcanoes."

"Well, that sounds different," I said. "How do you like it?"

"So far, so good," she said. She reached over to pat Thatcher's belly.

I looked over at Matthew. He'd set his tent up and had gotten some of the stuff from his pack tossed into it before getting a text from a friend back home. He was lying on the grass atop his half-emptied backpack, double-thumbing the phone in his hands.

Since Justin had already hiked the entire path in front of us, I took the opportunity to pick his brain. He had more information than we could take in, but there were three practical items of consequence. First, we should quit cooking. Justin had taken to carrying just one packet of soup mix in case of emergencies. Instead of cooking dinner, he ate pasties (pronounced with a short *a*). A pasty is a cross between an American pot pie and a calzone, much like a handheld Hostess fruit pie, except filled with meat, potatoes, and veggies. They're cheap, convenient, and easy to find in every town along the path. I ended up eating a lot of them over there and came to believe they are Cornwall's greatest invention. History buffs may disagree, but even they would have to admit that it's so much easier to carry a pasty into camp than a steam locomotive, and that it's a much more enjoyable thing to eat.

Justin also told us it didn't rain as much at the other end of the path, the Poole end, as it did at this end near Minehead. The coastline there faces across to France and Spain, which were just then being roasted by a heat wave. The portion of coastline we were following was opposite to Ireland and Iceland, and our weather so far, squalls interspersed with sunbreaks or cold drizzle, certainly seemed more Icelandic than it was European. He also told us that we had a long stretch of flat trail not far ahead of us.

"That's where I'll get back on the path," Rhonda said. "I'll be recovered from your attempted murder by then."

***

Excited about what lay ahead, Matthew and I left early the next morning. A cross-country bicycle course marked with yellow flagging intersected our path, and as it appeared to run roughly parallel, we decided to follow it through some bushes, then up a hill to the top of a sheep pasture. The ocean views from the beaches and clifftops along the Southwest Coast Path are undeniably beautiful, but Matthew and I are Americans after all, and were beginning to find it a bit predictable. We were used to hiking in wilderness, where navigation was more crucial and challenging, and the path had led us to overconfidence. We even made up a little poem and recited it to each other, using our best attempts at Cornish accents:

"Looz yer maps? Tha's awl roight.
Keeps yer sheeps on yer left,
'n yer sea on yer roight!"

The bike course ducked into some brush, behind some cottages, across a camping field, then straight uphill through a sheep pasture before turning back on itself at the top of a headland. By the time I got there, where following the bike course further would put the sea on the wrong side, Matt was out of sight. He could have cut rightward, the quickest way to regain the path, or he might have gone left to travel the shortest distance to the day's destination. Or he may have continued straight on to the farm lane dead ahead. I couldn't see him anywhere. I tried texting, but was out of cell range.

At home, while I was researching the trip, I found a Verizon cell service map showing all of England fully covered. Field testing demonstrated that the map was criminally misleading. If you're out in the countryside along the coast in England, you probably don't have cell service, period. It's surprising. Emma told us that her cell service in Guatemala was better than what we could get in Cornwall.

I guessed that Matt would go straight into the lane, so I continued on. Once in it, the lane proved to have a lot more mud in it than it had appeared to from the top of the headland. It also had more tractor wheel ruts and sheep manure. What it didn't have were any other human footprints. Matthew had gone a different way.

I didn't know where he was, and as I was out of cell range, he couldn't tell me. It was concerning. I'd lost contact with a fourteen-year-old boy, on his own and by himself in a foreign country. Unbidden, a cowardly hope occurred to me. If he was lost and without cell service, at least his mother wouldn't know.

Well, I thought, rationalizing the situation to myself. *Maybe it's good for him to practice independence.*

In the run-up to the trip, I'd done some research about walking in England, and knowing that some of our time would be spent in town and along streets, had looked up pedestrian injury statistics. It turned out that Americans are almost twice as likely to get run over and killed walking around their own neighborhoods as Brits are walking in theirs. And because I'd only seen English driving done on television, by chauffeurs in Rolls or by Formula One drivers on closed tracks, it had made sense to me at the time. But being there and seeing with my own eyes the narrowness of English roads and their absence of shoulders, and how the sidewalks suddenly switch sides of the road or disappear altogether, and how the roadside hedges make almost every corner blind; and after spending time in the back seat behind Duncan and

Walking Wet

experiencing the Britons' head-on method of determining yielding etiquette by playing chicken, it forced a revisitation.

How could it possibly be safer?

Possibly it was because their cars are, on average, smaller than the ones we drive back home in America. It's demonstrably healthier for pedestrians to be thumped by a Fiat than pulverized by a Hummer. Or maybe, I thought now, it was their lack of cell service. People crossing roads back home are usually wrapped up with their phones, and quite possibly, many of the motorists who run them over are as well.

That just wasn't possible here.

I looked at the downloaded British Ordnance Survey (OS) maps on my phone. The path was just ahead. I climbed over a gate, around the edge of a barley field, and back onto the official path. A couple of miles later, my phone chimed.

"Ding! Ding! Ding!" I'd walked into a random patch of cell service, and my phone was downloading messages that Matthew had sent.

[Where are you?]

[?]

[Now where are you?]

[Cell sucks here]

[Crap I'm in a town]

[Phone at 2 percent]

A long timestamp gap and then,

[Meet us there]

I texted my GPS lat-long coordinates back, but got no answer. Either he was out of cell service again, or his phone battery had died. He hadn't told me where he was or what he was doing, but I could make a few Holmesian deductions. When he'd left the bike racecourse, he'd likely used Google Maps instead of the detailed Ordnance Survey maps, as Google is more interactive and tells you which direction to go. But it uses up phone batteries at an alarming rate, especially when cell service is spotty. That would explain his phone dying after walking him into a town when there shouldn't have been a village within miles of the route we were supposed to be following.

It was also likely that he'd been in contact with Rhonda, and that the two of them were the 'us' that I was supposed to meet. Rhonda must have told him where she had made arrangements for our next campsite, the 'there' where I was supposed to meet them. It would have been nice if one of them had thought to tell me where 'there' was.

I called Rhonda, and it went to voicemail. Wherever she was now, she wasn't in cell range anymore either. I texted them both, telling them that I was on the path heading towards Barnstaple.

The path led into sand dunes and past a golf course. I lost the track again but kept on, meeting the occasional friendly cow, and eventually stumbled into a World War II training site for D-Day. Concrete pillbox bunkers were built against sand dunes to practice storming, and empty shell casings still littered the ground around them, even after eighty years. The site didn't look well-visited now, and the cows were using the pillboxes to scratch themselves on. I imagined that there must have been a road built into the area to get that much concrete hauled in. I found it and followed it for a while, but before long, it disappeared under a sand dune that had shifted onto it.

When I heard boat motors, I turned right and climbed over a series of loose sand dunes to the beach and then followed the shoreline to Crow Point, a sand spit nearly reaching across the estuarine mouth of the River Taw. If I'd had a raft, I would have paddled a short five hundred yards across to Instow, the town on the opposite bank. Keeping to the path, Instow would be a good twenty-two miles around the bay.

A long way around just to get over there, I thought. I needn't have groused about walking twenty-two miles to get to a town just a par five fairway across the water. As it turned out, I would be inefficiently off route for most of my way there anyway. I got myself there in fifty.

In the lee of the spit were a handful of small boats, just partially decked over dinghies and skiffs, really, each tied to a cinder block mired in the tidewater goo. Incredibly, people lived in them. The tide was out, and the boats had deep footprint tracks squelched into the mud leading away from them. Some also had parallel tracks returning to them, these sporting knee-high and goo-caked rubber boots on their bows.

I encountered the path again at a car park and was glad to be back on it. I hadn't been lost exactly, but being off the trail added to the anxiety of being out of touch with Rhonda and Matthew. Just past the car park, a construction detour sign had been placed on the dike, saying that it was closed ahead for work, but a look on my phone's OS map showed the trail veering right and following the shoreline anyway.

The embankment above the beach had been armored with what could only have been hand-placed rocks. I walked the whole length of it, almost two miles. It was about fifty feet wide from the foot of the armoring to the top of the slope, paved with dark gray rocks, roughly the size and shape of hat boxes. The rocks had all been placed on edge and fitted tightly together. It was difficult to walk on, but the dike at the top of the embankment was worse, grown over with tall, sharp-bladed sawgrass and rosehip brambles.

The dike armoring was impressive and must have been done before hydraulic-powered equipment had been available. I wondered how many workers had been on the job, how long it took them, where the rock had come from, and how they had gotten it there. It was impressive work, not just in scale but in quality as well. The rocks were similar in size and shape, but not uniformly identical. Fitting them together took not only hard work but skill, and a job so large would have required the kind of perseverance that only comes from professionalism and pride.

Hand laborers today are rarely afforded much respect for their work, and no one expects them to build anything that lasts, let alone endure a century of tides and storms. And it's a shame, really. Because right there was proof that they can.

The embankment hooked leftward, following a smaller tributary stream, and then abruptly ended where it had been removed. The island farm that the dike had protected for so many years had been converted to a tidewater nature preserve. Both OS and Google maps showed the trail continuing across the four-hundred-foot-wide breach, straight through the mud and an obviously deep and unwadeable channel.

Stupid maps. So much for being back on the path, I thought. I turned around to retrace the last two miles of progress, my anxiety rising again like the tidewater beside me.

This time, I walked past the 'Trail Closed Ahead' sign and found a guy in a mini excavator, nonchalantly mowing the sawgrass atop the inner dike that doubled as the new path. Past this minor hiccup, the dike continued around to the Tarka Trail, once a railroad line but now a paved bicycle path following the estuarine shoreline.

Lining the path was a motley parade of old boats, from modest sailboats to hulking tugs. They were immovably beached, their bows pulled up along the tidewater margins of mud. It was obvious that decades had passed since any of them had weighed an anchor, but they were all lived-in now. Some leaned in the mud at awkward angles, their battered undersides exposed, while others, in better shape, had solar panels, potted garden vegetables, clotheslines, or children's toys on their fore or aft decks.

I thought of Matthew and his possibly serious plan to live in an old school bus, and it made me wonder if these boats' inhabitants were content. Had they chosen to live this way, or were they adapting to a tough housing market? Compared to the little boats tied to cinder blocks miles back at the spit, I could see how families could live on these derelict vessels. These boats didn't look so lonely. It was at least as easy to imagine Matthew starting a family in one of these bigger boats as in an old school bus.

The path ahead was paved and dead level, and the monotony of its surface made my feet ache. But nervousness washed over me again and quickened my pace. Being out of touch with Matthew, who was just fourteen and alone in a foreign land, was a constant worry.

He's safer being lost here in England than he would be back home, I told myself again, but it didn't alleviate any stress. The source of my anxiety wasn't just where he was, but who he was. Matthew is the kind of kid that, if anyone posted a video of brain surgery on YouTube, would watch half of it and then cheerfully start in with it on one of his buds that he'd just talked into being his patient.

"I *got* this," he'd reassure them, revving a bone saw above their skull.

It had been several hours since I'd known definitively what he was up to, and by this time, he could have taken a stab at almost anything.

The path squeezed through a narrow strip between mudflats and grounded boats on my right and a traffic-laden highway on my left. A double-decker bus passed by, and I thought, *Matt could be on that bus right now.*

I watched it go around the corner ahead, and nobody was surfing up on its roof. I grimaced, wondering how many other parents would have felt compelled to check.

Finally, I got a return text from Rhonda with the name of the farm campsite I was to meet them at. To get there would be another four miles on the path, then three more uphill through town and into the countryside. I sighed. I'd walked twenty-five miles that day already.

Rhonda and Matthew were gone when I got to the farm, but I was relieved to see their backpacks dropped off in the camping field. I was greeted by Charles, the dairy farmer-turned-campsite-host/owner, who told me that they'd arrived and left again in a taxi.

Being an ex-dairyman myself, I was looking forward to chatting with him. But with thirty miles of sand, mud, rock hat boxes, gravel, and pavement just behind me, something else was top of mind.

"You wouldn't sell beer here, would you?" I asked.

"You're needin' a beer, are ye?" Charles asked, his right eyebrow arching in amusement.

"Just now, yes."

"I don't drink beer meself. Maybe a bit o' wine now and then, but not much for a pint."

"Me neither, usually."

Charles and I chatted about dairy farming and his farm's transition from milk production to an RV park and camping site. The changes in dairy farming in the United Kingdom were surprisingly similar to those back home in the United States. Dairy farmers deal with a lot of uncontrollable variables, a challenge that Charles and I had accepted. Working with and depending on animals for your livelihood just isn't a safely predictable means of making a living.

Livestock, besides being hungry and expensive to feed, can injure themselves or maim their keepers, succumb to infection, jump fences, or get spooked and run off in a stampede. Once, my entire herd broke out of the barn and rampaged down an unlit street on a moonless night straight into a pair of

Walking Wet

oncoming headlights. The motorist at first mistook their eyes for twinkle lights bobbing on a trailer in front of him, then slammed on his brakes as the herd came onto him out of the darkness.

Thankfully, he'd been able to stop his car before plowing into them, but he couldn't avoid the collision. The lead cows broke over the car's hood and windshield, pressed on by stampede physics and their fellows running full-tilt from behind. Had they been wild bison, they would have continued over and around, eventually to thunder off into the distance. But dairy cows don't have that kind of stamina, so my herd's stampede pretty much fizzled out at their first distraction.

Not that it did the driver or his wife any good. The first chaotic moments of tumbling bovines denting in the hood and cracking the windshield had abated, but my girls weren't finished. They were panting and belching when I got there and had the vehicle surrounded, which they were casually and systematically vandalizing. I pointed my flashlight at the windshield, but it was difficult to make out the couple still trapped inside.

"You can lay off the horn," I yelled through a kaleidoscopic curtain of cow slobber and shattered safety glass. "It only encourages them."

Charles' herd had treated him to an adventure much the same, except that his farm is closer to a busy town than mine was, and his girls ran through its streets during the daytime.

There's a lot of great and desirable things about living the life of a farmer. It requires just about the perfect mix of intellectual and physical exertions, and it's probably the best environment for raising an active and industrious family. Farmers are self-directed, self-motivated, self-supervised, and largely worthy of respect. Apart from all the sensual things like the smell of hay ready to bale, or the sight of distance across property I owned, or the methane smell of camaraderie from a herd lying in the shade chewing their cuds, that respect is what I miss the most.

I didn't get out much when I was a farmer, so I was home on the farm for most of my interactions with people, usually sales reps for fertilizers or feedstuffs, equipment and electronics consultants, veterinarians, or accountants. They would ask me to consider proposals, wonder if I'd ever thought of something, or ask if I'd like to do them a favor, a softly respectful approach to conversation that I became accustomed to and adopted as my own preferred method to converse.

But I'm not a farmer anymore, and people tell me what to do, where to go, what to think. I don't get, 'Would you consider's' anymore; instead, I hear 'You need to's. The reverence and a lot of the politeness are gone, and it gravels me.

The closest I get now is a neighbor who steps into my yard and asks, "Hey, you know what you ought to do?"

And each time he does it, I think, *Yeah, kick your butt off my property*. But I just hang my head and listen, knowing it wouldn't do any good as I'm no longer a farmer. He could be well off my property, and I'd still see and hear the man.

Lord, I miss farming sometimes.

Our accents may have originated five thousand miles apart, but Charles and I understood each other perfectly because we talked in the style farmers do with each other, a style that most everyone else may wish to consider. We shared experiences of episodes: crop failures, equipment breakdowns, no-show hired help, and how we'd handled them. Maybe not always with perfect equanimity exactly, but knowing that they were things we could learn from and make adaptations for. But some things are just harder to adapt to.

Advancements of all kinds have pressured not just dairymen, but farmers of all commodities, and the public's common but understandable misconception about it all is that advancements winnow out the farmers who can't change with the times.

My non-farmer friends, now a majority in my life, seem to picture a stodgy old stubbly white guy in bib overalls and a baseball cap, standing in a bean field maybe, and struggling with a probe attached to a computer tablet.

"Dod derned techno-logy!" he shouts, shaking the tablet. "Back in the day, I'd just TASTE the dag-gummed dirt and spray whatever danged fertilizer on it that I wanted to. Dern this devil contraption to all tarnation!" Then he chucks the tablet onto the ground and stomps it in with an unlaced muck boot. "I quit!" he says and putters off into the sunset.

But really, it's not that simple. For farmers, it's usually not a matter of what they can do, but what they can stomach.

The advancements made compulsory by the economics of farming aren't always good for the land farmed, and almost never for the farmed animals. I was dairy farming when the technology for extended shelf-life milk emerged, and that advancement required milk that only young cows could produce. All my girls over five years old had to be culled for hamburger. I loved dairy farming, but that made it a love too costly.

I may be an old white stubbly guy, but I'm no Luddite. And neither is Charles. It's as one of the most profound thinkers in our time has observed:

"I would do anything for love, but I won't do that."

Truly, we old farmers are a bunch of Meat Loafs.

Charles' land, a family legacy for generations, was a source of pride for him, but he sometimes felt unfaithful to it, hosting campers like me on it. Especially around four in the afternoon, when he should have been milking cows, as it was then.

Walking Wet

"Yep. I'd rather be milking cows right now myself," I said.

"Beats sitting here talking to each other," he agreed. We sat together in silence for another long moment.

"At least you still have your land and a place here we can sit together," I said.

"Had to sell out of your place, did ye?"

"Something like that. My ex-wife is on it." I looked around at the dairy barns and tractor sheds that Charles had repurposed for holiday campers. "There are dog kennels and an airstrip on my farm now."

Charles barked out a laugh. "Sorry not to be havin' that beer for ye," he said.

Our conversation meandered into politics, something I often avoid at home. "Explain to me your Mr. Trump," Charles demanded.

"I'm not sure how it works here, but we have two parties in America. One has all the answers, but mostly for the wrong questions. The other is asking some of the right questions, but their answers are wrong." I shrugged. "What do you do?"

Charles wouldn't be mollified. "But how could he bamboozle you lot?"

"It's not so much that he fooled everybody. A lot of folks voted for him, knowing all about his faults. They just want things to change, to go back towards the way they used to be."

"They want horses and buggies?"

I shook my head. "Not that far back. But quite a bit back, I think." I paused, trying to think of a way to explain. Charles waited, without a trace of impatience.

"We had this old TV show back in America that centered around a sheriff in a country town, and the storylines were about the townspeople doing mostly everyday things. It was relaxing to watch."

"I'll bet it was," Charles said.

"Anyway, if you watch an old rerun of it today, what's really striking is just how relaxed and unhurried they all were. A mechanic might spend the whole day adjusting a carburetor. A barber could spend an afternoon sitting on a bench in front of his shop. And everyone was fine with that, they felt secure, and it was respectable. Nowadays, there's gig work, performance quotas, requirements for overvalued degrees, people living in their cars. Holding any of those Mayberry jobs today and doing them how they were portrayed in that show would lead to an opioid overdose or worse."

"People voted for Trump because they want to sit around like the characters in Mayberry?"

"Really? You've seen the show here?"

"Sure. We traded 'Benny Hill' for it," he laughed.

"Funny! Yeah, well, they'd like to be able to, anyway."

"Don't wanna work hard for your American dream, do they?"

"They don't want to work hard for nothing. It seems like today, there isn't an American dream for anyone with a Mayberry job. You could bust your hump and never afford a house or support a family."

"There be more posh Americans on holiday here than there are Brits in America," Charles pointed out.

"Right, but it's not that way for everyone. And if they're not posh already, it's hard for them to imagine they ever could be. And that's tough to take if you're exhausted because you've spent your day pressure washing engine blocks or something, and then see other people riding bikes after work for exercise. Or watch actors on TV talk about how hard they'd worked on their last movie role. Really? They'd just been paid ten million dollars. Would they have rather shoveled rocks for it?"

"Or milked cows, eh?" Charles said.

"Exactly. So, a lot of people back home were thinking things like that while they voted. For all the talk of equity in America today, they think life is less equitable than it was in Mayberry. And they'd like a return to it."

"I'll bet there are lots who wouldn't. Women, minorities, gays, lesbians, shooting victims…"

"True enough. But economy-wise, dignity of labor, wealth division, local manufacturing jobs, and home ownership. That's what motivates a majority of them, I think."

"You think? You mean, you hope. You hope they're not Nazis and bigots," Charles said, not laughing at all.

I'd had a long, long day. I was five thousand miles from home and had just walked more than thirty miles. And I found myself somehow defending my country's collective wisdom and morality to a Briton who clearly had his own opinions about us. I wondered how this would have gone if he'd just given me a damned beer.

"Okay, you're right," I told him. "That is what I hope. But I don't think that hope is terribly misplaced. Because most of the people I live with in my country just aren't Nazis or bigots, or misogynists. And from what I've seen so far on this trip, it's not the case in your country either. How would you explain Nigel Farage?"

Charles could see how tired I was, and he put his hand on my back. He inhaled a big breath into his chest, and it squared his shoulders. He held it a moment, then let himself deflate. "Don't know that I could," he said. "I don't think I could explain Boris Johnson to you either, or Brexit, or Liz Truss."

We just sat there quietly together for a moment.

"I wish you had beer here."

Charles barked his trademark laugh again. "Right now, I wish I did meself. We'll just have to do what me grandmother always told me."

"Which is?"

"Trust in God and keep your bowels clear."

I asked Charles for an interpretation, of course, which he readily supplied.

"Means ye mind to what's ye's suited and leave the rest to God."

It was my turn to put a hand on Charles' back, just between his shoulder blades. "Plain and simple wisdom is rarely followed," I lamented.

"That's a problem for Him," Charles told me. "Just ye mind your bowels is clear."

And we just sat there together like two guys in Mayberry, talking a little and doing even less, a couple of old dairy farmer Meat Loafs.

Trust in God and Keep Your Bowels Clear

Walking Wet

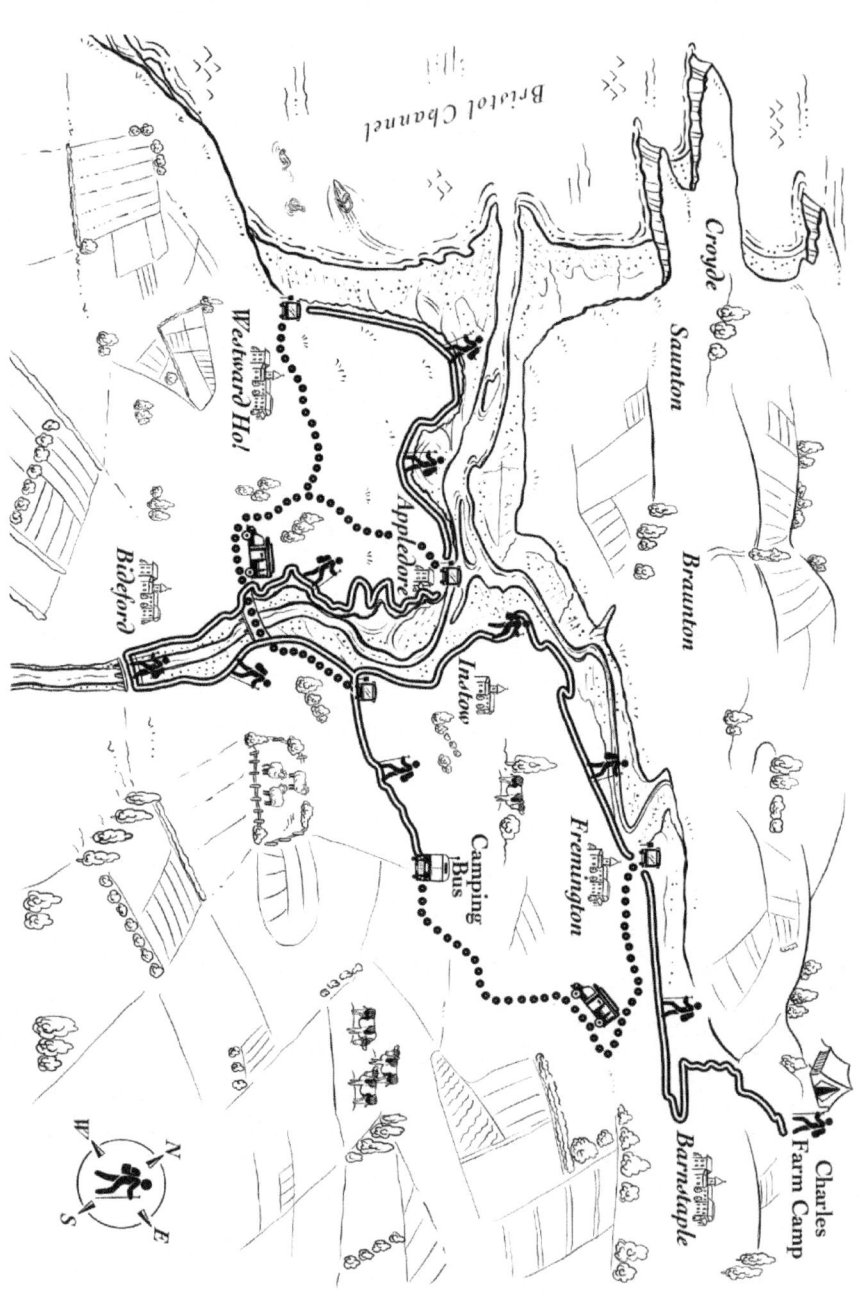

A Victory Over Smugness

11 ··· DAYS WALKING
102 ··· PATH MILES WALKED
137 ··· TOTAL MILES WALKED
https://www.southwestcoastpath.org.uk/walksdb/142/

A taxi drove through the farm gates and into the camping field, and Rhonda and Matt got out, burdened with takeout dinner boxes and brown bottles.

Charles stood and stretched his back. "There's ye beer," he said and walked off, marking the end of our conversation. I opened one and sat back for an update.

It turned out that Matt had been on buses a lot that day. His phone battery had gone dead searching for cell service when we had none, so he had no map to get back onto the path after he'd lost the trail. He was walking along the side of a road when a bus came up from behind and stopped for him.

"The bus driver knew I was an American somehow and told me I should walk on the other side of the road. 'Everyone will tell you to stay on the left,' he said, 'but if you are walking, you can't see cars coming up behind you. And that's not nice, innit?' Then he asked where I wanted to go."

"What did you tell him?"

"I told him that I would be going somewhere up ahead, but I didn't know where exactly because my phone went dead before my aunt texted me where to go. He told me to plug in and charge my phone there on the bus, but I didn't have a phone cord. So he drove a few more stops, and said, 'Curly, you go in there and buy yourself a phone cable. Then wait right here for the next bus to pick you up. You'll be able to plug in and call your auntie then, right?' So that's what I did."

"He called you Curly?"

"Uh-huh. But before he picked me up, a truck driver called me Muppet."

"Interesting," I said. "I was a little worried."

"Ha! There's nothing to worry about over here in England, remember? You said nobody would shoot me."

"Yes, but just remember you are a foreigner in a foreign country, and there are bound to be some things that are different here. You could get into something over your head. Understand?"

"Uh-huh," he said again, nodding. But it wasn't an 'uh-huh, I understand that I need to be careful' uh-huh. It was an 'I understand you're an old worry-wort ignoramus dumdum' uh-huh.

England, what we'd seen of it so far anyway, seemed somehow gentler or more civilized than back home. The cars and trucks were smaller and less intimidating, the houses and shops seemed cozier and homier, and the dogs we'd met here in England seemed friendlier and better behaved. Even the vegetation around us, including the roadside weeds and hedgerows, seemed softer, less prickly and thorny than the plant life back home. Matthew had invented a game he called 'Nettled or Not', where he'd walk alongside hedges and repeatedly stick his hand into them to find nettles.

"Not. Not. Not," he'd say." Then, "Nettles," when he got stung. And then he'd keep right on walking and sticking his hand back into the hedge. "Not. Not…, .." Even the nettles had less sting than the ones back home did. I worried that Matt would be lulled into inattentiveness and over-confidence, a twin threats for which he was especially at risk.

"Just be careful and try not to be over-confident," I said. "We're new here and there's things here you don't know, and you just don't know what you don't know."

"Duh. Nobody knows what they don't know."

"No, I don't mean that. What I mean is that there might be things here, like culture or customs or laws that are not only unfamiliar to you, but that you didn't even know existed."

"Uh-huh. It's hard to be familiar with things that don't exist."

That last 'uh-huh' meant 'You're not only an old worry-wort ignoramus dumdum, but now you are boring me as well.'

My brain was weary. I'd carried it thirty-two miles that day while it worried about my kid's whereabouts and the stress had it frazzled. Then it got shoved into a political debate before finally getting rehydrated with beer. Matthew's brain had spent most of its day riding buses around and playing video games on a smartphone. There may be times when my brain doesn't know what it doesn't know, but this wasn't one of them. This sparring with a cocky teenager's brain was chronically familiar, and it knew exactly what to expect. It expected defeat.

A Victory Over Smugness

"Just-" I said.

"Just, what?"

"Just trust in God and keep your bowels clear."

Matthew looked back at me, his face deadpan.

"Uh-huh," he said.

We set up our tents, and after dinner, I washed my clothes in the calving shed-turned-shower blocks. But the day's overcast sky gave way to evening rain, so I hung the laundry to dry inside the dome tent I shared with my sister, further crowding the already cramped space.

We lay there under damp socks and underwear, Rhonda catching up on news from home and scrolling Facebook, while I listened to the rain pelting the tent fabric. It sounded like we were under a gentle cascade of raisins.

This is summer in England, I thought. There had been rain showers each day on the trip so far, and heavy dew each morning. I knew my clothes weren't getting dry enough and would turn rancid sooner or later. I sniffed the air.

"It wasn't me," Rhonda said.

"No, I was wondering if my clothes were starting to stink."

"Starting? Your nose is a little slow to the party. They've been there."

"Well, I've always said there's no incentive to be the best-smelling person in a tent."

"Obviously. And you've no longer a reason to keep proving the point."

I fished my phone and reading glasses out of my backpack.

"The weather forecast is for more of this," I said. "For the next sixteen days, actually."

"You got a sixteen-day forecast?"

"Yeah. On the British Met Office site."

"Hmm. I'm thinking that tomorrow is downhill to the path, and then it's flat," Rhonda said. "So, I'd like to hike tomorrow, and then find an Airbnb place or something to stay in for a couple days. We could use that as a base camp and make forays onto the trail from there."

"Sounds good."

Rhonda showed me the map on her phone screen. "The path leads around this bay, in sort of a big 'S' shape. We should make our base around here," she said, pointing.

We found another camping farm almost exactly where she'd placed her finger, and this one had an old bus that they had converted to a living space.

"Matthew's going to love this," Rhonda said. "He always says he wants to live in a bus."

***

We expected the flat and monotonous Tarka Trail to be kind to Rhonda, but it wasn't. We had made the five miles downhill from Charles' farm and through the town just fine. But once back to the shoreline path, Rhonda began having problems. Maybe her feet had seen how we had abused her heart on our first day out and they were afraid to be next on our hit list. They protested by cramping up and hobbling her to make sure they'd come to no harm.

"Maybe you can watch me walk?" she asked hopefully. "My feet feel like someone's put them in a log splitter. Maybe give me some pointers."

I watched her take a few steps, paying close attention to her gait. A Geisha girl came to mind, possibly constipated.

"Well?"

"You should add fiber to your diet and maybe buy yourself a kimono," I said.

"I so appreciate your expert advice."

"Or you could pull up your panties instead of walking with them down around your ankles."

"I'll just suck it up," she said. "How awful can it get?"

Pretty awful. I watched her shuffle another five miles to Fremington, a testament to my tolerance for witnessing pain. Fremington is a former train station on the old Tarka Line. The ticket office and waiting rooms had been quaintly restored and converted to coffee and pastry shops. Fronting the bay, the old switch yard and sidings had been smoothed over and planted with lawn and adorned with flower gardens and park benches. We stopped and were afforded long views across the bay.

I'd passed dozens of inhabited derelict boats beached along the shoreline the day before, but today we'd passed only one. I'd thought that derelict boats would have grounded themselves more or less randomly along the shore and be distributed evenly, not absent on this side of the bay and stacked almost shoulder to shoulder on the other.

"Where do you think Matthew is by now?" Rhonda asked.

I texted him. "He's in Instow," I said.

"So, he's almost to the camping bus already," Rhonda said. "Let's call a taxi."

***

Over the next few days, I made bus forays to finish walking the sections between Fremington and around the bay through Bideford and Appledore and back out to the ocean coast and the exuberantly named town of Westward Ho!, which didn't appear to be a town at all. It looked to me like a bunch of developers in the fifties or sixties had slapped up high-rise hotels and condos on a buildable strip of land along the beach, but nobody came. I was greeted only by a binman in a hi-vis orange jumpsuit and a security guard when I got there. But it was raining cats and dogs, and the wind was howling, so it could have been that we three were the only ones dumb enough to be outside in it.

While I was stitching the path together with lonely wet slogs and bus rides, Rhonda and Matt made touristy taxi forays, enabling them to chat with the reasonable population of folks who weren't outside in the rain. They found an interesting explanation about the boats.

Under maritime law, a boat that breaks free of its moorings or otherwise drifts off with no one aboard is considered an abandoned vessel, and as such can be claimed (with reasonable efforts to find the owner) by anyone that can salvage it. Virtually all the liveaboard boats I had walked past on the north side of the bay hadn't actually been washed ashore there as I had thought. The strongest winds and storms came out of the north, so boats with lost moorings or snapped anchor chains most often would find themselves blown to the south side of the bay, where we saw but one. Boats left to flounder on that side of the bay wouldn't survive long. Storm winds and waves would batter the boats against the land with force enough to stave in their hulls.

There were local marine salvage operators that claimed these unlucky boats, plucking them from danger with barges and cranes. Afterwards, they would find a spot to safely beach and tie them up on the north side of the bay. To hold possession of the boats, the salvage men would fix them up and install renters. When I had walked past the boats earlier, I had assumed that I was walking past the homes of squatters. Maybe some tenants didn't pay rent for a time, trading labor to repair, remodel, or otherwise make the boats more attractive and livable. But they weren't living in them for free.

Ownership of the tidewater mudflats that the boats were resting on is sort of an iffy thing. It's classified as property of the Crown, which I gather means it belongs to everyone or no one, depending possibly on whether the tide is in or out. It seems that functionally, the ownership of the mud under the boats is mainly determined by the resoluteness of the claimant. At any rate, it's an acceptable place to ground boats. And the ownership of these boats is well-established. They belong to the people that who saved them from destruction.

I'd come back from my forays and hang enough soggy gear and smelly clothes around the bus to give Matthew a taste of what living in a school bus with seven children could be like. I thought maybe he'd reconsider and recalibrate his ambitions. But I should have known better, having underestimated his optimism many times before.

"Living in a bus will be great, Dad," he said. "But definitely, I'll have a tent set up outside for the kitchen. That would make it perfect."

"Maybe you'd like living in a grounded boat?"

"Nope. Chickens, remember? Chickens can't swim. And how would I move it? Think about it, Dad."

***

Our last morning in the camping bus, I set off early to catch the transit bus to Appledore, thence to Westward Ho!, leaving Matt and Rhonda to catch me up

Walking Wet

later at a camp yet to be determined further along the path. The weather was playing its usual game, toggling between rain and brief dry spells.

Westward Ho!, with its condos and festive beach paraphernalia, was still almost eerily deserted. Even the security guard and binman from the day before were gone. The beach at Westward Ho! runs out of sand not far away from the mouth of the River Taw and Bideford Bay, and in front of the hotel, it's a solid rock shelf, cracked with fissures and tide pools. One of these tide pools had been chiseled out to be quite large. A solitary swimmer was in it, braving the cold water under the drizzle. It took five or six strokes for her to cross the pool. I watched her reach the edge, where she made an Olympic-style flip to make another lap.

The trail veered off the promenade and onto the frontage service road, then wound into woods broken by farmland, with sheep on the left and the ocean, steadfast and gray, on my right.

The path descended into the village of Buck's Mills, old buildings mostly, perched precariously on rocks and stilts driven into cracks in the rock bench, being washed by wind-driven waves. A youngish man wearing a tweed jacket with professor's elbow patches had a clipboard in hand and was lecturing an older group of citizens holding umbrellas about the nuances of building engineering and risk assessment. His face was wet but looked cheerful. The citizens were dry, but looked gloomy.

The path led me up and through more woods and, in a few miles, curiously, to a sewage treatment plant in the middle of nowhere. Its main pond was about the size of a pickleball court. I got out my phone, but the OS map didn't show any towns nearby. Maybe it was farm waste? I guessed at the pond's depth, did a volume estimate, and tried Googling how many pigs, or sheep possibly, it would take to make that much slurry. But I had no cell service, of course. I stood there in the drizzle for a while, staring stupidly at the raw sewage being churned and wondering why I was so annoyed.

The path became a lovely walk on an old lane, cobbled over with smooth softball-like rocks. A porcelain commemorative plaque identified it as Hobby

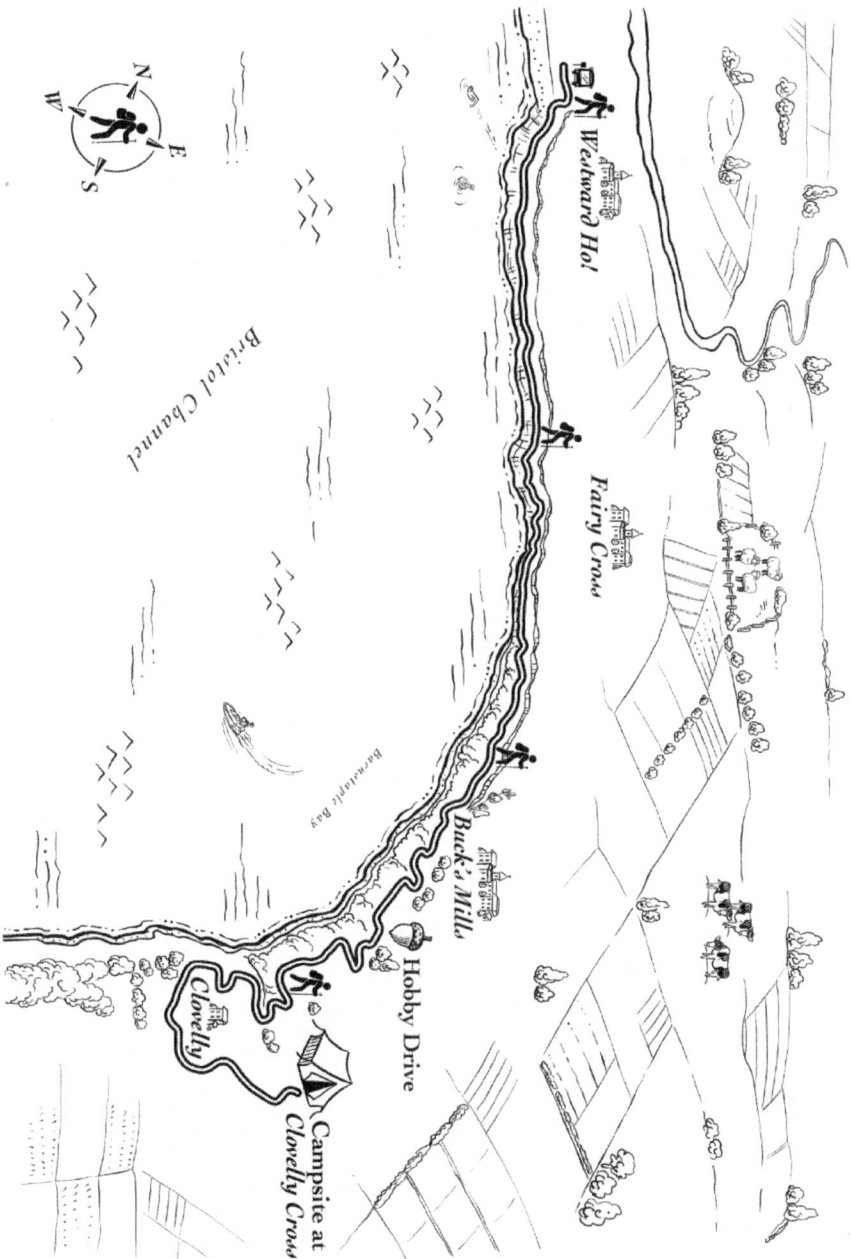

Drive. An older couple came up the Drive from the opposite direction and we

stopped to chat. The man warned me against buying the Clovelly Tour up ahead which, in his opinion, was ridiculously over-priced.

"They're out to gouge the tourist, so they are," he said, "they'll be tryin' to sell ye the tour. Don't take it. We walked around outside by ourselves. Saw everything there was to see without paying a penny." They both looked proud of themselves.

I thanked them and asked where they were from.

"Scotland, o' course," he said as if it was perfectly obvious to anyone else less dim. "Drove our own campervan down. Got us a site nearby for fifteen quid a night."

As I continued along Hobby Drive, I cautioned myself against the 'cheapskate Scotsman' stereotype. But the way the man had presented himself seemed calibrated to conform to the caricature to a tee, and I wondered if the stereotype was a source of pride for him. On the other hand, maybe he knew I was an American and was just having me on.

The episode with the frugal Scot unearthed a memory of Dr. Claus, my old excitable wildlife biology professor. I'd asked him why, since he had such a great sense of humor, he never included jokes in his lectures.

"I grew up in Denmark," he explained, "then went to university in the Netherlands and had Dutch professors who assigned us textbooks written in German. And then I went to Canada for my PhD and wrote my dissertation in English. There are things that translate well and things that don't, and jokes... they don't. No one outside Denmark thinks my jokes are funny. I have learned not to tell jokes."

"I'd like to hear one," I said.

"No."

"Come on. I'm curious now."

He shook his head.

"Love a good laugh, I do." I cocked my head, trying to look eager and jocular.

"Well... okay," he said. Then, "How do you know when you are looking at a Scottish fishing boat?"

"I don't know. Just how do you know when you are looking at a Scottish fishing boat?" I asked.

That I followed the formula and repeated the question back, he took as encouragement, and it infused him with a shot of mirth and hopefulness. Overcome with a nerdy case of giggles, he struggled to blurt out the punchline, "Because there are no seagulls!" He slapped his thigh and surrendered to an uncontrollable fit of laughter. I remained mute while it tapered off to a final wheeze.

"It's the seagulls, see?" he said as the bright hope in his face began to fade. "The seagulls have altered their behavior patterns in a specific response to an inadequate food source. Get it?"

"Not really."

"Scottish fishermen are frugal and keep all the target species' viscera as well as all by-catch mortalities!"

"So?"

"So! So, nothing is tossed overboard, and seagulls have nothing to eat!"

"And?"

"*And*?" he spluttered. "And? And seagulls have learned to identify fishing vessels sailing under Scottish registry!" He was almost panting, exasperated at my obtuseness, a sight, (being his student) that I'd seen many times.

"So…" I said. "What I hear you telling me is…"

"Yes?" His panting had subsided, though his face was still red.

"…you should not tell jokes."

The path brought me to the doorstep of an airy, modern visitor center. A fresh-faced and earnest young docent offered me a ticket to tour Clovelly, but I had been forewarned, so I shrewdly declined, even though the offer came with the use of an umbrella. It's a sin of pride to feel self-satisfied and smug, and I knew it. Still, I couldn't help how pleased I felt with myself. I walked around behind the building to see for myself what there was to see for free.

There wasn't much. I stood outside, there in a parking area between a bus garage and a plastic barrel full of used cooking oil. Presently, the drizzle turned to a steady rain, and I savored my latest victory over smugness, letting it soak in.

Not long after William the Conqueror took over England, he gifted the entire village of Clovelly and its surrounding land to his wife Matilda, and because of that historical oddity, the picturesque fishing village overlooking a rocky shore has been privately owned ever since. All the cottages and shops in the village are original and in excellent condition, even though many of them were built nearly a thousand years ago. The town's current owner lives nearby in an estate between the town and a church that was built in the twelfth century. I know all this because later, when I walked back into cell service, I looked it up on Wikipedia. But I never saw any of it while I was there, having not purchased a ticket and saving myself £8.75.

I walked the roadway uphill to Clovelly Cross, the intersection at the main A39 highway, to cell service and a campsite. I texted Matt and Rhonda my whereabouts, and they shortly arrived by bus. We pitched our tents, but the wind came up, and we were forced to unpeg and drag them to a sheltered spot snugged up to a hedge.

It was a full-on gale when a young couple arrived, drenched through and shivering. They got their tent set up next to Matthew's, and once inside, struck

Walking Wet

up a conversation with him through the wind-driven rain and a couple of layers of flapping tent fabric. When they mentioned that they'd run out of food and were hungry, Matt upended his chow bag onto his sleeping pad and began listing its contents to them, offering to toss them over. But each offering elicited a request to read aloud its list of ingredients, which earned each of them a rejection, accompanied by ethical and dietary diatribes shouted back through the wind and weather. They couldn't and wouldn't eat anything he had.

Back in our tent, Rhonda and I squeezed in amongst my damp clothes hanging inside. After the previous few nights of luxuriating inside the roomy bus, the cramped dome and incessant sound of wind and rain pattering against the tent's fabric was an irritation.

"I'd almost forgotten what you smell like," Rhonda said.

"Ha. You just think the stink is me," I told her. "But you're wrong, and I know something you don't."

"Listening."

"The bus dropped you over there, but I walked up from the other way, and I know what's behind this hedge."

"Still listening."

"A pigsty. There are eight hogs just upwind of us, there on the other side."

"Hey, Matt," Rhonda shouted through the tent wall on her side. "Your dad says there are hogs on the other side of the hedge."

"Yeah, so?" asked Matt.

"Just thought you'd want to know."

"Yeah, and why would you think that?"

The snark in his tone surprised me until I realized that the two of them had spent most of the last three days together entertaining themselves while I was out walking in the rain. Rhonda shared a point of information with me under her breath. "You're raising a little shit," she said. Then, raising her voice to be heard through my wet clothes and driving rain and flapping tent fabric between her and Matthew, she addressed her nephew.

"Why? In case you want to join them, that's why!"

It was calm the next morning when I set out again, early and alone. As I got to the street, I woke our neighbors from just around the hedge. "Wakey, wakey, eggs and bakey!" They'd been lying in their shed sleeping peacefully

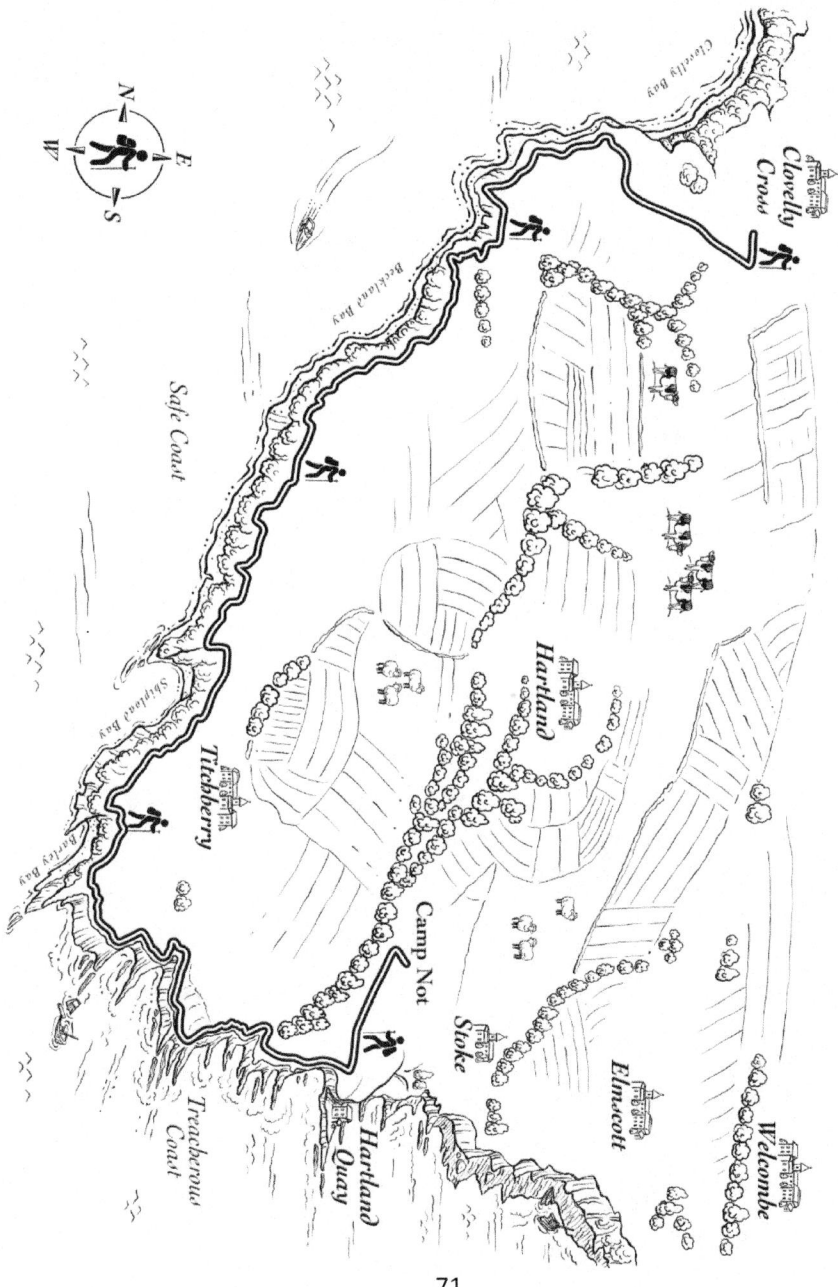

together, snug as a seal's fingers, and I felt guilty when they startled. It was a thoughtless thing to do, mentioning a breakfast of pork to a slumbering bunch that would be sizzling in fry pans themselves soon enough.

I walked past the Clovelly Church, a stone edifice set in a square patch of granite headstones behind a wall of quarried rock. It looked picturesque but unremarkable, until I pondered the fact that everyone who had built it and the stone walls around it, and everyone under the headstones in its cemetery had lived and died some hundreds of years before Columbus sailed across the ocean.

I thought of going straight overland towards saltwater, passing through the back yard of the estate. It was just after six, and workers were already there preparing for a wedding reception, setting up chairs and tables under sparkling pavilion tents. They were all dressed in background-black, like stagehands in a Broadway production. I scuttled through, across a pasture, and onto the path.

The trail took me due west to Hartland Point, where the character of the coastline took a dramatic turn. Bedrock is jointed, that is, it's typically fractured into horizontal layers and vertical cracks. The rock underlying the coastline I'd been following since Westward Ho!, the Devon formation, has its hidden layers laid down mostly horizontally, but tilting downwards a bit as I walked. The cracks that run vertically into the formation, the ones you can see at the surface, are aligned east and west. At Hartland Point, the coastline comes to an abrupt corner, making a ninety degree turn to the left. This brings the erosive force of the wind and waves to bear on the rock's joint planes from a new direction, and it makes all the difference.

I had been walking along a coast where the sea had carved the bedrock to make rock shelves and tide pools along the shoreline. Remember the swimmer at Westward Ho! in the tidepool and the overhanging buildings at Buck's Mill supported on stilts driven into tidepool cracks in the bedrock shelves below? Rounding the point, the ocean's power came in from a different angle, and instead of making wide shelves and tidepools, it hewed the exposed bedrock into sawtooth jetties and rock fingers that jutted far out into crashing waves. It was a more dramatic coastline, and one that must have struck fear into early mariners who could only rely upon wind, wits, and luck.

I was way ahead of schedule and would be arriving at the campsite we'd agreed upon well short of noon. There was cell service atop the point, so I checked in with Rhonda and Matt. They had just gotten off the bus and would be there even before me.

We had a sunbreak, and our first thought was to set up the tents before it started raining again, but what would we do after that? None of us were excited about doing anything that any of us could think of; moving on a bit further down the trail, sightseeing in Hartland, or looking for a laundromat.

A Victory Over Smugness

We decided on a change of scenery. Justin had told us that the other end of the path, at Poole, because of its location and shoreline orientation, had a different climate. The weather we'd been enduring came to us by way of Greenland and Ireland. Poole was closer to the European mainland, still broiling in a drought and heat wave. At the time, I had listened to Justin with skepticism. Poole may have been at the far end of a six-hundred-mile path, but the path was curved like a horseshoe, and as the crow flies, it wasn't far away at all.

Only seventy-five miles. How different could it be? But I'd just seen how quickly the character of the shoreline could change with just a turn to the south.

Besides, if we spent the rest of the day in buses and trains, we'd at least stay comfortable and dry. Doing what we've been doing, me walking along outside in the rain, with Rhonda and Matt killing time and making short bus hops to all meet up to crowd inside domes of damp fabric. Well, none of that was especially conducive to good cheer and understanding.

Google mapped a route for us back to London and then on to Poole, a sizeable city of a quarter of a million people. Our transfers were smoother and less panicky this time, as we were becoming accustomed to the hustle of train stations and platform changes.

We made it to Poole by early evening and walked to our least expensive choice for accommodation, another Travelodge. Their website showed vacancies, but they wouldn't book us a room when we got there. All bookings had to be done online.

"Isn't that a computer right there?" Rhonda asked the man behind the counter. "Why don't you go online and get us a room?"

"Using the hotel computers to book rooms for our guests is against hotel policy," he explained.

"Uh, what? How does that even make sense? What kind of policy is that?"

"It is hotel policy. You may use your phone to book a room."

"Thank you," Rhonda said, "I'll do that now."

We enjoyed our stay across the street at the Holiday Inn, which had a nice restaurant and lounge. Dinner entertainment was provided by a man sitting alone at a nearby table conducting a business meeting via his Bluetooth headset. If there was any substance in the conversation, it was coming through his earpiece only, because everything going into his mic was meaningless nonsense. "We're turning the ship." "Let's put a name on it." "Break it down for me." "That's a positive direction." We figured he was lonely and was just putting on a show to attract attention. But Matthew and I pretended he was legit so we could trade guesses about what business he was in.

"He's in sales for a company that puts wheels on pogo-sticks," I guessed, "or maybe they put bingo daubers on them."

"No way," Matthew said, "it's a YouTube channel where they drive tanks and things and squish cans of corn over and over. Haven't you been listening?"

Rhonda was having trouble moving on, apparently. "He's a support specialist for online hotel booking software," she said. Little things affect her longer than they should sometimes.

The man was looking our way, pretending to listen to his plastic earpiece. "I think we're headed for a breakthrough now," he said.

There was a television in our hotel room, the first one we'd seen since starting the trip in Minehead, and we stayed up late watching. And in a bizarre replay of our last TV night at the other end of the Salt Path, Rhonda found another installment of *Bare Attraction*. This time, all the contestants were non-binary, which the host was making a big fuss about. Again, we were treated to suggestive banter and innuendo, and eventually the frosted glass doors were raised to their navels. The camera panned across from one contestant to another, then pulled back to show the four of them that were left.

"They all look binary to me," Rhonda said.

That's what I saw, too, honestly. But it's something I'd rather not be looking for.

***

Our target campsite for the next night was an average day's walk away, but it was raining heavily again, so we resigned ourselves to taking a bus there. The bus turned out to be an open-topped double-decker, from a line called the 'Sun Coasters.' It was crowded. No one was sitting in the upper deck, and passengers near the staircase opening were getting drenched. Pools and rivulets of water sluiced around the floor under the seats, splashing against various sides of the passengers' shoes depending on whether the bus was nearing or leaving a stop or which way it was going around a curve.

"Looks like people usually expect sunshine here," Rhonda said.

The bus slowed for a stop up ahead, and everyone lifted their heels up off the floor in front of the rush of water, including us. "Or maybe people here are just nuts," Matthew said.

It had just quit raining inside the bus when it got us to Herston and the bus stop in front of the grocery store. We got some staples, then walked uphill to our campsite, situated on a farm above the town.

This camping farm was nothing like Charles' farm. The soil below his farm in Barnstaple was rich and fertile, and the farm's buildings and stonework fencerows seemed to spring from it with purposeful precision.

Here, the vegetation was scraggly and weedy, the rock wall fencerows were jagged and haphazardly constructed, and the outbuildings were spindly and skeletal lean-tos. Farming couldn't have ever been prosperous here. Back home, we have a term for these unfortunate and infertile plots of inarable land that settlers had tried to clear and farm anyway: stump farms. This was a stump farm, minus the stumps.

The bedrock underlying the hills above Herston is a rich brown limestone, and its consistent color and hardness made it a building material perfect for street paving or erecting brownstone buildings. When I met the campsite's owner, she showed me a map of the area and made particular mention of the streets' alignments and told me about their origins. From the seawalls of Swanage to the hilltops above Herston, several streets run straight up the fall line. We'd walked one of them to the camping farm, straight uphill from the grocery store. After the Great Fire of 1666, London was rebuilt to be more fire-resistant, and much of the brownstone used for the effort had been carted directly downhill from the hilltop quarries to the port.

And for centuries before that, she told me, these hills had been quarried. The limestone is jointed with horizontal cracks about a foot apart. To quarry the rock, all that's needed is to wedge off big slabs of the stuff, then chisel or cut out regularly sized building blocks. There's still rock being quarried there today. Just behind our campsite was a massive pile of limestone slabs and a pole barn under which loaders and forklifts attended a screaming rock saw. The sheet metal had been left off the sides of the pole barn to help let the dust and noise out.

So our campsite, like much of the land in view, wasn't on farmland soil at all but rather a mix of mine tailings, chiseled rock spalls, and overburden. The campsite itself, though, went beyond mirroring the shabby. Recycling barrels overflowed with beer bottles and spent fuel cannisters, and we picked glass shards and broken mason jars out of the tent pitches she assigned to us.

I found the toilet and cinder block shower building hidden in the woods off a muddy footpath. The wooden doors squeaked on rusted hinges and were largely unpainted, cobwebs blanketed the fluorescent lights, and the mosquitoes and black flies trapped in them made the dim lights even dimmer. On the men's side, one of the fluorescent lights was out completely, and the other buzzed and flickered incessantly.

It happened to be a Friday night, and around ten o'clock, two cars rolled in perilously close to our tents while their drivers shouted at each other through the rain in some Slavic language. They decided to set up camp just beside us, beginning, apparently, with lighting up a bucket of coal for a campfire. The acrid smoke seeped through our tent's fabric, stinging our eyes. They were a noisy bunch till about midnight, when they began adding marijuana smoke to the coal fumes.

We'd been in England for two weeks, long enough for my body's clock to adjust itself to the local time and to resume its usual habit of waking me up at four-thirty in the morning, regardless of how much sleep it had gotten. I walked past the rickety toilet blocks, venturing out of the woods and into the fields above the coast. It wasn't raining, but the air felt wet, and the dew was heavy. A small group of cows was clambering through a break in a rock wall that had been put together with spalls and other quarry rejects, and they froze for a long moment when they saw that they'd been caught in the act.

"Looking for greener pastures?" I asked them. They were bony and thin-skinned and could have used some greener pastures, but there weren't any around.

The one closest to me started making a cow pie without lifting her tail high enough. "Happy hunting," I said and moved off before she could flick it at me.

I called home, where it was 9:30 at night, and had a FaceTime conversation with Monica, who was hosting some of our couple friends on our back patio. The sun was setting, and the light made them look tanned and golden, especially Monica. It made me wish I was at home on the patio with her and our friends with a cocktail and wonder why I was in England atop a landscape of weeds and quarry spoils with a poopy cow tail instead.

I tried at first to be light and cheery, but she knows me, what I need, and when I need it. And just then, I needed to vent about the trip. It was a relief to speak candidly for a change.

"I probably shouldn't have taken Rhonda here," I said. "This trail is harder than I'd expected."

"But still easier than the Pacific Crest Trail, though, right?"

"No, it's harder, I think. The PCT, most of it anyway, was built for horses and pack trains. It takes you higher up into the mountains, but it does it gently for the most part, with long gentle gradients. Once it gets you up into the mountains, it keeps you there for a good long time, winding around mountains and headwaters and leading through mountain passes. It was made for horses to carry miners' provisions into the backcountry. The Southwest Coast Path was made for customs officials, for sneaking up on and ambushing smugglers in steep, rocky coves."

"So, the Coastal Path doesn't use the topography to its advantage, then."

"Well, if the purpose is to keep from killing horses, then no, it doesn't. But if your purpose is to drop down onto smugglers like a bowling ball, it's laid out great."

"I can see how it might not be ideal for rehabbing heart patients," Monica said. "But at least you don't have to carry much food, so your packs aren't as heavy as they were on the PCT. So that's good, right?"

"Well, true, we're not carrying as much food. But everything else we have weighs more, because it's damp. Tent, clothes, sleeping bags, and even the packs themselves weigh more. And when things are damp, or you're wearing rain gear, nothing seems to move or ride comfortably. It's harder going. And..." I trailed off.

"And? And what?"

"And it's annoying. I hate to say it, but hiking here can get a bit annoying."

"Do you think Matt and Rhonda are annoyed?"

"Absolutely. But for different reasons. I keep comparing this trip to what it could be, a hike on a smooth trail in fine weather, and I get annoyed because it isn't. They're just annoyed because they followed me here."

"You can't blame them there," Monica said.

"I don't." Two of the bony cows came around a bush behind me. They just lurked around, pretending to look for grass, but kept their ears swiveled towards me, the least competent eavesdroppers I'd ever been lurked by. And strangely, that annoyed me, too.

"Why don't you do something different?" Monica suggested. "You're there as tourists, why not explore something else?"

"The whole idea was to hike the Southwest Coast Path," I replied. "But with the weather like this, I'm the only one doing it. Matt and Rhonda aren't having much fun with it."

"Doesn't sound like you are either."

"Fair point."

Monica has found that after illuminating a point, it's best to give me a moment to re-align my thinking and adjust to it. We looked at each other's faces on our phone screens while I did that.

"Okay," I said finally.

"Okay then. Why don't you take Matt to see those English car guys he likes or something? Or go to London and see Big Ben and the palace guards with the tall hats. You guys are in England, after all. Be tourists. At least for a while, till it quits raining."

"That could be a long while. And by the time we get back onto the trail, there may not be enough time to finish it."

"And that's important, why exactly?" she asked.

We looked at each other's faces on our phone screens in silence again while I re-aligned and adjusted.

Walking Wet

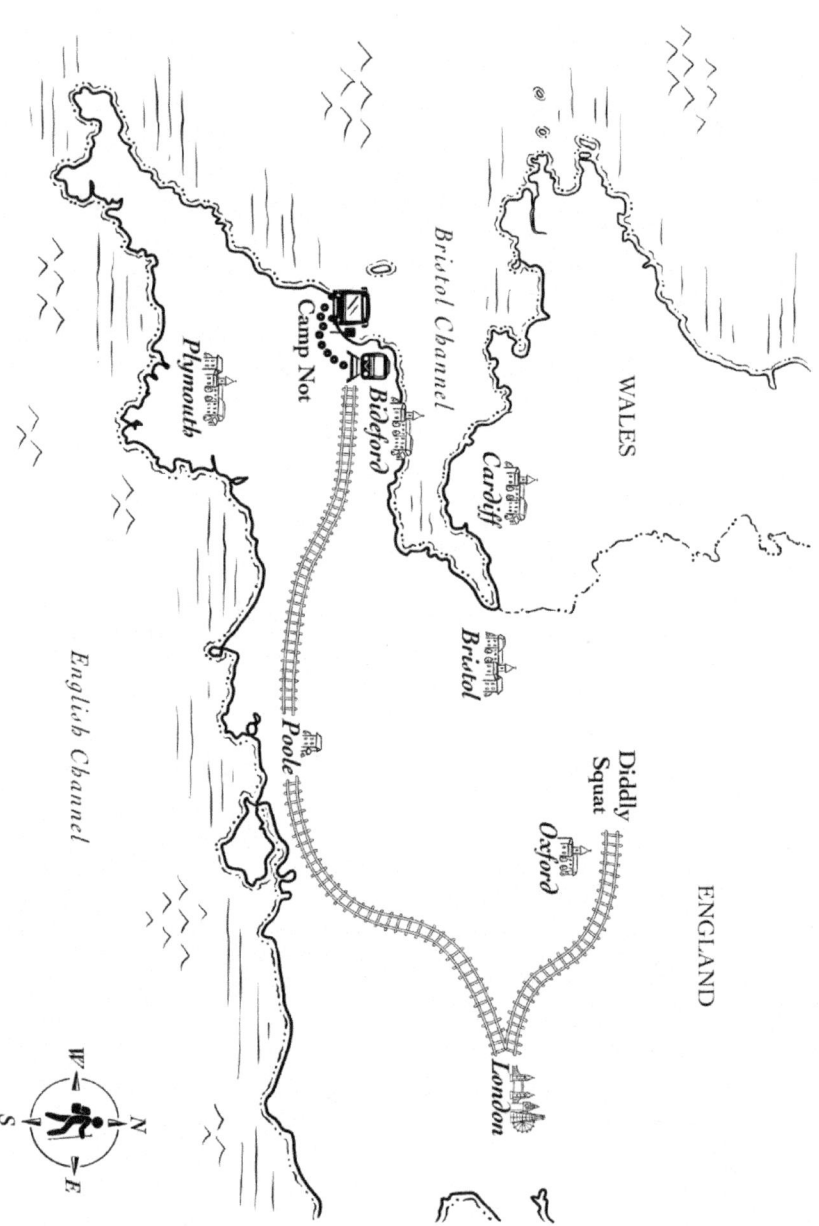

Diddly Squat

15 ⋯ DAYS WALKING
104 ⋯ PATH MILES WALKED
158 ⋯ TOTAL MILES WALKED

When Matthew and Rhonda woke up, it didn't take much to persuade them to go for another adventure.

"I'm out of here," Matthew declared before I'd even finished the proposal. We packed up and retraced our steps, walking downhill to the same grocery store as the previous day for the bus back to Poole. It wasn't actively raining this time, so the puddles were missing from our bus's floor, but it was chilly still, and we sat on the lower deck all the way back to the train station.

This time, navigating train schedules and platform changes was even easier and less intimidating to us, and we found ourselves enjoying the journey without any stress or anxiety.

From Poole, we hopped on a train to the Bournemouth Station, transferred to Redding, and then an overland route to reach the English Cotswolds and Charlbury. We had a short walk from Charlbury Train Station, followed by a long wait for our next bus connection. The bus stop was in front of a brick tenement building, and I had time to explore around back, discovering a short trail that led to a welcoming community recreation center.

The place was a gem, complete with a library, tennis courts, ball fields, and playground equipment. I looked inside the library windows and saw children and moms busy with finger painting. The rec area outside was impeccably maintained and playing host to families enjoying their Saturday afternoons. The weather had taken a turn for the better here, with the sun shining through broken clouds.

We eventually boarded the bus, and it took us to an RV and tent camping site adjacent to the Diddly Squat Farm Shop. In England, a farm shop is a produce store that sells only locally sourced food products, typically grown on the farm itself. What made the Diddly Squat Farm Shop special was its owner, Jeremy Clarkson, known for hosting Britain's *Who Wants to Be a Millionaire* game show and as one of the three auto enthusiasts featured on *Top Gear*. Matthew was an ardent fan of Jeremy, having streamed all the British *Top Gear* episodes.

Clearly, the farm shop was a popular destination. The parking lot was overflowing with cars, and vehicles lined both sides of the road, a tricky prospect for a bus when there are no shoulders. The driver had to maneuver through people walking the road to and from the shop, avoid the ones stepping out from between car bumpers, and abstain from removing car doors when they were carelessly and without warning flung open. The queue to the shop began at the road, curling back on itself several times between roped dividers for the hundred yards or so to the shop, a modest, wood plank-sided building about twenty feet square. It seemed an inordinately large crowd looking to buy bread or beans.

Parked out front near the street was a striking white roadster. Stainless flex pipe headers emerged from the vented engine cowling behind huge old-style headlamps. They fed exhaust pipes mounted below running boards that blended into fenders curving over spoked wheels. It was an odd-looking hulk, like something Al Capone might have ridden in had he hired Liberace as his chauffeur. Matthew instantly recognized it as the vehicle Mr. Clarkson had driven in the latest *Top Gear* episode. Matthew had already watched it several times.

I left Matthew and Rhonda to set the tents up at our campsite and went next door to join the queue, an exercise I typically avoid practicing whenever possible. But Matt had been a good sport to give up a summer vacation he could have had back home hanging out with his friends, instead of coming to England with me and his aunt to camp in the rain. The plan was for Matthew to come find me in the line after he had settled in and to take my place.

The farm shop had two doors, one for entry and one for exit, with an employee stationed at the entry door. As shoppers inside finished up and left, she would wave in another group of people. The line moved faster than I expected, and I was on the verge of reaching the entry door when Matthew came to take my place. I went to leave, but the people I'd been chatting with in line insisted that I stay, in essence, allowing Matthew to cut. Their kindness surprised me, especially considering they had already waited in line for over an hour.

I was struck by how pleasant everyone in the queue had been. They had all traveled considerable distances to get there, then struggled to find parking and waited patiently in line for an hour or more to enter a building the size of a two-car garage. Inside, they would buy items they could have gotten for themselves cheaper at their local Tesco. None of them appeared frantic or irritable; they just seemed genuinely patient and kind. Maybe, I thought, those virtues are characteristic of the British culture in general.

Or it could be that the English are accustomed to standing in lines for things, and just another hour-long wait was nothing out of the ordinary for them. Either way, it made me wonder why I was so childishly impatient, when here was a whole nation here that knew how to behave.

Then again, everyone else in line was a Jeremy Clarkson fan. Maybe Mr. Clarkson attracted especially kind and patient people to his fan base.

That would be ironic, I thought. I'd watched several episodes of *Top Gear* as well as *Clarkson's Farm*, another show he'd featured in, and from what I've seen, Mr. Clarkson is at least as irascible and childishly impatient as I am.

Inside the shop, we bought a loaf of bread made from Diddly Squat produced wheat, and a half quart of milk produced on a neighboring dairy farm. Matthew had seen the dairy farm's owners while watching *Clarkson's Farm*, the TV show that chronicled life on the Diddly Squat Farm. He assured me the dairy farmers were good people. I confirmed this for myself because I wake up and wander around in the mornings earlier than sane people, and met one of them myself when he stopped by the farm shop to restock it with milk.

Just beside the farm shop was a larger building, a grain and equipment storage shed that had been made into a welcoming space with about a dozen picnic tables and a few more on the apron outside. At one end of the shed, they sold plastic pints of Hawkstone beer, brewed from barley grown on Diddly Squat Farm. A food vendor's trailer stood outside, offering pretzel bun sliders. The line to the bar was shorter, so I got a pint. It was good beer. Matt, being a fan of Mr. Clarkson's shows, had a sip and declared it the best beer he'd ever tasted.

It was busy around the farm shed's picnic tables, cheerfully crowded, and with a cold beer in my hand, completely satisfactory and lovely. The sun was almost out by now, and the climate there in the Cotswolds seemed noticeably drier and friendlier than that on the Cornish Coast. The barley in the field across the way stood taller, with plumper heads of grain than the ones we'd been walking past in Cornwall, and were free from blight and rust.

The trees in the woodlands were taller, their trunks more robust, and their canopies more far-reaching than those along the coast. The rock walls between the farm shop and the campground weren't slimy or lichen-covered, and the fencerow hedges were taller. Everything exuded vitality, appearing well-watered but not drenched, and well-warmed by the sun as well.

The Cotswolds landscape offered sweeping vistas of gently rolling plains, punctuated by wooded copses and living hedgerows. I could envision stepping out of the shed, beer in hand, and walking straight into a painting. It was comfortable and soothing at the brainstem level somehow. I sipped my Hawkstone and drew my easiest lungfuls of air since I'd left home.

Walking Wet

We had booked a three-night stay at the campsite, and each day we explored minor adventures. There was a bridle trail near the campground, leading us through woods and farmlands, passing grand equestrian farms replete with polo fields and steeplechase courses. I was fortunate to spot deer and foxes along the trail one morning, and it became my favorite place to video call back home to Monica.

Matthew and I also discovered another trail, that, despite a rough time getting to it along a shoulderless highway and an uninviting start on a gravelly road, eventually transformed into a farm lane. From there, we took a detour straight through a lush barley field. On the other side of the field was another farm lane, and we passed a wooden gate with a yellow plastic warning sign that read, 'Bull in Field.' Matthew instantly recognized the sign, having seen it on *Clarkson's Farm*.

"I know this place," Matthew said, eyes wide. "Jeremy and Gerald put this sign up."

"Who's Gerald?"

"He's the guy with the accent that nobody understands. They had other signs that were funnier, but they used this one. They were here, standing right here. And now we are."

Just beyond were a couple of horses in a pasture. "I've seen those horses!" Matt exclaimed. Then the lane led us between farm buildings and a substantial brownstone home. I was admiring the colonnaded balcony off the second floor, but Matthew was electrocuted by something else.

"Oh my God, that's Jeremy Clarkson's customized Land Rover!"

"What?"

"I've seen it. That's his Land Rover. They customized it just for him. He was driving it when he found the dead badger and put it in a bag in the back."

"He drives around with bags for dead badgers?"

Matt put his hands on his hips. "If you're a farmer here, that's what you have to do," he said sternly. "They have to be tested for brucellosis, so they don't kill all your cows."

"How do you know about brucellosis?"

"Because Charlie told him about it on *Clarkson's Farm*. And that's his Land Rover. He must be home right now."

I peeked again at my phone's OS map. There we were, marked by an orange triangle atop a yellow line. Yellow lines meant public rights-of-way. But we were in his backyard, for Pete's sake. I remembered being led astray by the outdated map before, at the beginning of the Tarka Trail.

"Alright," I said. "I'm not sure we can be here, so let's keep it quiet and keep moving along. I don't want to be mistaken for stalkers or something and have the dogs turned loose on us."

"They have dogs, but they only chase deer," Matthew said. "Besides, they never do anything Jeremy tells them to."

"Uh, right, just in case, though, let's get out of this guy's backyard, okay?"

"Okay, but get my picture. Can you get the Land Rover behind me?"

We continued out the driveway, and it took us back to the road leading to the farm shop and our campsite. We turned left instead and walked into town. Chipping Norton felt very different from Charlbury. Charlbury had radiated vibrancy, with children and families enjoying outdoor activities, its buildings more inviting and less homogenous, and some were being actively refurbished, fronted by scaffolding. In contrast, Chipping Norton seemed moneyed, but stale and stiff. There weren't many folks outside, and the ones who were outside weren't doing anything with verve. Chipping Norton reminded me of a 'free range nursing home', though to be fair, I've never seen one. But its skin felt dry and crepey, like a place where old misers would bring their money to die.

On our last evening there, I wandered over to the farm shop after it had closed and everyone had left. It was peaceful without the tourists and lines, and I sat on a stack of pallets near the shop, noodling about on my phone. A little red Fiat pulled up, and a young college-aged couple stepped out.

The girl was dressed in secondhand store chic, and on her feet were mismatched flat-soled sneakers. Her hair was dishwater blonde, unremarkably styled and worn around a kindly and fresh generic face. Her eyes, though, looked old and wise. They gave the impression somehow that hers couldn't have been the first face they'd looked out from.

She fumbled around inside the car and snaked out a set of keys on a ring attached to a little stuffed animal of some kind and a long neck lanyard. She reached inside and rummaged for something again, and when she stood up this time, lit herself a cigarette.

Her boyfriend stood beside the car and waited. He could have just come to life and walked off the cover of a romance novel. His hair was slightly curly and framed a flawless face, and when I looked at him, I got the impression that he was probably better than me in any measurable way.

They walked over to where I sat on the pallets. "Are you alright?" the girl asked. 'Are you alright?' was a customary greeting in a lot of Britain, but her eyes made me understand that she really did want to know how I was.

"Yes. Yes, I'm okay," I said. "Just here enjoying the quiet. We're camped just over there." I pointed towards the RV park. "We're here from America- me, my son, and my sister."

"Quite the journey. Do you like it here?"

"Love it, so far. Could do with a little less rain, though. We're actually here to hike the Southwest Coast Path around Cornwall, but the weather there has been a challenge. We thought we'd come here for a bit, see if things clear up on the coast."

"You're fans of Jeremy's, then?"

"My boy is for sure. He's a real motorhead."

"In case you're wondering, I'm not breaking in," she said and held up the keys. "We're short on bread up at the house, and I need to go in and get some."

I learned that she was one of Jeremy Clarkson's stepdaughters. "It's too bad my son isn't here," I said, "he's a huge fan of your stepdad's."

"Is he?" she asked.

"He's seen all the *Top Gear* episodes at least four times already, and the *Clarkson's Farm* series as well."

"So, he likes Jeremy's shows? How old is he?"

"Fourteen, and he's itching to get behind the wheel of something. Of anything, actually."

"That's the way," she said. Then, "And what do you think of the shows?"

"I think they're pretty good," I said, "especially the farm show. There's nothing that explains better what it's like to be a farmer, I don't think. At least nothing better in the U.S."

She looked at me as though I wasn't done talking.

"And it's strange for me personally as well. I mean, for the first half of my life, I was a farmer, but my farming life was over before my son was even born. He's never known farming life at all, and it's a shame because the most important lessons I'd learned in my life came on a farm. And that's what your farm show here does. It provides those lessons. Know what I mean?"

"Perfectly."

"I think I saw you on the farm show once. Did I?"

"Yeah, my sister and I were on when they wanted horses on the show. Very briefly." She shook her head slightly, but at what, I didn't know. "I'm curious," she asked, "what do you Americans think of Jeremy?"

"We like him okay, I'd say."

"Do you?"

"I think when we see him on television, we feel comfortable. We can get a little intimidated by all the suavity, you know, like Rolls-Royces, butlers, and all the British sophistication we see in James Bond movies and the like. But when we see Jeremy, we don't feel looked down upon. He's more relatable, a crusty and curmudgeonly old Brit."

"How do Americans feel about the latest controversy?" she asked.

I liked the way she pronounced 'controversy.' "What controversy?"

"You don't know what I'm talking about?"

"No, but that might be because I don't keep up on everything like I should."

"Well," she said, "he's made some incredibly unfortunate comments lately. It's led to some embarrassment and pain." Her expression made me wonder if some of that embarrassment and pain had fallen to her. I wanted to do what I could to lessen it.

"I was standing in line here the other day," I told her, "chatting with a retired cabbie from Sheffield. He'd asked me the same question you just did. To be polite, I told him that we Americans were all fans. He told me then that he loved Jeremy just like a lot of the Britons do because he was the only one brave enough to say what everyone else was thinking."

I could see that what I said didn't reassure her at all.

"See what I mean?" her boyfriend said. "It's like I've been telling you, there's an upside to this. It's actually kind of..."

She groaned and turned to her boyfriend. "Now, don't you go egging him on yourself. There're enough people hanging around and winding him up already, trying to get him to say more outrageous things. He doesn't need any more encouragement."

She finished her cigarette, snuffed it out, and dropped it in the bin beside me. "It was nice to meet you," she said. The second key she tried in the lock opened the farm shop door, and she went inside.

She left her boyfriend outside with me, and we chatted a bit about the Cotswold scenery, comparing it to the Cornish Coast, and some of the expressions used in the United States compared to their English counterparts.

On the show, *Clarkson's Farm*, Mr. Clarkson had a youthful hired hand whom he constantly referred to as 'The Fetus.' I wondered if he'd monikered his stepdaughter's boyfriend 'The Specimen.'

She came out of the store with her loaf of bread. They said their goodbyes, and she wished me well. I thanked her, and her old eyes looked at me again. She started the car and backed out.

After they left, I Googled "Jeremy Clarkson controversial remarks" and saw what the matter was. Meghan Markle, who is Britain's new king's second son's wife, had complained publicly about how she thought she had been snubbed by the palace administration because she was the first person of color to marry into the Royal family. That was surprising, as I hadn't known Meghan Markle was a person of color until just then. Anyway, her comments rubbed a lot of the English the wrong way as they didn't like the implication that their monarchy basically was racist.

There was a noisy reaction against the duchess, and then a counter-reaction supporting her. And then Jeremy Clarkson suggested in a tabloid magazine that she be treated to a *Game of Thrones*-style public shaming. The ultra-conservatives apparently were giddy about the comments and happy to amplify them, while the progressives were angered and appalled by the line he had crossed. Unruly protests and online ugliness ensued. An apology was demanded, and he delivered one but added an explanation. And a dumb one at that, which was rejected, of course.

I read the comments and his apology. At first blush, they looked like the blatherings of a dumbass. But I doubt Mr. Clarkson is one. People making fortunes in the public eye generally aren't.

Mr. Clarkson may have, as his daughter lamented, hangers-on who wind him up and egg him on. I'm willing to believe his comments were, as he had said, the result of hurried carelessness. I don't have hangers-on to wind me up, and I generate plenty of boners myself. But I have an editor who goes over my stuff and protects me from my stupider self, a tough job he usually does very well.

Jeremy's editor didn't do that. And the magazine's publisher ran those remarks for no other reason than to simply get more views. It's careless and irresponsible, and it shouldn't be alright to duck responsibility by pointing and saying, "He said it, not me".

It may be profitable, but riling people up and manufacturing controversy is, as the British would say, not nice.

It's not nice at all.

Diddly Squat

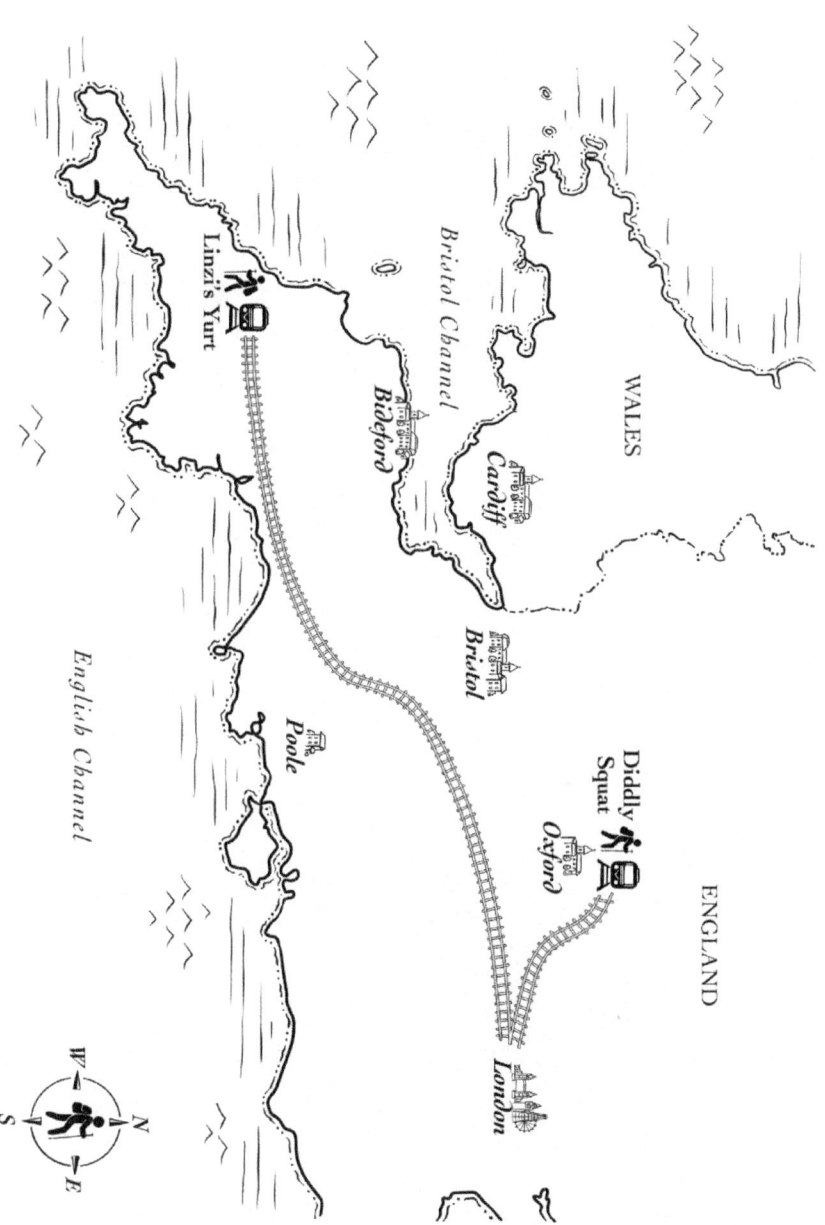

Walking Wet

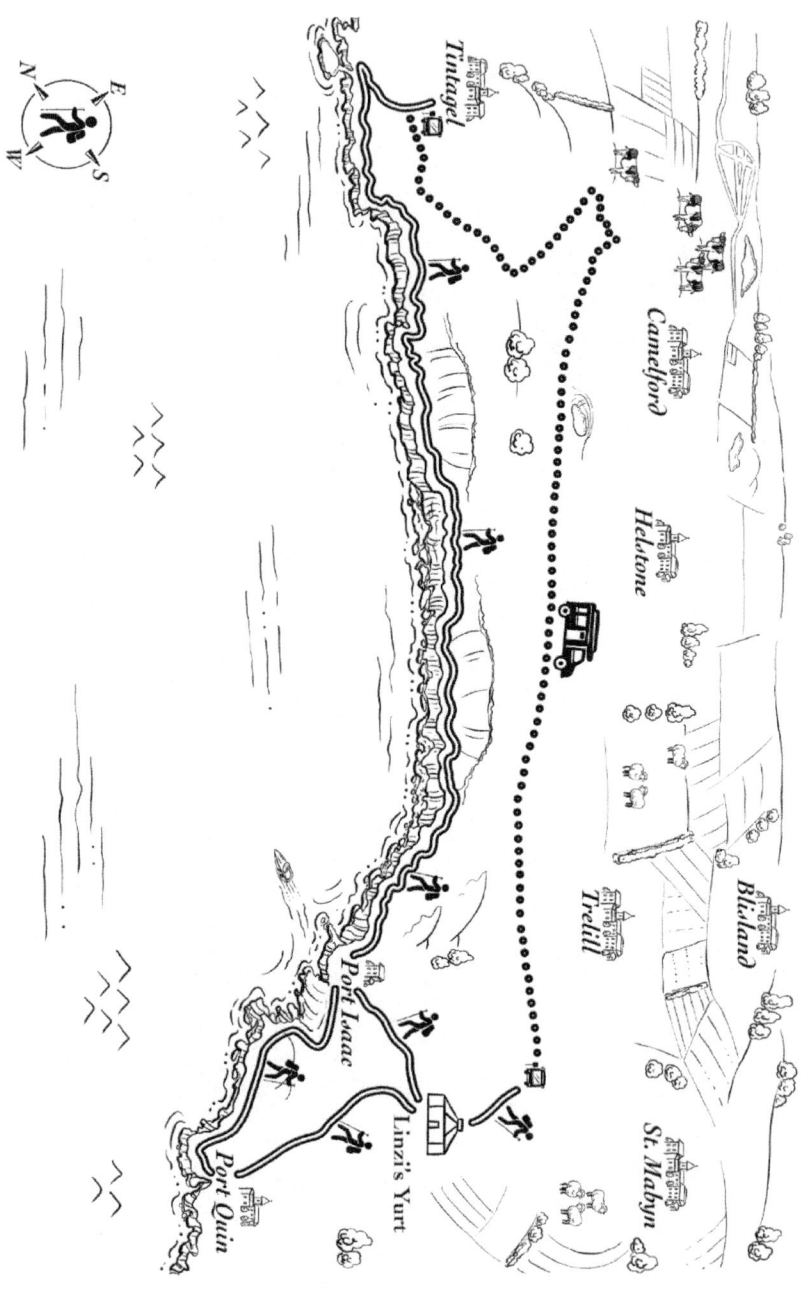

Dyin's Their Favorite Pastime

16 ··· DAYS WALKING
106 ··· PATH MILES WALKED
166 ··· TOTAL MILES WALKED
https://www.southwestcoastpath.org.uk/walksdb/148/

"This has got to be the stupidest thing we've ever done," Matthew said.

"I doubt that." It had already been a long day of trains and buses, and I wasn't feeling particularly agreeable. "We've done lots of stupid things together. This can't be the worst. You just said that because it's my idea, not yours."

"No. I just said that because this," he said, stamping his foot to mark the spot for posterity, "is a stupid idea."

"Look, these guys have got to know where they're going. Tourists must be coming through here all the time. All we need to do is follow them."

"They're a bunch of idiots. Big, dumb, smelly idiots."

"They can hear you, you know," I reminded him.

"Sometimes, I wonder if you're all too smart, either."

"Yeah, well, I may be following them. But I noticed that you're following me now, aren't you?"

We had gone back to the coast to continue on with the Southwest Coast Path. The weather hadn't improved during our absence. We weren't keen on spending more nights cramped in a damp tent under drippy clothes, so opted for the homebase-and-foray hiking method again. We'd rented a yurt set in a pasture on a working farm, and our host Linzi, an over-worked but amiable lady in her thirties, had told us that the trail to Port Isaac started below the barnyard. We went past the two main barns and through a gate between a shallow green duck pond and the lambing shed. A pair of Muscovy ducks were preening themselves and had made a little flotilla of down floating on the algae scummed surface. A gray gander stood on one foot and watched as we closed the gate behind us, as Linzi had instructed.

Instead of a well-defined trail, there were three diverging cow paths. We chose the left and most worn one, and it traversed us sidehill to another farm gate, this one beside a stile made of shale stone set into a weathered rock wall. We went over it and were met by a dozen half-ton steers. After their initial surprise, the bullocks, as steers are called in England, gave us a warm welcome. They snorted and burped, tossed their heads, and kicked their heels in the air, twisting like bucking broncos and bashing into each other with clumsy exuberance. They ran a couple circles around us, old-western-Apache-style, then lit off across the field. Partway across, they halted and turned around, waiting for us.

"Clearly," I said, "we're meant to follow them."

Matthew looked at me dubiously.

When we got to them, the bullocks ran a circuit round us again, then stampeded off, covering another stretch of pasture before stopping and turning to.

I was doubly thankful, both for our bovine trail guides and for the chance to show off to my suburban-bred and raised son the wholesome wisdom I'd absorbed in my earlier life communing with livestock. And it was there, in the middle of the field that Matthew insulted not only me and my farm boy wisdom, but our party of erstwhile fly-cloudy trail guides by stomping his foot and declaring the whole enterprise stupid.

The bullocks ran to the end of the field, leading us to another gate where they waited for us. When we got there, one of the steers was mashing his forehead against the gate, while the rest of them looked at us, panting and drooly. Just beyond was eighty acres of perfectly untrammeled and delicately ripened barley.

"Dare you to open that gate," Matthew said.

The bullocks followed us partway back, but lost interest before we got back to the slate stone stile. We backtracked to the goose and ducks again, and this time, took the middle path that snaked into bushes and squished along a creek bank. We enjoyed a couple miles of mud and brush before turning away from the creek and onto a paved, narrow lane. Ivy hung over a rock wall of shale rising on our left, and to our right, we looked down on cottages roofed over with shingles of shale, quarried and shaped for them on the spot.

Port Isaac doubles as the quaint and backward village of Portwenn in the British TV series *Doc Martin*, which features a stuffy surgeon turned village GP. The series ran for some eighteen years, and Monica and I have watched every episode at least twice. It was fun to walk into the village and recognize landmarks from the series, even though most of them were in surprising places.

The harbor slipway, Doc's surgery, and the Portwenn School resided where my mind's map had placed them, but others would pop up unexpectedly as we walked along streets lined with buildings that never existed on the show.

Across the street from Mrs. Tishell's pharmacy, which s an ice cream and curio shop in Port Isaac, was a pasty shop I'd never seen in Portwenn. Two men were behind the counter inside, making them from scratch. We dumped our packs and went inside.

"What would ye like?" the younger man asked us. He'd just taken a tray of them out of the oven, mesmerizingly close to our noses in the steamy confines of the tiny shop.

"Two of those, whatever they are," Matthew said.

He laughed. "Hope you like lamb and onion, then," he said.

"Think I will?"

"Know ye will, son. These be the best around. My partner has been right here making 'em in this shop for thirty years. He's the master."

His partner nodded and continued crimping the edges closed on another batch with his fingers.

We were chatting with the pasty man around mouthfuls of lamb, onion, and happiness, when the young European couple who had camped next to Matt at Clovelly Cross stepped up into the shop and leaned over the counter, still wearing their backpacks. It wasn't pouring outside, but raining enough still that they'd needed to put on their backpack covers. Water dripped off them onto the tiny tables and the patrons seated at them.

"Hey, there! Remember us?" I asked.

The young woman turned to face me, dripping her backpack onto a different patron. "No," she said.

Up close and in better light, I was surprised at how pale they were and how thinly drawn their skin was over their facial bones. They looked tired and skeletal.

They set to interrogating the pasty chefs about the ingredients they used and their methods of preparation, none of which they found satisfactory. They refused every item offered. I couldn't understand how they could be so choosy about something as inconsequential as pasty fillings and wondered if there was some kind of psychological abuse and control going on. Obviously, they were hungry, close to starving.

I listened and looked both of them over closely, on the lookout for any clues as to who might be abused or the abuser. But as far as I could tell, they were both zealots and equally perplexing.

Walking Wet

With their backpacks still on, no one could get in or out of the shop while they educated the pasty-making veterans on the differences between vegetarian and vegan diets. It was raining harder again out there, so I was happy enough to stand there beside them and finish off my pasty, which despite being neither vegetarian or vegan, was marvelously delicious. But Matthew had grown impatient for some reason.

He interrupted the young man's evangelizing and addressed the younger pasty maker. "Don't bother. I've met these guys, and they won't eat anything anyway."

The couple left the shop, and as the doorway cleared, one of the patrons who had been getting dripped on reached out and tapped Matthew's elbow.

"Well done, sir," he said.

When Matthew and I returned with groceries to the yurt, Rhonda was in the outside kitchen shed chatting with our host.

They were talking about sheep. "Yes," Linzi said, "that trailer is a portable sheep shearing station. We use it to shear our three hundred sheep and lots of others besides. One of our side businesses it is, sheep shearing. We go all over Cornwall."

"It must be pretty good, farming sheep," Rhonda mused, "you can graze them almost anywhere and you get paid for both wool and meat."

"There's no moneys in wool," Linzi replied. "We shear it off, and bin it. Wool's not worth nothing by the time you cleans it."

"So why shear them at all, then?"

"You have to for their health. They gets sick if you don't shears them. They gets heatstroke and die."

"That's hard to believe. We've been rained on every day since we landed here," I said.

"They still gets it. Or they get caked in mud and snarls so's thick on 'em so's they can't walk. Then they'll lay down, get sick, and die."

I loved the way she said the word 'die' with her Cornish accent. She pronounced it 'doy.' I wanted to prod her to say it again.

"But other than shearing them," I said, "it must be pretty easy raising sheep here. At home, we have bears and mountain lions; even wolves that kill a farmer's sheep. You don't have to worry about any of those, so sheep wouldn't die very often here," I said.

Linzi bristled. "You doesn't runs sheeps, does ye? If they gets a sore foot, they lays down, and doys. If they gets stuck in a fence, they doys. If they stumble into a ditch, they goes upside down and doys. They doys during lambing. They doys during shearing. They doys when you vax 'em, they doys when you trucks 'em. People's dogs gets loose and chase 'em till they drop and doys. Sometimes, they just lie down and doys for no reason. They just love to doy, they do. Doyin' is a sheep's favorite pastime," she said.

Jackpot! I thought to myself. I tried to hide my satisfaction from her with contrition. "Sorry," I said. "I had no idea."

"And now ye do," she said.

Linzi's family was one of three living on the farm, and it wasn't easy. Her parents-in-law lived in the main house, and her husband's brother and his wife in a converted bunkhouse. Linzi, her husband, and their three kids were in a single-wide mobile home, or caravan as they are known in Britain, that they'd parked between the equipment shed and the silage bunker.

There was another substantial stone structure on the homestead, previously a barn, now converted to upscale vacation rentals. "Those are managed by my in-laws, and my husband's brother and wife rent out the camping spaces down there. The yurts here are mine," Linzi told us.

In addition to the barley fields and the beef cattle that Matthew and I had met earlier, and their flock of three hundred sheep, the shearing side business, and the vacation rentals, they also did custom grain combining in the area. Linzi's husband worked an additional full-time job at a neighboring dairy farm, and Linzi herself managed a craft store in neighboring Woodbridge. Her brother-in-law repaired equipment and ran a welding shop out of one of the farm buildings.

"It's work," she said, "and we does what we needs to stay on the farm. Our two boys and daughter want to be farmers, and me brother-in-law and his wife have two boys who wants to stay as well."

"The work doesn't bother them?" I asked.

"Living here, they knows how to work. You have to work somewhere, and there's no better place for it than a farm."

"I agree with you there," I said. "I've worked a lot of jobs, but I'd have worked only one if I'd had my way. On my farm."

"The kids see what else is out there and decided there's nothing better."

I looked past the barns built of stone, towards the drystone wall enclosing the silly bullocks' pasture, and the barley fields beyond that. Tractors and equipment were parked sidehill below us in the field we were standing in, the way we'd done on my stepfather's hilly farm when I was a kid, in case the brakes or chocks failed.

"There really is nothing better," I agreed. The ground beneath our feet felt like good rooting soil, and I wondered again if I should have done more to stay on my farm, as Linzi and Charles had done to stay on theirs.

"Nothing better out there, but I don't know what more we'll do to keep thems here," Linzi said.

That night, Rhonda, Matthew and I listened to rain drumming against our yurt's canvas roof.

"That noise you hear right now, it's not rain," Rhonda said.

Walking Wet

"Sounds like rain to me," Matthew said. "Maybe you should go outside and look."

"Don't have to. I've got the British Met Office's weather radar map up on my phone right now. The nearest rain squall is at least five kilometers away from us. We have clear skies, and it's raining cats and dogs over there, see?" She held the phone out to Matt. "Not raining here."

"Can I see your phone?" I asked.

The screen showed rain squall blobs of pixelated blue, green, yellow, and red along a bit of coastline between Tintagel and Newquay.

"I've got us centered on there," she said.

Sure enough, the nearest blob was some distance off the coast. At the bottom of the screen were slider bars to choose how far out into the future you'd like to see your forecast. When I zoomed out the map and fiddled with the sliders, I could watch a scattered flock of blobs make a two-week trip towards us from Iceland. I slid the slider bar back and forth and watched their movements, the way a coach watches opposing players on game film. I couldn't see that they had any strategy, but there were a lot of them.

"It's ninety degrees at home right now," Matthew said.

***

I failed to cover all of the path between Hartland and our temporary Port Isaac yurt base, including the castle I'd been looking forward to at Tintagel. Still, I did enjoy some bouncy and jerky bus rides through the country and muddy tromps under unruly rain squalls in the attempt. My favorite outing, a loop walk to Port Quinn and back, didn't involve buses at all and featured a return walk through a herd of cows who behaved with a sophistication and grace totally unknown to Linzi's band of bullocks.

That night, I talked Rhonda and Matthew into repeating the circuit with me the next day. It wasn't far, and we decided to all stay together this time, a plan I was excited about.

I didn't know it would be our last walk together in England.

We were on the country road to Port Isaac early enough to see a hedgehog and, just around the corner, a family of stoats.

"Are there mongooses in England?" Rhonda asked.

"It's a bunch of weasels, and they're fat!" Matthew stage-whispered, reaching for his phone.

"Crepuscular mustelids," I whispered back. He rolled his eyes.

"Postulant muscle-heads?" I'd been too quiet for Rhonda to hear.

"Dad's pretending to be a wildlife biologist again. It just means you see them at dusk or dawn, and they stink," Matthew said.

There were four of them, siblings probably. They'd wrestle in a ball, then break out of it for a wild chase, only to ball up on top of each other again. They saw us but didn't seem concerned, and that, as well as the rainbow dewdrops around us and the sunbreak sky above, put us in a good mood. We snapped a few pictures before their game took them into the hedge and out of sight. A public path cut across a barley field, then back to the road just as it steepened over and dropped us into Port Isaac. We turned left at the fish house and climbed steeply along the clifftops ringing the harbor.

"I'd always thought there was countryside past Doc Martin's house," Rhonda said as we came abreast of it. "They always show him driving uphill from here, but we're almost at the end of the road."

We stopped and looked back out over the harbor and the village. Portwenn, Port Isaac.

"Actually, this is the end of the road. We need to turn back," Rhonda said.

"It's just a little more uphill to Bert Large's bench, then it sort of levels off till we drop down into Port Quinn," I said.

Matthew had spent more time with my sister on this trip than I had. "Aunt Rhonda says we're done, so we're done," he said. He started walking back down the hill, Rhonda beside him. Down below, the tide was coming in, and the boats behind the breakwater were just beginning to float. I took a mental snapshot, then followed, staying well behind.

Back at the yurt, Rhonda and Matthew told me they were cutting their trip short and would go home together the next day. They were calling friends and family back home, making plans for a real summertime vacation upon their return. I wandered out to the pasture to be with the rest of the silly bullocks and called Monica.

"Were you surprised Matthew was so protective of his aunt?" she asked after I'd recounted the day's events.

"Not especially. He's spent more time with her on this trip than I have. And it's like I've said, this obsession I have to get back onto the path and make miles annoys them."

"Well, like you've admitted before, you can't really blame them."

"But flying back home, though. That surprised me. They must have discussed it before," I said. "It must have been their backup plan already, and today's outing just decided it for them."

"I'm surprised they stayed with you this long," Monica said. "It was your dream, not theirs, you know. You're relieved to start walking alone, though?"

"'Ambivalent' describes it best, probably. But yes, I want to keep walking, and I'm looking forward to being able to really get on it."

"Then I'm glad you're doing it."

"What surprises me is that Rhonda is taking Matt with her and how much she is paying for the airline change fees. You know, I've never really known before how much people are willing to pay to get away from me. But it's been quantified now, and it's a lot."

"Does that bother you?"

Walking Wet

"Yes, it kind of does."

"Look, you're a good person. Don't let it get you down. Most people won't pay so much to be rid of you..."

"Thank you."

"... only those who know you best."

"And how are you with it? "I asked. "With Matt staying at Rhonda's for the summer?"

Monica thought for a moment. "Again, 'ambivalent' might be the best description. I know Rhonda's town is Matthew's birthplace, and he feels a pull and connection to it. It's important that he visits. But the culture of the area concerns me sometimes."

"I know," I said. "They don't exactly lean forward on every topic."

"They don't exactly lean forward on any topic."

"They're good people, most of them," I said. "And my family, some of them."

"Oh, I know that. But you know what I mean."

"Yes, I do."

"And you're not worried?"

"A little," I said. "But he should be exposed to different perspectives. That's one of the reasons he came over here with me."

"Kids are impressionable at his age."

"Yeah, well," I said, "as far as I can tell, Matt and his teenage friends don't believe anything for very long anyway."

"That worries me, too," Monica said.

That last night in the yurt, I looked at maps and possible tent sites for the path ahead, while Rhonda and Matthew planned family gatherings and summer adventures for themselves back home. I had some four hundred and fifty miles of the path left to walk, but it seemed they had more to do than I did. They were still making plans and bouncing ideas off each other the next morning while we waited at the bus stop in front of the church. When the bus came, I hugged them and, after watching it take them away, pointed myself back towards the path and started walking.

Dyin's Their Favorite Pastime

Walking Wet

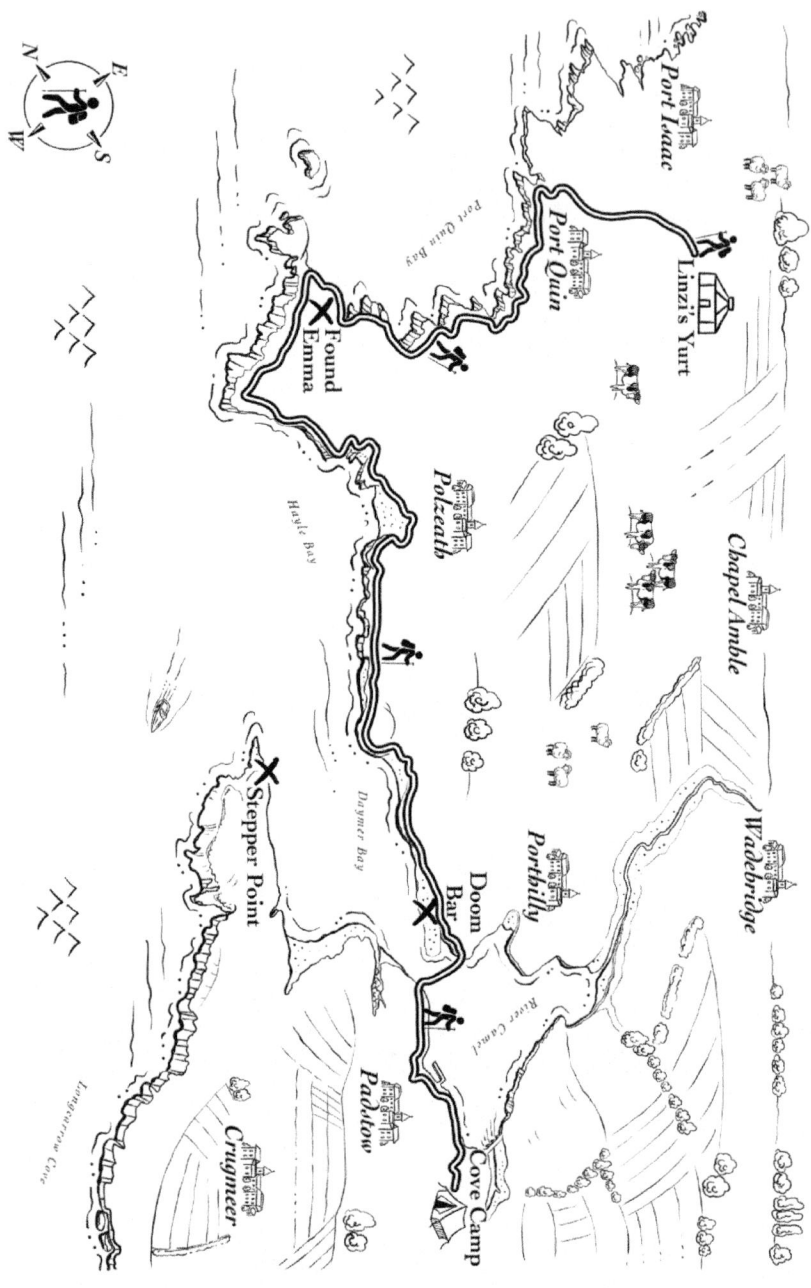

Walker's Brain

17 ⋯ DAYS WALKING
118 ⋯ PATH MILES WALKED
180 ⋯ TOTAL MILES WALKED
https://www.southwestcoastpath.org.uk/walksdb/149/

I was sitting and killing time at the ferry landing on the oddly named Rock Beach, which has absolutely no rocks on it, across the water from Padstow. Not long after seeing Matthew and Rhonda off onto the bus, I'd found Emma again on the trail. Unlike us, she'd stuck to the path despite the rain and had been wondering what had become of us. She'd gained a new hiking partner, Leanne, a game youngster studying to be an elementary school teacher on summer break from college.

They invited me to camp with them in Padstow for the night, and I had fully intended to walk with them the rest of the day. But then Emma told Leanne about how strong Matthew and I were and how fast we negotiated the hilly parts, so I felt obliged to scurry ahead to protect our reputations. Silly, I know. At any rate, it gave me time to noodle the internet for local stats and history while I waited for them to catch up with me.

The ferry would take us across the mouth of the River Camel, about a mile to the other side. But just a few days before, I'd ridden the bus with Rhonda and Matt across the River Camel just upstream at Wadebridge, and there it was a pipsqueak of a stream, something you could throw a newspaper across. Google told me now that its drainage area was barely a hundred and sixty square miles.

Such a half-pint of a river couldn't have delivered material enough for the king-sized sand dunes behind me, the broad beach in front of me, nor the sandbar stretching out across the river's mouth.

So, where did all this sand come from? I wondered.

The internet told me it was dredged up from the sea floor and washed along the coastline by ocean currents. Surprisingly, some sixty percent of the sand in front of me was composed of ground seashells. Across the bay, a rocky point jutted out into the sea and into the current that flowed up the coast, and this created an eddy behind it where the current slowed and dropped the pulverized seashells and seafloor dredgings it had been transporting. It deposited a sizable sandbar there, nearly damming off the entire river mouth. The sandbar is exposed at low tide, and I could almost walk across to the point on the other side. When the wind blows on warm and sunny days at low tide, the sandbar's surface dries out. Dried sand is loose and mobile, so individual grains of sand are blown across the bar to the beach I was sitting on, or blown further up, into the big dunes behind me.

The sandbar was aptly called 'Doom Bar', and was a nasty place in the days of wind-powered boats. It captured and wrecked over six hundred of them.

Padstow Harbor was practically the only refuge for ships along the hundred and forty miles of rocky coast between Land's End and Hartland Point, especially when gales blew out of the southwest. But when the sailing boats of old sought shelter in the harbor and rounded Stepper Point, the rock promontory across from me, they'd suddenly find themselves without wind, and no way to steer or make headway. And once rendered slack-sailed and helpless, the swirling currents of the eddy inexorably drove them onto Doom Bar.

In the early 1800s, enterprising interests quarried the tip of Stepper Point away, converting the last three hundred feet of the rock point into a breakwater rather than a tall bluff. This extended the area of fair wind for boats just enough to sail around the point and to reach the navigable channel at the head of Doom Bar, which was situated tightly up to the lee side of the rock promontory. Lookouts would fire rockets trailing a line to the boats as they entered the passage, and provided with this initial lifeline, the sailors could then 'warp' their way along a series of hooks and rings into Padstow with capstans, manually pulling their boats up to the harbor and safety.

When Emma and Leanne arrived, we got on the Padstow ferry, a flat, powered barge about thirty feet long and ten wide. The front deck was open, with benches along the gunwales, and we rode over in the open with our backpacks in front of us, sitting close to be heard over the motors and the wind.

Leanne and Emma had done some internet research as well and were looking forward to visiting a shop in Padstow that featured GMO and gluten free vegan pastries and ice cream. They tried to stir up some enthusiasm in me for the place, but they just couldn't, given the abominations inherent in making ice cream without real cream.

At low tide, the ferry goes ashore about a quarter mile downstream of town at the delightfully named Chiddleypump landing. I saw a rusted iron ring anchor-bolted into the rock about six feet above the waterline, and became excited at the thought that it may have been one of the warping rings of old.

I was pointing it out to Leanne and Emma when one of the ferry crew gave me this admonishment: "We are coming in to land and will be maneuvering the craft up against the rock wall. It's very possible that we will crush or sever any heads or limbs extended past the rails. You may wish to keep them safely aboard if it please you, sir."

I looked at him dumbly, so Emma pushed my arm down and spoke up. "Thank you," she said. "That would well please us all."

We walked with the rest of the ferry passengers into Padstow together, and the place was thronged with tourists. We stopped in front of a restaurant, The Shipwright's, as a white pickup truck and a couple of black SUVs with carbon-tinted windows worked their way through the crowd. They parked on the quay just in front of us, and people popped out and got to work. Most were wearing black denims and polo shirts, some unloading wooden crates and lobster traps from the truck and arranging them in a stack, while others attached lenses and readied camera equipment on folding tables they'd set up under the opened hatch doors of the SUVs.

There was a couple, a middle-aged man and woman, wearing outdated hiking clothes that were worn and tattered but weirdly clean. The woman, a diminutive pigeon lady, began consulting with the crew dressed in black, while the fellow, lean and bearded, chatted up the crowd of onlookers.

Two women in everyday dress walked over to the restaurant, where we were standing. The older woman chatted with the restaurant's owner, who had come outside. The younger woman saw the three of us wearing backpacks.

"Are you three hiking the Salt Path?" she asked.

"We are," Emma told her. "We've been at it three weeks now."

"And how are you finding it?"

"Lovely," Emma said.

"Beautiful," was Leanne's response.

"Kinda wet," I told her.

The young woman looked at me, frowned, then turned to Leanne and Emma. "How would you two like to be extras in our film shoot?" she asked.

She led them over to the bearded guy talking with the circle of people gathering around him and the lobster pots. A crew member was going around the circle, passing out money.

"Isn't this all so exciting?" the restaurateur asked me.

No one was giving free money away where we were standing. "It's exciting over there, anyway," I allowed.

One of the black-shirted guys carried a camera on his shoulder to stand next to me and the restaurateur, and another of the black-shirted guys waved at the bearded hiker guy and said, "Okay, we're ready."

The pigeon lady pulled a woolen cap over her hair and shouldered in to disappear into the crowd, and the hiker guy walked over to us, turned around,

Walking Wet

and walked back to the lobster pots. He had suddenly developed a pronounced limp.

He took off his backpack, pulled a wooden crate off the stack, and stood on top of it, shouting for everyone to gather around closer. He'd fished a leather-bound booklet from his pack and was waving it over his head.

The crowd quieted, and he began reading a passage from *Beowulf*. He was a gifted orator, his voice clear and strong. It was all staged, for sure. To attest to that were cinema cameras and a big fuzzy microphone held on a boom above him. But there was nothing inauthentic about the way he captured and mesmerized the people around him.

The pigeon lady hiker woman emerged from the crowd, took off her woolen cap, and held it out in front of her as she worked the arc of listeners. They started putting money into it. I saw Leanne and Emma make donations as well.

The man finished his reading, thanked and blessed the crowd, then stepped off the crate and hobbled back towards me and the camera to my right. The pigeon woman joined him, showing him the contents of her hat. They looked to be having an earnest conversation as they passed me, but they weren't really. They were nodding to each other and moving their mouths without making any noise, as if they were lip-syncing.

They carried on their silent conversation until they reached the quay and then came back. The man went back to chat with Leanne and Emma, and the other people milling around the lobster pots. The pigeon woman handed her hat to one crew member and then went to a folding table behind an SUV to review a laptop screen with another. Emma waved to get my attention and beckoned me over.

"This is our friend Rick," she said when I got there, "and he's hiking the whole Coastal Path as well. He's an American, and he's already hiked the Pacific Crest Trail, the long path over in the U.S."

"That is so amazing. I'm Jason," the man said, shaking my hand. "Just how long was it on the Pacific trail?"

"It was about five months," I told him. "About twenty-five hundred miles."

"I can't..... I have trouble imagining what would prompt a person to do something like that. I mean, just what motivates a person to keep going on such an arduous journey? What event happens in a life to make a person decide to take on a challenge like that?"

"Uh, I just did it because I'd always wanted to."

"What?"

"Well, I met a couple of people who had just gotten a divorce, a few who had lost their jobs, and a lot of visiting Europeans. One guy I met had shot himself in the knee, and after all the surgeries and rehab, he just wondered if he could do it."

"That fellow must have been American," Emma said.

"Yeah," I admitted.

"So, what about you three?" Jason asked. "What motivates the three of you to hike this path together?"

Leanne answered promptly. "We're not together," she said, glancing pointedly towards me.

Emma said, "I grew up in a village near the path, and now I've been several years away from home in the travel and eco-tour industry in Central America. I came back to walk and visit family here, so this is a homecoming of sorts for me."

Jason looked at me.

I shrugged. "Beats heck out of working. And I kind of like walking."

"I've gathered as much," he said. "Still, there must have been something specific that brought you here, so far away from home, to do this particular trail?"

"Well, there was this book, but I doubt you've heard of it. *The Salt Path?*"

Despite being half-covered in a grayish beard, Jason's face was exquisitely expressive, so his impression of me was plain: equal parts pity, confusion, and annoyance. He turned to Leanne and Emma. Leanne just shrugged.

"It's called Walker's Brain," Emma explained. "It happens to all of us long-distance walkers occasionally. It's the fatigue, the stress of homesickness, low blood sugar, or something, that from time to time, just makes us really stupid."

Jason looked me over again. "Fascinating," he said. "The fellow's walked a long way, he has."

A crew member tapped Jason on the shoulder and took his backpack. "It looks like we've got it," he said. He handed Jason a colorful fiver with Winston Churchill's portrait on it, saying, "Here, had some extra in the hat." Then he left to help load the lobster pots back into the truck.

"Oh, dear, this must be the little girl's money," Jason said. "I saw her put a bill in the hat. We only gave the prop money to the adults."

"What? It wasn't real money?" I asked. But Jason was ignoring me, standing on his tiptoes and looking over my shoulder.

"Oh, she's gone now," he said.

He was still holding the five-pound note and looking for her when the crew had the lobster pots tied down in the truck and the cameras put away in the SUVs. Jason was the last to get in before they worked their way back through the crowd and out of town. From the outside, the side windows were completely opaque, but I imagined Jason inside with his face pressed up against the glass, still holding the fiver and looking for the girl who had given it to him.

I turned to Emma. "Walker's Brain?" I asked.

"Do you not know who that was?" she asked. "That was Jason Isaacs."

My walker's brain had never heard of him.

"Captain Hook? Lucius Malfoy?"

"That guy is Lucius Malfoy? No way. He's so nice. That Malfoy is a total, well, a total you-know-what."

"Actors? Movie stars?" Leanne asked. "Ever hear of those? What did you think they were doing here? His costar is Gillian Anderson."

"That pigeon lady was Gillian Anderson? I thought they were shooting a gag for a reality show. They did the whole thing in one take, and nobody said 'Action!' or 'Cut!' It was just Jason reading poetry to a random bunch of tourists. I was surprised how much you all enjoyed it. I thought you Brits were famous for being sharp hecklers."

"We're not all Monty Python over here, you know," Emma said.

Leanne wasn't finished with me. "I was absolutely mortified when you told Jason Isaacs that he'd never heard of *The Salt Path*," she said, "just after he'd finished a scene from the MOVIE they are making from it."

"No one told me they were doing that."

"The producer's assistant didn't tell you?"

"That girl? All she said to me was that I'd make her 'ever so happy if I were stood over there and out of the way.'"

Emma jiggled one of my backpack straps. "Don't worry about it too much," she said. "Walker's Brain happens."

Just out of town and past the National Lobster hatchery, the Cove Camp office was situated by the entrance like a toll booth, but it looked more like a cozy wood-framed garden toolshed, or maybe a smallish espresso stand. Inside was an energetic earth child. She wore her hair in beaded dreads under a faded headband. Woven leather bracelets were on her wrists, and rings on a couple of her toes. She assigned me a tent pitch for the night and marked the arrangement in a worn binder.

"So, you're all set for the night. How are you finding Cornwall? It's a long way from America, innit?"

"It is. But how do you know I'm American?"

"For starters, I just rented you a tent 'site' instead of a tent 'pitch.' That alone makes you Canadian or American."

"And what made you guess American?"

"I didn't at first. You asked if I had any tent sites available instead of telling me direct that you wanted one. So, I thought 'Canadian' because your gentle manner of speech. But then you paid for your tent pitch like it was a business transaction you had to close."

"It wasn't?"

She laughed. It was infectious.

"You've got me pretty well pegged. I'm from the west coast of the United States, near the Canadian border."

"That explains it," she said. "I'm Sam."

A young man came through the back door of the hut. He too had dreads under a headband, and his shirt and shorts sported the threadbareness and stretched wrinkles that come from enduring regular handwashing and wringing. His eyes seemed to take in everything at once, and when they rested on me, he smiled through a curly and blondish beard.

"Ah, Trevor, perfect timing," Sam said. "This is our American visitor. I just rented him a tent pitch."

Trevor offered me a hand to shake. "What about you two?" I asked. "Are you locals? Grow up here in Cornwall?"

"Sam and I are both from Bristol, though we didn't meet till university."

"How far is Bristol from here?" I asked.

"It's a good day by bus. Far enough to be a different world, but close enough to visit," Sam said.

"So are you and Trevor here year-round?"

"Not quite. The camp here closes for the winter. In October, just as mushroom season begins. We do some foraging, sell some mushrooms for cash, visit our parents back in Bristol, and then spend our winters in Spain."

"Spain? I'd imagine it rains less in the winter there than here," I said.

"That it does. It's also less expensive," Trevor added.

Sam explained, "We found a small tent community not far outside of a town. With what we make working here and the mushrooms, we get on until spring, when the camp here reopens."

"So, where do you live when you're working here? You all rent a place in Padstow?"

They both laughed.

"What?" I asked.

"Nobody lives in Padstow," Trevor said.

"I just walked through there. It was packed with people."

"Yes, but none of them live in Padstow. They're all on holiday, visitors like you. It's too expensive to live there."

"We have a yurt here at the camp," Sam explained. "It comes with the job, and it's perfect. We ''ave everything we need and we're right here in case anything comes up. This is our fifth year here. It's ideal."

She spoke cheerfully, but I wondered if their semi-nomadic lifestyle, without plumbing, and shuttling back and forth between patches of ground owned by others, had ever been part of their life plans. Maybe it was just the best balance they could strike between necessity and desire. I risked prying.

Walking Wet

"When you were growing up, did you ever dream you'd be gypsy adventure travelers, or did you picture yourselves putting down roots in a country bungalow and having children?" I asked.

Sam looked at me thoughtfully but didn't answer.

"That's my parents' dream, there," Trevor said. "But doing that brings serious tradeoffs. We're not about banging on just to make a quid, and I don't see us doing the whole 'nine-to-five' thing, and all the rubbish that comes with it."

"I see what you mean. But are your folks some disappointed then?"

"I wouldn't say disappointed. They's eternally hopeful, I'd say."

"His mum keeps texting me baby emojis," Sam said.

"You're kidding. That's hilarious."

"A right nagger, she is," Trevor said, laughing.

"Well," I said, "I have a teenage boy who doesn't see himself doing the whole 'nine-to-five' thing either. He wants to roam around in an old bus with a partner, surf a bunch of waves, and make a bunch of kids."

"There are aspects that don't seem especially practical," Trevor observed.

"Exactly," I said. "I can't see a bus as a viable home."

"Really? Buses are right difficult to keep on the road, I was going to say," said Trevor. "And if it's parked, there's nowt more freedom than a house."

"Especially if it's filled with kids," Sam added.

Walking Wet

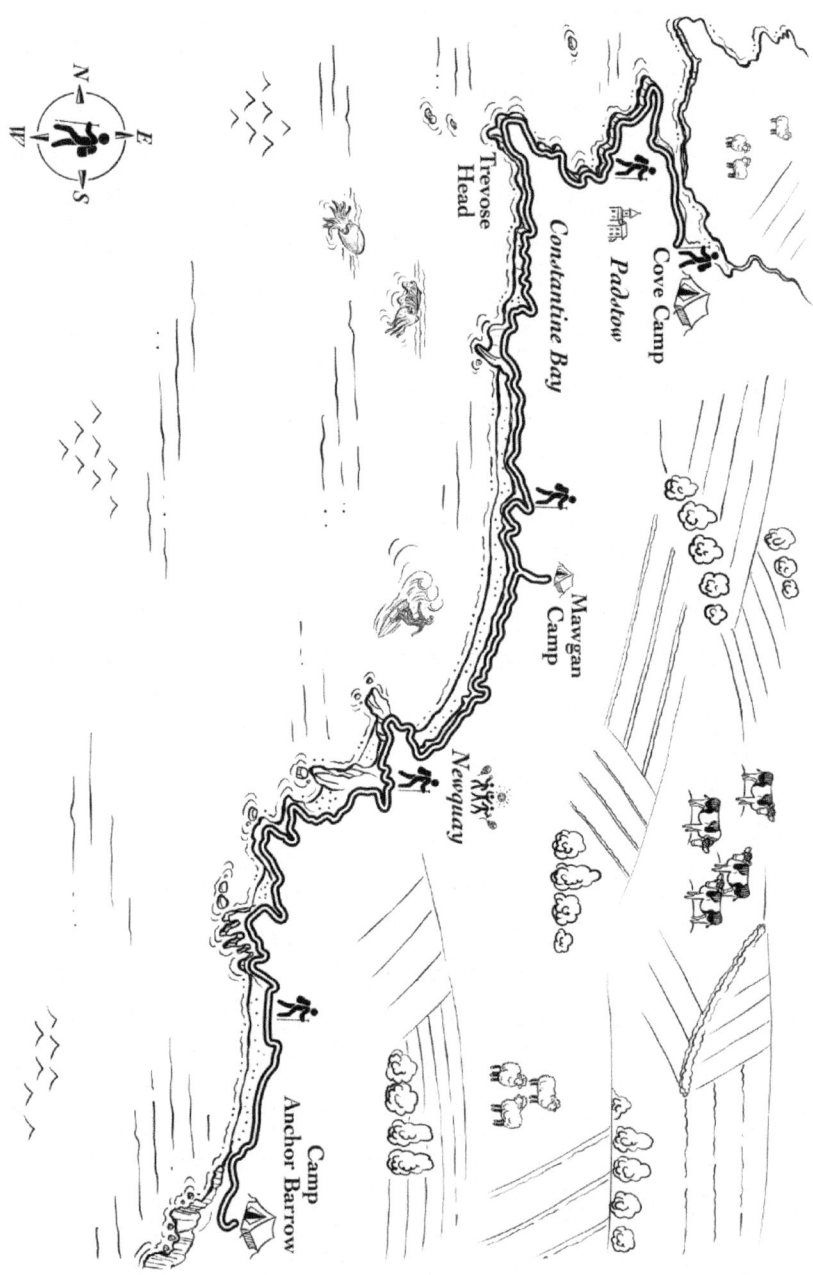

Cuttlefish Skeletons

19 ··· DAYS WALKING
155 ··· PATH MILES WALKED
219 ··· TOTAL MILES WALKED
https://www.southwestcoastpath.org.uk/walksdb/150/

The next morning, I was walking back through Padstow to the path well before six. The sailboats in the inner harbor were peacefully afloat even though the tide was out. A pair of ingenious heavy wooden gates, called half-tide flap-gates are mounted at the inner harbor entrance. They're hinged like old west saloon doors so they can swing freely, except that they're built too long to swing past each other so when they close, they jam against each other instead.

They hold seawater behind them when they're closed, keeping the sailboats docked inside afloat, even as the tide recedes. Outside, the commercial vessels anchored in the greater harbor were stranded on the exposed sandflats. When the tide comes back in, the water pressure jamming the gates together would be equalized, and they could be opened so boats could enter or leave at will. The gates' heights are set so they're over-topped when the tide was about halfway to full height, or half-tide, and then flap themselves closed again as the tide ebbs down to below that half-tide elevation.

The gates didn't make a perfect seal, and small jets and trickles were leaking from the seam. I noticed a handful of silvery mullets, mackerel-looking fishies, swimming below me and grazing on the algae growing on the watered, inner sides of the flap gates.

There's some smart cookies, I thought.

Some years ago, I'd been involved in an effort to count fish in an intertidal harbor much like that of the River Camel. The sand floors of these intertidal harbors can be extremely flat-bottomed. At one of our test sites, it was a two-mile trek across exposed sand when the tide was out from the high tide shoreline to the water's edge at low tide. That fish can live in intertidal zones is remarkable enough; twice a day there's no water over them. But what really surprised me was how at home the fish that live there can be. Territorial, even.

The fish counting project worked like this: At high tide, a crew of us would wade out to our test sites and set up 'fyke' nets. Imagine a volleyball net, except that it's four times as wide, the fabric it's made from is softer, and the grid openings are pea-sized. Tie cork footballs onto the top edge so it floats and then weave a weighted line onto the bottom, so that edge sinks. Now, make a windsock from the same fabric, and attach a ten-gallon bucket to its small end. Sew the wide end of the windsock onto a hole you've cut in the center of the volleyball net, and that's basically a fyke trap net. The volleyball net wings are staked out to create a broad 'V', with the opening towards shore, and the pointy end with the fyke bucket away. That way, as the tide goes out, the intertidal fish get funneled into the 'V' and are trapped inside the windsock's fyke bucket.

As the tide lowered, we'd upend the fyke into a series of smaller buckets and start sorting and counting fish. Most of them, we could toss back into the water so they could continue to be carried away by the tide. But some of them, the species we were especially interested in, would be treated to special privileges. These guys, we dropped into a bucket of anesthetizing solution that knocked them out so we could pump their little stomachs empty and see what they'd been eating. Then we'd mark them by cutting their fins with nail scissors. For each site, we'd cut a different pattern of little slits or notches into their fins. Then we'd put them into recovery buckets, tickle them with aquarium bubblers, and once perked up, would carry them out to the ebbing tideline to pour them out. There could be a hundred or two of them in a set.

The next day, we'd go to the same sites to do it all again. Now here's the crazy part: if we'd marked up a hundred little fish at a site the day before, we'd catch maybe sixty of them back there again the next day. Consider that for a minute.

What they had done, in order for us to catch them again, was to ride two miles out with the tide, and then, as the tide turned, pilot themselves back again to the same patch of sandflats. And most of them were small enough that you could scoop them up with a credit card.

And they hadn't done it just once. Because tides cycle twice each day, they'd done it twice. They'd swept over eight miles of tide flats. Presumably, it's something they do each and every day. You would need to line up seventy of them nose-to-tail to be as long as an average-sized human. So, scaling up the intertidal fishes' feats of swimming and homing to our size, one of us humans would need to comport ourselves over five hundred miles each day to match what those minnows routinely do just to stay home.

I have my doubts about any of us humans being able to do it even once, especially if we'd gotten our stomachs pumped out and our limbs sliced up just the day before.

So yeah, I took note of the mullets poking around the inside of the flap gates, because I knew what they would have to be doing out on the intertidal flats if they hadn't found themselves a niche to claim as home. I'd roam over more shoreline this day than they would.

Even though I'd been on holiday in England for almost three weeks, it was the first morning I'd been given where I could do exactly and only what I wanted to do. I didn't know where I'd spend the night, but as there was no one else to consider, it didn't matter.

Matthew and Rhonda were in a hotel near Gatwick airport and would soon be flying home without me. I'd enjoyed camping next to Leanne and Emma the night before, but they were at least as independently equipped as I was, and we needn't walk or camp together again. All I owed them was a little peace and quiet as I packed my tent and things. Which I did, without waking them. I'd left and walked past the lobster hatchery, gulped down the last of my two breakfast bars, and had been presented with a wide-open and seemingly deserted town to walk through. It was beautiful.

For me, walking early when the world is calm brings balance, Zen even, and I cherished these mornings as divine gifts. And gifts so precious ought to be shared. But it's difficult to roust a reasonable person out of a warm sleeping bag that early, and I'm grievously misunderstood when I try. Likewise, when I insist they eat cold granola bars on the move instead of having themselves a hot coffee or chocolate in camp. My morning mantra, "Early miles are easy miles!" grates on their nerves. Matthew, for instance, won't hear it anymore and mocks me with retorts like, "Early miles are *stupid* miles" or just tells me bluntly, "You suck." People don't seem to notice how eager I am to share early mornings' divine gifts with them, concluding instead that I'm irritatingly impatient.

Well, I have news for them. I'm not impatient. They should all just hurry up and realize that.

Especially my loved ones. But when they aren't into early walking as much as I am, like because it's raining maybe, or it's giving them heart attacks and such, my enthusiasm gets misidentified as a monomania, or thoughtless pushiness, or possibly chronic cluelessness. However misinterpreted, they find it irksome. I love them and they love me, but it makes things stressful.

Strolling solo past the lazy mullets and through an empty Padstow, it wasn't lost on me that I'd likely be alone for the rest of the Salt Path. I resolved to be open, observant, thoughtful, and tranquil. I'd have no one to share the adventures with, but I decided to still allow the path to fill me with contentment and quiet joy.

Walking Wet

It had drizzled overnight, but patches of promising blue were above me, peeking through the clouds. I smiled and looked up at them, and as I leaned back, some of the chilled morning dew that had been on my tent as I broke camp in the morning found its way through the bottom of my backpack to dribble down my butt crack.

I hiked around the partially quarried point I'd admired the day before, and beyond were a lot more cliffs and a few isolated beaches. One of which was signposted as Butterhole Beach, a name I found at once delightful and disturbing. The beach was roundish and surrounded by cliffs, was a long way down, and when seen from above, had sand of a buttery yellow hue.

The path stayed mostly on the cliff tops as it went out and around another point, Trevose Head, before dropping down to a properly long and wide beach with breakers coming in from the open ocean.

The Coast Path walks along the entire three-quarter mile length of the beach fronting Constantine Bay. A stiff breeze came off the ocean, but the sun was out and almost warm. The beach was made up of perfect sand, and I took my shoes and socks off to feel it between my toes. There was nothing squishy to avoid, like kelp or seaweed strewn about, but there were thousands of brittle little husks tossed up onto the beach.

They were hollow, about the size and shape of a bar of soap half gone, and a little wider at one end than the other. They were thin-walled, yellowed, and translucent, and partially open at either end. You could put one upright in a shirt pocket to hold your pencils. They must have been some kind of sea creatures at one time, or maybe parts they'd discarded. I'd never seen them before.

Partway down the beach, a silver-armed old driftwood oak lay half-buried in the sand. I stopped and dug the tent out of my backpack, along with everything else that had gotten wet, and tied it to the gnarled branches so it could whip and dry in the wind. I sat and leaned back against the log and watched a lone figure working his way up the beach towards me. He was about my age, wearing Bermuda shorts and a polo shirt, and had headphones attached to a metal detector.

"Hi there," I said when he came close to me. "Find anything yet?"

He pulled his headphones down to wear them like a cervical collar and smiled. "So far, nought but a nice day," he said. "Enjoying the beach, are ye?"

"Yes, it's good to get dried out. Hey, I'm wondering. You're a local guy, right? Do you know what all these things are?" I put one of the little husks to my lips like a kazoo and hummed the first few notes of 'Norwegian Wood' into it.

"Them's is cuttlefish skeletons. All at's left o' them when they dies."

"Really? Which end was I blowing on?"

"Rear end, I think. The cuttlebone used to sit inside there."

"I've seen cuttlebones in pet stores and parakeet cages, but I'd always thought it was a made-up name for bird suet."

"No, they's real things. When cuttlefish are alive, the cuttlebone is porous and they controls their buoyancy with it, like a fish's air bladder."

"There are a lot of them here. Do cuttlefish migrate here to spawn or something?"

"No. They must have lived close by, just out there," he said, waving towards the surf. "They don't migrate or move. They lives only a year or two, and muck about in just a small bit o' seafloor, below the waves and currents. Their whole lives they does in an area about the size of a football pitch, if I remember right."

"How do you know so much about cuttlefish?"

The man shrugged. "David Attenborough," he said.

"I haven't seen these skeletons on any other beach. Why are they only right here?"

"Sir David didn't say." He shrugged again and put his headphones back over his ears. "Have a good day, now." He swept the metal detector in an arc over the sand, then stepped into it. He made another arc, stepped into that, then another.

Emma and Leanne still hadn't arrived when my tent and things were dried, so I packed up to leave, setting out without them for the second time that morning. I didn't know where I'd end up camping that night, nor who I'd be camping with. And I didn't know about the next night either, or any of the other nights ahead of me till the end of the path.

I'd hiked the Pacific Crest Trail a few years earlier. It had taken about five months of walking and camping, and most of the time I didn't know exactly where I'd be camping nights either. But there, it didn't really matter. On the PCT, pitching a tent is allowed almost anywhere beside the trail. Choosing the next campsite had less to do with where it was than it did with how many miles it was from the last one. You would decide how many miles you needed to walk that day, and then camp just about wherever you happened to be when that was accomplished.

It was different in England, where the Coast Path is almost entirely on private land. You are welcome to walk along it, but camping on the trail is considered trespassing. The citizenry in England is woefully under-armed to deal properly with trespassers, but I'd decided to be respectful anyway and to camp only in approved, pay-for-pitch sites. And these were usually some distance from the path.

On the PCT, I needn't choose a campsite before I was tired of walking. Here, it made sense to plan ahead. I'd been relying on Rhonda for that until she left, and then I attached myself to Emma and Leanne. But for this day, there was no plan, no reservations. I didn't know how far I'd get before I got

Walking Wet

tired of walking, nor how much further I'd need to go to find a campsite when I did.

It was weird, not knowing these things. At home, I was a respectable little cuttlefish and enjoyed a healthy level of predictability and security. But now, I knew less than those whose skeletons were all around me. I knew less even than the mullets behind the flap gates in Padstow, or their friends riding the tides out and back across the flats. I'd be going with the flow all right, but unlike them, at the end of each day, I would wash up somewhere off my path, and each time, someplace different.

Walking Wet

Red Right Hand

22 ⋯ DAYS WALKING
196 ⋯ PATH MILES WALKED
268 ⋯ TOTAL MILES WALKED
https://www.southwestcoastpath.org.uk/walksdb/156/

Despite not knowing where I'd wash up each night, I settled into a routine of sorts and made good mileage over the next couple days. It wasn't as difficult or as inefficient as I had feared it would be. I made nineteen miles on the path that first day out of Padstow, and only had to walk another mile and a half to find a camp that night. The next day, I put another seventeen miles of path behind me and camped only a half-mile off the path. And the day after, I covered ten miles of path with another six miles of off-path travel.

On average, I walked an additional three miles or so off the path at the end of each walking day getting to or from campsites. The path was still beautiful, but I'd seen two hundred miles of it walking along cliff tops, through cove villages, and astride beaches, and the coastline had begun to lose its novelty. I started to gain a special appreciation for the miles I walked inland on my way to and from the campsites. My feet were sore by the end of the day while I was doing them, but those "inefficient miles" that I initially considered wasted energy became daily treats I looked forward to. The camps and miles off the path were where I ran across the most interesting experiences and people.

One was Jane, who rented me a room in her house in Hayle. She made ornate wedding dresses from used tea bags, stitching them together with handmade thread she'd spun from nettles. They were exquisitely beautiful. She also advocated for and rescued industrially farmed chickens.

I wondered how that worked, practically and logistically, and imagined her sneaking onto the grounds of chicken farms at night, dressed head-to-toe in black and opening the big rolling doors that kept the chickens inside. I imagined her screaming, "Fly! Fly away for your lives!" and then being knocked down by a violent hurricane of blindly panicked chicken flappings, loosed feathers, and a gale-force pelting of wet chicken poo.

"That would be stupid," she informed me. "It wouldn't do anyone any good, least of all the chickens." What she did instead was occasionally go to a chicken farm with cash in hand to buy a few washed-up chickens to take home for a while and find them new homes in suburban backyards.

Factory farms manipulate every aspect of chickens' indoor environments to accelerate egg production, but it only works for so long. Laying hens only eighteen months old are already 'washed up' in that system, but taken outside, can be healthy and productive for another seven to ten years.

It unsettled me that I hadn't before appreciated the mistreatment chickens endured at the behest of agribusiness and food production technology, especially since I'd walked away from dairy farming for much the same reasons.

Initially Jane's altruism struck me as kooky, and I thought her endeavors would likely lead to nothing more than a couple of stoats and foxes in the suburbs getting chicken dinners. Her efforts on behalf of chickens' well-being were surely too small to move the needle, so why bother?

There is no shortage of serious problems and injustices in the world that are more serious than chicken welfare, and precious few of them that can be resolved by any one person. But meeting Jane made me consider again if that was a valid justification to stand by and do nothing. After all, it's not just a few lucky chickens that benefit from having Jane in their world, because it's our world too that she's laboring in. Compare Jane to most of us, and she is a bit kooky. But compare most of us to her, and we're stingy.

That I'd rented the room from Jane in the first place was due to Emma staying in touch with me through WhatsApp and sending me occasional weather warnings and updates.

Back home, I follow a local weather blog that laments NOAA's lack of funding and access to supercomputers and claims that the British Met Office uses a more sophisticated forecasting model and more powerful supercomputers. Their forecasts project further into the future and are rendered at finer scales than ours. Their forecasts tell you exactly what to expect in fifteen-minute intervals out to sixteen days in advance, differentiated down to parcels of land no larger than a movie triplex's parking lot. They are incredibly detailed, but I found them to be virtually unusable.

The forecasts are chronically and perpetually incorrect, as if they had been generated by ChatGPT's socially backward cousin. But whenever I complained to a native about the obvious and undeniable discrepancies between the weather forecasted and the weather we were actually standing in, they'd explain that we were 'stood here in a local microclimate zone,' and that viewing a sunny forecast while being poured upon was not only perfectly acceptable but to be expected.

Being American, I sensed a state-sponsored propaganda and brainwashing campaign, a governmental conspiracy perpetuated by England's Meteorological Office. Every Brit alive today genuinely believes they live in a micro-climatic zone and that the bogus forecasts generated by the Met Office are flawless. I know this to be true, but to what purpose I've no idea.

So, I had stopped reading the weather forecasts altogether, which kept my mind safely insulated from their deep-state control, but led me, admittedly, into walking through downpours more often than completely necessary. Emma noticed and took it upon herself to read the Met Office weather forecasts, tea-leaf style presumably, and to interpret and summarize them for me whenever something remarkable was on the horizon. The 'British Weather Forecast for Dummies' text messages she sent were practical and to the point. [Get tent pitched before 3:00 p.m.] her message might say, or [Find a roof to get under for lunch.]

Emma's forecasts were uncannily reliable. And she didn't seem, though one can never be certain, intent upon brainwashing me for some nefarious purpose.

***

I left Jane's house before full daylight the next morning and had walked through the old explosives plant and sand dunes behind her house to get back onto the path when another of Emma's weather updates reached me.

[Stay put until 1:00 p.m.] it read.

Too late for that, I thought. I kept moving.

I was walking through Saint Ives by 6:30, and except for a guy driving a street sweeper and a couple of binmen, had the town to myself. It was enchanting, and I made a video call back home, where it was 10:30 at night, to share the experience with Monica. We climbed and twisted through the narrow cobblestoned streets together, flanked by buildings of five-hundred-year-old stonework.

The ground floors hosted touristy curio shops, or pastry and pasty shops, still closed but perfectly suitable for window shopping. King Charles had been crowned not long before, and above us were Union Jacks and colorful pennants strung between the tenement balconies above. We traversed the entire town, and as the path left the streets of Saint Ives for the brush-lined and muddy track beyond, Monica signed off as well.

The skies were dark gray, and the winds blustery, but it wasn't raining yet. I wondered if Emma's forecast was mistaken or if I had indeed stumbled into a genuine microclimate zone that eluded even her predictions. Presently though, spatters of rain arrived. Then it began to pour. Heavily.

As the weather deteriorated, so too did the path I was on. In the brushy sections, veg and brambles encroached and covered the trail, and the wind commanded the wet branches and leaves to lash at me and my pack. I held my hands over my face, as if holding binoculars, to keep my eyes from being gouged. Where the path broke out into the open, rain driven horizontally by a ridiculous wind blasted cold water through my rain gear. The track itself turned into a mud-bottomed, knee-deep rut liberally strewn with rocks resembling bread loaves in size and shape, which rolled about haphazardly when stepped upon. In places where the path turned steep, the track became undefined, morphing into a slippery scramble over slime-slicked and lichened wet boulders.

At one point, sure that I had wandered off the trail, I fished my phone out of my side pocket and the Ziploc bag it was sealed in to check my location on OS Maps. I could see the little yellow triangle representing my position overlaid perfectly onto the dotted line of the Coastal Path under the rivulets of rain washing my phone screen. I looked around again but couldn't discern a path any more than I had before taking my phone out.

I pulled an earbud out of the Ziploc, stuck it in an ear, and chose suitable music for the endeavor before resealing my phone back into the bag and stowing it away again in the hip belt pocket.

I carried on in generally the indicated direction, over boulders, through brush or sideways rain, on the lookout for the deep ruts and tumbly bread loaf rocks marking the path proper while contemplating the real possibility of wrecking my knees or hips, or maybe tumbling over a cliff to my death onto the rocks below, with the wind howling in one ear and the movie soundtrack from *Dumb and Dumber* playing in the other.

Emma's message had intimated that the storm should be passing by early afternoon, so I could look forward to improving conditions in three or four hours. Not so long then, but on the other hand, plenty of time to arrange any number of routefinding or limb-altering maladies. I slowed down enough to avoid making calamitous missteps, but not so much, I hoped, to slide my core body temperature any further into hypothermia. I picked my way along while Nick Cage sang "Red Right Hand" into my left ear...

"Take a little walk to the edge of town and go across the tracks. Where the viaduct looms like a bird of doom as it shifts and cracks.

"Where secrets lie in the border fires, in the humming wires, 'Hey man, you know you're never coming back..."

A sheep-sized tunnel appeared in the brush on my left, spitting a rivulet of silt and mushed leaves into the water, mud, and bread loaf rocks I was walking on. I stopped for a quick peek at the OS map. It was a 'public walking path' and it led to a farmyard nearby and the highway just beyond. I crouched down into the tunnel and followed it up.

"Past the square, past the bridge, past the mills, past the stacks.
On a gathering storm comes a tall, handsome man in a dusty black coat, with a red right hand..."

The sheep tunnel, after boring through a half-mile of brush, opened up into a stone-walled cow lane, but a rarely used one. As the way widened, the overarching brush that had made the tunnel's roof pulled away, allowing the thistles and stinging nettles to find daylight enough to grow face height. At the lane's first opening in the rock wall, I went through it and found myself behind a herd of dairy cows huddled together, tails to the wind and chewing their cuds as calmly as my old girls ever had.

It's instinctive for cows to huddle close against the weather if a storm is miserable enough, and this one definitely was. I wedged myself between a pair of cows' rumps and wriggled my way into the herd between warm and paunchy bellies. Warmth seeped back into me as I looked over the tops of their streaming backs and drooping, dripping ears.

"He'll wrap you in his arms, tell you that you've been a good boy. He'll rekindle all the dreams it took you a lifetime to destroy..."

I was warm again by the time I'd made my way through the herd. My feet hadn't been stepped on much, and as an added bonus, I hadn't been pooped on at all. Beyond the farm was the highway where I could flag down a bus. Public transport in England apparently has no interest in brainwashing people, and forty minutes after leaving the cows, a bus came by, exactly as scheduled.

It was already filled to standing-room only, cram-packed with damp and disappointed tourists, but the driver stopped to let me squeeze on anyway. A few of the riders objected to the operation, but they were in the minority and much easier to move off their marks than the cows I'd just been through anyway.

"You'll see him in your nightmares, you'll see him in your dreams.
He'll appear out of nowhere, but he ain't what he seems..."

The bus driver told me he'd take me to the next town, Pendeen, where I could duck into a pub and get 'owt 'e rain.' And as the plan I'd made for myself had included no more than surviving for the day, and seeing that I had already mostly accomplished that, adopting the bus driver's plan for me sounded reasonable enough.

"You're one microscopic cog in his catastrophic plan,
designed and directed by his red right hand..."

The pub he dropped me off in front of had a big fireplace hearth inside, the kind they used a couple hundred years ago to boil cast iron pots of stew in, but it wasn't lit. A couple of locals sitting on barstools were, though, even though it was barely past noon. Behind them on the wall was a plaque that read, "Get pissed and talk shite!"

I disobeyed, however, and the barman made up a pot of coffee for me instead. I stayed inside, nursing my coffees and noodling my phone, but the cell service kept dropping out on my web browser. The rain began tapering off at about 1:30, and bless Emma's kind heart, the sun showed itself through a kettle-shaped hole in the clouds. I went outside and had a look around.

About a mile behind the pub, a hill sporting a low beret of granite looked down on the town. Improving weather or no, I'd had enough of the Coastal Path for the day. I hiked up the hill to find some better cell service, and once there, it was short work to find another Airbnb for the night.

When I'd come down from the hill and walked back towards the north end of town, Ted, my night's host, pulled his car over to the curb and waved me in. He brought me to a new terrace-style home and opened the door in the left unit. His wife Margaret was just inside to greet us, and I could smell warm biscuits and freshly brewed tea coming from the kitchen behind her. We settled ourselves around a tea setting on their kitchen table. An expansive wooden patio deck was just through the sliding glass doors, and out beyond, I could see the hill above town that I'd climbed to get cell service.

"Nice view out the back here," I commented. "I was just up there when I made the booking for your place."

"We saw you up there, while you were texting us then," Margaret said.

"I was trying to guess which house was yours. The village is beautiful from up there." I looked around the well-appointed modern kitchen. Their kitchen looked American, resembling mine back home more than it did Jane's or Sandy and Duncan's, the other English kitchens I'd visited. "It's beautiful inside here, too. I like the flooring and the countertops."

"Thank you," Ted was visibly proud. "The contractor what done the refurbishing suggested we go for a New World style when we chose the interiors. Makes you feel at home, does it?"

"That it does. How long have you been here, then?"

"We just moved in six months ago," Margaret said. "We sold our place in north London to come here. We've never lived in so much space before. There's drawers in this kitchen with nowt to puts in them."

"Our London house, we paid ten thousand pounds for it in 1975," Ted said. "Last year, we sold it for fifty times what we'd paid for it."

"Whoa. Who bought it, then?" I asked.

"Never met the bloke who bought it. Our agent said it was an investor buying homes to let. Isn't that crazy? I was a cab driver with a wife pregnant when we bought that house. The older couple who sold it us had raised their family in it, and I'd always imagined selling someday to another young couple when it came our turn."

"Well, if the buyer is renting it out there could be another young family under its roof right now," I said.

"Yes, but they be renting," Ted pointed out. "How can a young couple starting a family afford to buy a house now? The prices are so bad, young people can't even get into the market. We have two grown children with good jobs who can't afford them a house. Our daughter is an office manager, our son a policeman in London. Their spouses have good jobs, too, but still they be renting."

"You know?" I said. "Come to think of it, since I've been here, I've met only old coots like us who own the homes they live in. Younger folks I've met, they're renting, or they live in a van, or a yurt, or they've parked a caravan someplace. I even saw families living on derelict boats pushed up in the mud and tied up along a shore."

"It's a shame," Margaret said. "Young people needs them a place of their own, and it be near impossible. They can't gets a home to lives where they'd grown up."

"So are youth here in Britain moving out of the country?" I asked.

"Don't be soft!" Margaret admonished. "Where woulds they go for better? The U.S.?"

"Well, maybe," I said. "It's better in some places back home, I think, than London."

"People with money started buying property for investments even here in Cornwall, never minds London," Ted said. "It's not nice. Here we are, me, a retired cab driver and me wife, a retired pastry baker, sat here in a lovely new home while our children with university educations and good jobs struggle to rent anything half as nice. Now, how did that happen?"

I was beginning to feel jangled and jittery. Margaret's tea was stronger than I'd expected, especially after having downed a pot of coffee earlier in the pub. I shrugged. "My smartest friend back home says it's because we've allowed an essential human need to be commodified," I said.

"Did you ask him what that means?"

"I did. It's like investing in art, where what determines a painting's value is how rare it is and how many people want it."

"And the more valuable it becomes," Margaret said, "the more's the people who wants it."

"Exactly. Add mortgage options and tax rules, and homes become really good investments for people who don't really need them, like paintings in art collections."

Ted pointed a finger at me. "You lot should work on that."

"You guys first, Ted. My country is kind of big and slow, and it's always seemed that we're following you Brits anyway."

"Really? I always thought it was us following you."

"Naw," I said. "Rolling Stones. Gay marriage. National healthcare. You do it first, then send it over."

"McDonald's," Ted said, "Starbucks, skateboarders, box stores, drug overdoses…"

"No fair, that last one you got from Holland!" I protested.

Margaret got us back on track. "If homes hadn't got so expensive, we couldn't have sold in London or got this house we be in now. Neither would you be here on holiday, eh?"

"Right, that," I said.

"If we work hard, we deserve to have a nice place to live in someday. Just like we have here," Ted said, "or your place back home. That shouldn't change."

"But it has changed," Margaret said. "We worked hard and saved. But our kids, they work hard as we did, and can't save enough. We can't tell them to be more frugal and work harder than we did."

"Kids don't work hard today," Ted said. "They don't commit to real work, anyway. When I started, cabmen had to learn the Knowledge. We had to learn every street and every landmark in London and pass the Knowledge test before we could even charge a fare. These days, they just follows an app on their phone."

"Now, that was just new technology, Ted," Margaret said. "You can't use that as an example."

"Oh, I'm with Ted," I said. "I think that may be a perfect example. The Knowledge is still essential to get around London. But now, cabmen get an app and use it to rent a tiny piece of the Knowledge for each trip. It's easier and cheaper for cabmen to use an app than spending years mastering the Knowledge, so they can undercut the price of a fellow that does."

"Still charge more than they're worth," Ted groused.

"That may be, but the point is that the Knowledge is still essential, and it's still being paid for. But instead of the money going to the cabmen who learned it, it's going to whoever owns the app the drivers are using."

Ted thought about that for a moment. "They be raking in a lot of money," he said.

"Probably buying up property with it," Margaret mused. "Do you have any children?"

"We do, a teenage son," I said. "We had ours relatively late in life."

"He be scrimping and saving forever to gets him into a house. Best wait for youse to die and inherit the house ye boughts while it was still affordable, eh?"

"Ted!" Margaret admonished.

Ted put his teacup back on the table shakily and grabbed at his chest, feigning a heart attack.

"And yours won't be long in waiting either, dear, if you don't start walking more," Margaret scolded.

"Oi! But me knees is bad," he croaked. But he looked at us and then shook his head, all clowning aside.

Walking Wet

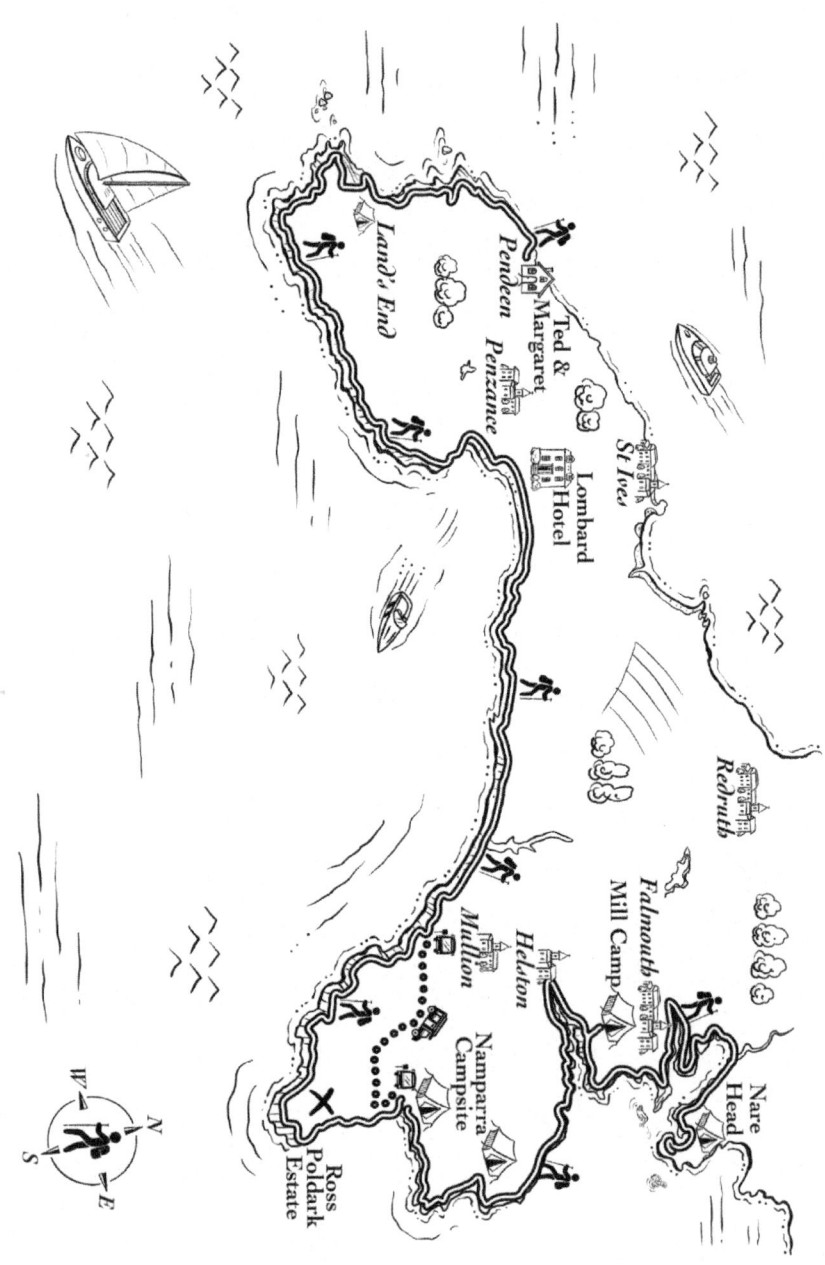

A Right Bloody Wanker

31 ⋯ DAYS WALKING
319 ⋯ PATH MILES WALKED
416 ⋯ TOTAL MILES WALKED
https://www.southwestcoastpath.org.uk/walksdb/157/

I set out the next morning, backtracking to walk the section of the path I'd bused around the day before. It was weirdly uncomfortable with the ocean on my left instead of my right. I could hear waves crashing onto the rocks below me through the wrong ear, and the wind buffeted the wrong side of my face. Somehow, it made my feet uneasy.

The path was different here. Gone was the mud from the day before, as were the ruts with the bread loaf rocks in them. There was no brush encroaching over the track, nor steep sections with boulders to clamber over. All around was heather growing through gravel, except for the tread itself, where there was only gravel.

Tin has been mined in the area around Pendeen almost continuously since the Bronze Age. The last mine quit in 1990, the Geevor Mine, situated right on the Coastal Path where I'd started my day of wrong-way walking. It's open today still, but now as an educational landmark and tourist attraction.

In prehistoric times, the ore was exposed right on the surface, and people used sticks and deer antlers to stab and pry it loose. But the ore-rich veins ran deep, and as time passed, the ore was extracted from tunnels dug underground. Most of the tin production came after the 1700s when Cornishmen got their hands on dynamite. Some four hundred fifty thousand tons of tin were mined and smelted from the shafts they bored and blasted through the solid rock, chasing after those veins.

The tin ore in Cornwall was some of the world's richest, but the veins were usually no more than a couple of feet wide. To mine them, the

Walking Wet

Cornishmen had to tunnel through a lot of granite that bore no tin at all. If the mines were close enough to the shoreline, miners wheelbarrowed the ore-less rock to a cliff to dump into the sea. As those mines got deeper, they'd sometimes bore tunnels horizontally out through the cliff faces to dump the waste rock out of. Some of them are still looking out over the surf below, and you can easily see them today.

But most of the mines weren't that convenient to the shoreline. I walked through the mining district for the next few days and trod over a lot of waste rock that hadn't been so easy to get rid of, granite that had been blasted and pulverized into craggy little walnuts and spread over the ground.

Later, I was to be stuck in a hotel room to wait out yet another storm, and I calculated how much rock had been brought out of the tunnels and mineshafts. Starting with the four hundred fifty thousand tons of tin production purported on Mine Greevor's educational placard, and making reasonable estimates, about three million truckloads of waste gravel and tailings had likely been dumped over the district in the last three hundred years.

That's a lot of gravel, and spread evenly, would cover the mining district's forty-eight thousand acres six inches deep. That walnut-sized granite mulch makes it tough to grow anything other than heather and low grasses. But for mud-free and crunchy walking with unobstructed views, it can't be beat.

The path lost its gravel and became muddy and brushy again just before I reached the sheep tunnel I'd bailed out through the day before. The friendly herd of dairy cows were out standing in their field, but with no rainstorm to huddle against, were dispersed and grazing. I doubt any of them recognized me. Few of them even bothered to look up.

The wait for the bus was pleasanter this time and the ride less crowded. I rode it back to Geevor Mine, and after a brief self-guided tour of the interpretive signage, got my feet back onto the path, this time pointed in the proper direction.

***

The next morning, the path took me round the bend of the westernmost tip of England at Land's End. At 6 a.m., as the timing worked out, and I had the point to myself. For a brief period on that Friday morning, I was the nearest human on English soil to everyone I knew back home, and to everyone else in my country. Standing there alone and looking out over the gray ocean, I could feel it. If ever a debate breaks out between cosmologists over the existence of a fifth force, one that governs magnetic forces among culturally connected humans, I'd join the ones arguing for.

There was a strange little farm there on the tip of the Land's End peninsula, and I took a photo of England's westernmost pig and sent it as a digital postcard to my loved ones across the ocean. Matthew, who was at my sister Rhonda's house and apparently not in bed yet, texted back.

[Nice selfie, Dad.]

I stuck to the trail around this iconic part, but my feet hurt. I'd been walking in England for nearly a month, and for most of that time, my shoes were wet. It had degraded the shoes' footbed material, effectively converting my once-rugged trail runners into flimsy moccasins. My knees and hips appreciated the path's gravelly non-slip surface through the mining district, but I could feel each and every one of the jagged little walnuts underfoot.

I went inland away from the coastline to get outside the mining district and found trails with kindlier tread. In England, public pathways are everywhere, even across private property. Back in the Middle Ages, knights and lords and such routinely trampled across any lowborn's garden or pasture whenever they wanted. These paths became rights of the Crown and apparently still are. And they're well-used. It seems everyone in Cornwall has at least one dog, and all these dogs take their humans out for walks. The trails are lovely, and one more thing the British have that is better than ours.

I recorded and posted a video of my favorite traverse across a sunny pasture via a public pathway, playing Pied Piper to a frolicking herd of Holstein heifers. Just as I was getting used to the sunshine, Emma sent me a text.

[Find someplace to hole up for the next few days] it said.

I did what she told me to, ignoring the pleasantness of the day, and made reservations at a hotel up ahead.

The next few days, I listened as gale-force winds outside the hotel room window whistled and howled through the masts and riggings of the boats moored across from me in Penzance Harbor, when it wasn't actively raining, anyway. When there were raindrops in the wind, all I could hear was furious pelting on the windowpanes.

The Lombard Hotel first opened in 1833, some decades before England came to know toilets. They had added one to my room, however, and a shower. It also had a television. The first time I switched it on, a cheerful young woman was standing beside a wall-sized weather map with a cyclone on it. But it was the middle of July, and I wasn't in the mood for that nonsense. The second time I turned it on, translucent shower doors were rising to expose another set of unclothed kneecaps. I shut it off and put the remote in the mini fridge, where it stayed till I left.

Strangely, Emma had gone against her own advice. The night after sending me the text, she'd tried camping in Pendeen. The wind blew her tent stakes out of the ground and collapsed a wet sack of billowy fabric around her. She gathered up her drenched gear and spent the rest of the night shivering with it inside the camp's toilet facilities, 'a right dingy loo,' as she aptly described it. She texted me when daylight came, then bused to Penzance and the Lombard

Hotel and took a room on the ground floor. Leanne got on a bus too, but she'd had enough of the Coastal Path. She went home.

Emma, as far as I could tell, spent her time at the hotel waiting for the storm to pass productively, organizing her trail notes and writing in her diary. Not me, though. I wrote grumpy emails to friends back home. One afternoon, I ventured out into the tempest to explore Penzance and buy some shoes, but found instead the Lloyd's of London branch that must have inspired the Gringotts Bank façade in the Harry Potter films. When I took my phone out to get pictures, an open umbrella that had been loosed into the wind yard darted the back of my head. I spun around, intending to thank the person responsible appropriately. But nobody behind me would take credit for it, or even admit to seeing any flying umbrella, the fakers.

"Did you say umbrella? A flyin' umbrella, mate?"

"You've got to be kidding me," I said.

I recounted the episode in a woeful email to my friend Mikey. Venting to chemical engineers is a pointless exercise because, well, they will never get the point. He promptly wrote back confused, asking why I'd rather get harpooned in my face.

I sent my former boss Gina, an email complaining about the locals asking me, "Are you alright?" instead of "How do you do?", or my preferred greeting, a simple and cheery "Hi there!"

"Nobody actually cares if I'm alright or not," I groused. "Next time someone asks if I'm alright, I'll tell them, 'No, I'm not alright. No one here is. We all wring buckets of rainwater from our knickers, innit?'"

Gina replied promptly as well, thanking me for representing the culture and maturity of my countrymen while traipsing about England. It didn't help that they had both mentioned the perfect weather they were enjoying back home without me. I sent them photos of England's westernmost pig, with whom I'm sure they felt cosmologically connected.

My phone chimed with a text from Emma, which also annoyed me.

She's sending me a text when she's just down the stairs, the lazy-butt, I thought.

[You may quit sulking and go back to the path in the morning] it read.

***

I left the next morning before six and had a video chat with Matt as I walked. He was enjoying his time over there at Rhonda's place, engaged in doing what he described as 'man things.' He'd been working with his older cousin and his friends, rebuilding diesel engines in the shop during the days and moving bales of hay out of fields when it cooled off in the evenings.

We talked about how the summer was turning out. Monica was following through with the visits she had scheduled with her out-of-town friends while Matt and I were supposed to be in England together. With me in England and

Matt at his aunt's, this was the first time we'd all been apart from each other since the day he was born.

I'd walked all the way around the bay and was on the opposite shore from the Lombard when I got another text from Emma.

[On bus back to the path at Pendeen now. Stopped by your room to say goodbye. You weren't there.]

This is the second time I've done that to her, leaving early in the morning without a goodbye, I thought to myself, feeling suddenly remorseful.

I'd been so eager to get back onto the path that I left without thinking. We would likely never see each other again. We should have hugged it out, or at least fist bumped and wished each other well.

She deserves better, I chided myself.

I'd hiked the Pacific Crest Trail a few years before, and while doing that, I'd left dozens of people behind in the mornings without saying goodbye. It seemed to be a pattern, and I wondered what kind of character flaw it was about me. I don't feel like I have abandonment issues or am especially shy about goodbyes. It's just that I'm always waking up before anyone else, and it doesn't occur to me to say my goodbyes the night before. I think about it sometimes the next mornings when I'm set to leave, but by then I would have to wake them up to do it.

I texted Emma back, telling her where I was and added some banal comment about how the sea foam smelled sulphury on the wind. Then, [Let's try to meet up in Poole], which was stupid as I didn't really see how.

The sulphury sea-breeze smell seemed to give me a sour stomach all day. It rained a couple of times while I was walking, which was nothing new, and as I got further away from Penzance and into more remote countryside, I lost cell service. That also was nothing new, but for some reason, I had extra trouble finding a campsite that day.

I'd read of people on the path 'wild camping' at night, setting up their tents and camping without permission on private property. I wanted to be a respectful visitor to the country, and it seemed like finding campsites and paying for them would be a better way to go about it than squatting.

Here's what I'd been doing to find campsites: Around early afternoon, I'd take my phone off airplane mode and use UKCampfinder.com, a no-frills website that displays your current position and the nearest campsites. But the maps on UKCampfinder were so rudimentary and featureless that they were useless for navigation, so to pinpoint a campsite's location, I'd use Google Maps. That most of the public footpaths were neither shown nor recognized by Google Maps was problematic. Also problematic was that Google's directions for those of us on foot often point towards grisly deaths and other unpleasant surprises.

Walking Wet

So once the target was pinpointed on Google Maps, I'd open a third app, the OS Maps (British Ordnance Survey) maps app. The OS Maps app didn't show many of the campsites, or anything else less than about forty years old, but it did include all the public footpaths one could use to get themselves anywhere. It was incredibly useful, especially since it could keep working if, on your way to the camp, you lost cell service. And in Cornwall, that happens more often than not.

So once my knees started hurting, about fifteen miles out from the Lombard, I followed the procedure to find a campsite and a route to it. I found a place, a couple miles up the path and an additional three miles away to the side. When I got there, I learned it was exclusively for members only. I repeated the apps and maps procedure and walked three more miles to another campsite. This one hosted only RVs or camping trailers, so I walked another two miles to a third camp that turned out to also be member-exclusive. On the OS map, there was a beach marked with public bathrooms back on the coastline, now two miles away. I was thirsty and out of water, so I headed there.

The bathrooms had been closed and replaced by portaloos, which are lousy places to get water from. Further up the beach was a horse trailer-turned-beach-food-stand catering to surfers and sunbathers and they were kind enough to let me to pay them eight pounds for a couple of bottles of water. They had deli sandwiches on the menu board, but they'd sold out. I bought a bag of potato chips to go with the water.

My stomach was still sour, and I was tired of walking. The girls in the horse trailer pointed to where they occasionally saw people camp behind some beach grass nearby. It was an unattractive place to pitch a tent. To me, a guy adept at strategies to cope with a diminishing storage capacity for renal output, it looked like a place people would use who couldn't make it to the portaloos. I consoled myself that it had been raining cats and dogs for most of the last three days, and that sand is permeably washable.

Because their food was sold out, I bought some beer, rationalizing that it was made from grains like the outer parts of sandwiches are, and resigned myself to pitching my tent on the urea sand after all the surfers and tourists left.

Halfway through my second beer, a bus appeared. It jockeyed itself around the hairpin curve at the top of the hill and began working its way slowly down, bullying cars and drivers into the hedges lining the narrow road to the beach. I finished my bottle of Newcastle, grabbed my pack from the picnic table, and jogged out to the road.

A kind Swiss girl on holiday got on the bus with me and recommended a camping farm she had stayed at near a bus stop up ahead. When the bus rolled into cell service, I called and reserved a spot there. It was another fifteen miles up the coast, done easily enough on a bus.

At the Namparra Camp and Caravan Farm, I camped in a pasture replete with a burro and two alpacas. There was a tavern/cafe on the site with free Wi-Fi, where I had another pint of beer and a burger.

Opposite the cafe and next to the beer garden were pigs and goats in a wide pen. The goats had a trampoline to play with, along with a seesaw and other hand-built goat agility toys. The pigs had a soccer ball, a couple of lobster pot buoys to play with, and a mop suspended from a clothesline. As I watched, one of the pigs walked up from behind and lifted her head up into it. She posed for me there, looking like a magistrate.

Namparra was an oasis of surfers' vans and caravans in the midst of moneyed exclusivity. Most of the site's maintenance looked like it was performed by surfers, or at least by people with a similar sense of 'good enough.' I felt welcome there. You could lean a chair back on two legs if you wanted, or set your beer down without a coaster.

Andy, the husband of one of the sisters who owns the property, had finished his workday out installing countertops and backsplashes. He drew a beer for himself and another for me before joining me at my table. We talked about tile backing and grout, and other particulars only carpenters and inveterate do-it-yourselfers care or think about.

It was easy talking with Andy. Like most carpenters, the passion he had for his craft was small-scale and detail-oriented. Carpenters talk about making walls plumb, drain lines sloped, trim flush. They build things because they like working with their hands. There's nothing wrong with that, because somebody's got to do it.

I'd worked for twenty years in an office of fish and wildlife biologists, and the scope of their talk was usually more regional in character. They were idealists, or at least had started out as such. They wanted to mitigate climate change, prevent an extinction, save a forest, or restore a watershed. And there's nothing wrong with that because, God knows, somebody's got to do those things, too.

Now that our careers were in their later stages, Andy and I were more reflective about the broader impacts of our work. The conversation I'd had with Ted and Margaret about the exorbitant rise of home prices and gentrification still needled me, and I was curious to hear Andy's thoughts.

I asked him, "Do you ever worry that you've been helping outsiders come in and make houses here harder to buy, more expensive to rent? Do you worry that you have been helping to push out your own neighbors?"

My question didn't make Andy defensive at all.

"Look," he said, "I love living here in the Lizards, and the irony isn't lost on me. Sure, I've remodeled old local houses into holiday rentals for

Walking Wet

outsiders. But the outsiders is about the only ones with money, bringing it into our economy, and we need it if we are going to stay here."

"But doesn't the money they bring change the place into something else, something less authentic? It's definitely less affordable. Doesn't it make it hard for people who already live here to stay here?"

"It already was hard for people to stay here. The holidayers and vacation-homers didn't do that," Andy said. "Farming doesn't pay like it used to, and they had nothing to do with that. Fishing's in the dumpers, and they had naught to do with that. If it weren't for people coming here on holiday or to retire, we'd have hardly money coming in at all."

"But isn't that…" I sputtered a laugh and pointed over Andy's shoulder. The pig had turned around under the mop and was using it to scratch an itch on her rump.

"Vicki's doing the hula again," Andy observed. "Look," he said, "Cornwall has always exported natural resources. Mining, fishing, farming, and even timber. And so it is today, except now, we trade in natural wonders. Tourism. We export beauty and experiences, attitude and atmosphere. And that is something we have more control over and can make more sustainable."

I smiled. Andy had just reconfirmed an observation that I'd made long ago: that idealists are not the sole purveyors of idealism. Doers can also be dreamers.

"And when those tourists come to rent a holiday cottage," I said, raising my glass, "they'll have some right nice countertops and backsplashes in them."

"Damned straight," Andy said and drained his pint.

A couple of Andy's nieces and nephews came over. I asked one of them, an eighth-grader, if he had a choice between living in a London flat with lots of money or living with pennies in the Lizards in a caravan parked in a pasture, which he'd choose.

"Lizards, of course," he answered without hesitation, "gots to breathe, don't you?"

The next morning, I left my tent in the care of Tony Orlando and Dawn, as I'd named my burro and alpaca friends, to get back onto the path and pointed my feet the wrong way up the coast again, aiming to cover the ground I'd bused around the day before. Back home when we were looking at the route, this section was the bit that had Monica buzzing the most.

The Lizard Peninsula, the southernmost point of England, is gorse and heather moorlands and at its tip is Kynance Cove, the setting for the PBS series *Poldark*. The day turned out dry after some morning showers, and the views over the purple heather out to the cliffs and the ocean beyond were amazing. I played the historical romance's soundtrack in my left ear as I walked and shot videos of myself, doing my best to emulate Ross Poldark's gallant and confident stride over his land to send home to my wife Demelza. I mean Monica.

Kynance Cove, where many of the series' outside scenes were shot, turned out to be less developed than I'd expected. Going through Port Isaac, I'd been struck by how much larger the town was in real life compared to its size depicted on *Doc Martin*, the show that was filmed there. If it weren't for the bus parking lot and the hordes of tourists, Kynance Peninsula would have been just as wild and desolate as it had been depicted in *Poldark*.

I scooted through quickly, but even so, I recognized landscape features and a few of the buildings that featured so prominently in the show.

Just before reaching the horse trailer beach food stand where my walking had ended the day before, was Marconi's Telegraph Station, where the first radio signals were sent across the Atlantic in 1901.

The antennas are long gone now, but the concrete foundations for the towers that held them are still there. It took a massive amount of electricity and manpower in those days to broadcast a series of dots and dashes across the ocean through a sea of radio static. A hotel was built nearby to house all the telegraph and power plant workers needed. The hotel is still there, but today is a stately assisted-living facility.

The stretch around the Lizard was all mining territory and gravelly, and I walked on jagged walnuts again the whole day. That night, I complained about it over a couple of beers in Namparra to Andy.

"A pair of shoes lasts a thousand miles on the Pacific Crest Trail, the hike I did back home. Your trail here, though. These shoes have less than four hundred on them, and they're shot already. Killing my feet."

"Take the bus to Helston. Buy yourself some shoes," he said. Andy made time for a lot of things, but complaining wasn't one of them.

***

The next day, I did just as Andy had recommended, again leaving my tent's security under the care of Orlando and Associates. Helston was middle-sized, peaceful, and real. I didn't see any place to buy touristy curios or quaint mementos, but for everyday items like the things I needed, a pair of shoes and a haircut, the town was perfect.

Surfers were filtering into the Namparra bar when I came back, trying to decide whether they wanted to do karaoke or not. Their children went into the adjoining room with the pool table in it. I took my beer outside. An old nanny goat was trying to get some rest on the trampoline while her kids bounced and frolicked on it around her. I finished my beer, took my pint glass back inside, then went back to my tent. It was just as I'd left it. Mr. Orlando and Dawn had watched over it well.

I went inside and called Monica, who was still home alone and just starting her day.

Walking Wet

"So, how'd you like the *Poldark* country videos today?" I asked.

"Absolutely loved them," she said. "It was the first time I wished I were there with you. It's getting lonely here without my boys, you know."

"Matt seems to be enjoying himself at my sister's."

"Yes, I talked to him last night too," she said. "He seemed in good spirits. He told me he got another job working evenings as a pole dancer. Thought he'd get a rise out of me, the goof."

"Yeah, he told me that, too. He's been with his Uncle Ron in the diesel shop during the day when it's hot and started working at the neighbor's ranch evenings."

"Doing what? He's not pole dancing, surely?"

"That's what they call what he's doing there, a bit of fun."

"So what is he doing, really?"

"The rancher has this big machine he drives around alfalfa fields to pick up hay bales. It arranges them on a tilt bed, and he drives it back to the barns, backs it up, and tilts it up into a stack. Matthew runs around with long poles to brace against the stack so the farmer can unclamp and drive away for another load."

"Is it dangerous?"

"I suppose he could get run over or maybe crushed under a falling haystack if he does it wrong. But it's more likely he'd just have to restack it by hand."

"Hmm. I'd feel safer if he was working at McDonald's or Jamba Juice or something."

"I know. But he's gaining experience he wouldn't get making burgers or slurpees."

"Smoothies," Monica corrected. "And no one's ever been crushed by a smoothie. Plus, 'Pole Dancer' won't read well on a resume."

"You have a point there," I said. "But I know the guys, and he'll be okay. Matt loves it. Makes him feel manly, working on engines and stacking hay."

"As a parent, I'm not so sure 'feeling manly' is worth the risk of our son getting crushed under haystacks or machinery," she said.

"As a parent, I agree with you," I said. "But as a man and a father, I can assure you it is."

"That's dumb," she said.

I remembered again that all four of Monica's siblings were sisters. "I know," I agreed.

"I just hope he doesn't get squished," she said.

***

With new shoes and leaving the mining district behind, there was less need to leave the main trail and travel inland to save my feet, but I did it once in a while anyway, so I could visit cows. I even escorted a retired fisherman through a herd that he was convinced was out to kill him one afternoon. It was strange to see him so nervous about a bunch of cheerful jelly-bellies after surviving and retiring from an occupation that features so many things that really were out to kill him. It's all about what you get used to, I guess.

We made it through intact, but my new shoes attracted a lot of extra attention from the girls, which was terrifying for the old fisherman. The shoes I'd bought in Helston were sturdy and comfortable, but they squeaked annoyingly whenever they were wet, which was almost always. The cows, though, loved the noise they made.

Shortly after escaping the freckle-nosed killer cow and her friends, the path took me down the fairway of a busy golf course. A foursome of cigar-smoking seniors waved me through, and a short hike inland brought me to my camping farm for the night just outside Falmouth, a sizeable city with a university and shipyards around a busy harbor.

The next morning, I walked along a beach hosting an event by the Bluetits Chill Swimmers and was surprised at how many people were in the water so early. More than a dozen were a mile from shore, at least. That, to me, really would be terrifying.

I walked around Pendennis Point and visited Pendennis Tower, a naval battlement built by King Henry VIII. I'd gotten into the habit of posing in front of castles or grand estates, pretending they were mine for the PODs (pictures of the day) I'd been sending to my wife since the trip began. I stopped here and took a selfie, posing in front of the tower with my arm outstretched as if it were another possession I could offer her, and sent it on, attaching to it this text:

[Milady, I am pleased to present to you my Tower of Pendennis!]

But just after I'd sent it, I saw that Google's spell checker had removed from 'Pendennis' four of its interior letters, changing the tone and intent conveyed in my cheery caption into something else entirely. Before I could type out and send a correction, Monica's short and sardonic response pinged back:

[Just like every day. Handle it yourself.]

Hmm, maybe I'll just leave it there, I thought and zipped my phone back into its pocket without sending a correction.

There were two cruise ships in Falmouth's harbor, and the shipyard held gray navy vessels. A ferry took me to a peninsula across the harbor, then another to jump across a connected inlet.

Earlier that morning at the beach before Pendennis, I'd met a middle-aged hippie couple who had just finished their Bluetits swim and chatted with them a bit. They asked if I had a tent in my backpack. I told them I did.

"You need to wild camp at Nare Point," the guy told me. "It will change your life."

"Spiritual," his partner added.

They described the point, where to load up on groceries for a wild camping overnight, and where to fill up with water before the point.

You shouldn't shop for groceries when you're hungry, but when I got to the Spar store (England's version of 7/11) I was. Maybe that was why I bought a chocolate cake with frosting for the next morning's wild camp breakfast and put it in my backpack.

When I got to the water stop the swimming hippies had told me about, I filled up and then started up the steep trail to the point. It was solid work. It was hot, the first day without rain since I'd started the path, and my pack was heavy from the extra water and poorly balanced as well, having hung some of my gear off the sides to make room for the cake.

The point had a glorious 270-degree ocean view and would undoubtedly become spiritual as sunset came. There, around an upright boulder, was one small flat spot, so I took off my pack and sat on it to wait. But I noticed, sitting there waiting, just how bad I smelled. Deprived of its daily rain shower, my T-shirt had turned mean.

I took the rancid thing off and flung it over a bush. That was better. I'd stopped walking earlier than my usual routine, and it became obvious that spiritualism, if it came to me at all, would only come after some boredom.

I had cell service, so I used a little battery power to document my stinky shirt on Facebook. I was pleased with my droll wittiness, but still bored. And boredom, as so often happens, brings cravings. And in the top of my pack was a chocolate cake.

That evening, I learned two things: that there was a road within a short walking distance of Nare Point, and that it was a favorite sunset destination for local lovers.

I was surprised when that first couple came around the boulder, but not as surprised as they were to see an old shirtless stinky guy sitting on a backpack and eating a chocolate cake, holding it with both hands like an oversized hamburger.

"You alright?" I asked.

I'd asked, "You alright?" because it seemed to be the locals' greeting of choice, but with my mouth muffled and filled with cake, what came out sounded more like, "Mmm. Alright!" which made me sound friendly enough, but also, regrettably, voyeuristic and creepy as well.

The guy just stood and stared blankly down at me, stiff upper lipped and all with a wine bottle wrapped in a beach blanket under his arm, obviously shaken and at a loss for words.

But his partner's ability to vocalize thoughts hadn't been disrupted at all. "This is shite," she said. "A right bloody wanker 'e is," then turned on her heel and left.

The two of us watched her leave, dumbfounded.

"Want some cake?" I asked her boyfriend, holding out a gooey hunk of it to him.

My presence there disrupted two more couples' evening plans, but it was too late to hike on to the next commercial campsite. I could see another spot that could be flat enough to pitch a tent about a quarter mile up the path and downslope of it, just before the rock rounded over into vertical sea cliff. I gathered my stuff and worked my way over, and it turned out to be a small crater of broken rock, covered over with grass and bracken ferns. It was a darned weird terrain feature, but it worked for the night.

***

I was packed up and off again at sunrise, and an hour down the trail, came across an old World War II bunker and a placard explaining Operation Starfish. Falmouth had extensive shipyards, valuable bombing targets. Operation Starfish situated lights on and around Nare Point, so from the air at night it looked like Falmouth's town and harbor. And the decoy worked. The Luftwaffe hit Nare Point with seven hundred and sixty-eight-night raids over the course of the war, each time thinking they were bombing the bejeebers out of Falmouth. Operation Starfish, by getting the Germans to drop bombs onto Nare Point, saved dozens of navy ships and hundreds of British lives.

And one of those bombs dropped on one of those nights hit and exploded on a granite rock shoulder just before it rounded over into a vertical sea cliff, leaving a crater just big enough to pitch a tent in.

Walking Wet

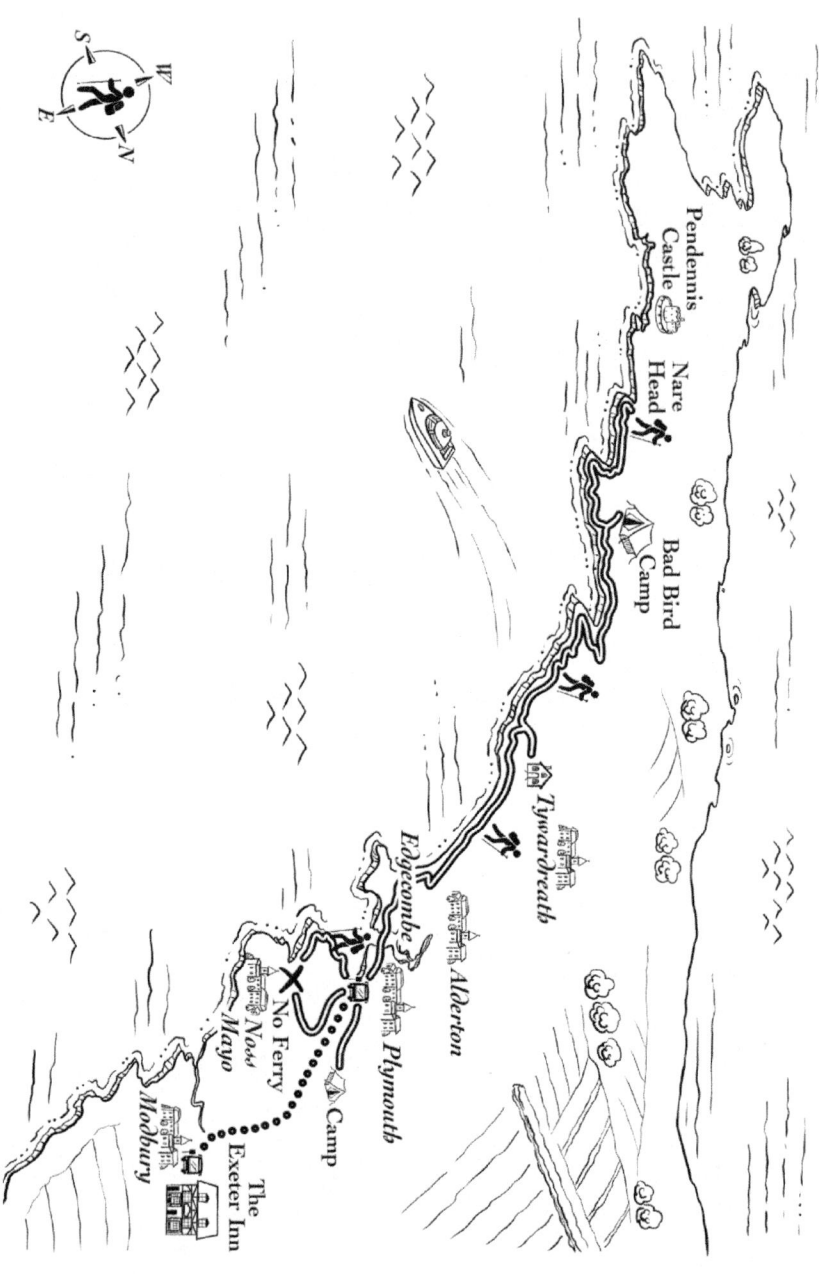

Aren't We the Eloquent One?

37 ⋯ DAYS WALKING
390 ⋯ PATH MILES WALKED
508 ⋯ TOTAL MILES WALKED
https://www.southwestcoastpath.org.uk/walksdb/166/

On the cobblestone pavers between the ancient rock walls shepherding me up the steep and narrow road to Mevagissy, one pigeon was killing another.

At first, I thought it was an awkward attempt at reproduction, a meeting of instinctual desire and a lack of experience. But I saw in a moment I was wrong. I'd stumbled onto pure evil.

The one had the other pinned on his back, standing on the underside of his outstretched left wing, high up near his 'armpit.' He was pecking and tearing at the throat of his target, who was squirming weakly to get away and making ineffectual swats at him with his free wing. The aggressor bird's appearance was as silly and ridiculous-looking as any of his kind, but made terrifying and macabre by the sure method and intent of his assault. He concentrated on a specific part of his target's throat, right where, on a human in an emergency, a doctor might perform a tracheotomy. If the downed pigeon tried protecting himself by pulling his 'chin' lower to cover his throat, his assailant switched targets and pecked at his eyes.

Both of the injured bird's eyelids were bleeding, and a featherless nickel-sized patch of skin was pulpy on his throat. Feather down was spread around them on the cobblestones, as if they'd been making a snow angel together, and bits of fluff were stuck to the killer's lips and beak. I grabbed him up off his victim, intending to throw him over the rock wall opposite, but couldn't. If you've never thrown a pigeon before, you should know that it's more difficult than you've supposed. It took both hands to curtail his flapping, and the best I could manage was a shovel-pass motion akin to tossing a cat off the bed, or throwing sand on a fire.

He pecked at my arm just above the wrist, and just as I made my delivery, he clamped down on a beakful of rain jacket. So instead of going over the wall, he fluttered and knuckleballed himself into a gentler trajectory, landing lightly atop it just under a blooming hydrangea puff ball. He turned around and stared back at me with one eye, and then the other.

The bottom bird struggled to stand up, but his left wing wouldn't fold in properly, and his feet were too extremely 'pigeon-toed', even for a pigeon. His feet were still spasmed and curled like a stroke victim's as well, so when he tried to stand, he kept tipping over. I picked him up and found a resting place for him under some overhanging ivy. I'd had to carry him up the road a bit to where the ivy was growing, and was surprised when the evil one followed us up. He lit on the rock wall on his side of the road again, eyeballing his partially hidden mark, obviously waiting for me to leave him unguarded.

I used a hiking stick to shoo the evil bird away and stayed with the wounded one for a bit. He recovered enough to stand but was unable to fly. I'd read that pigeons are pretty stupid and that for them, things are forgotten rather quickly. For pigeons, something out of sight really is out of mind. Indeed, the wounded bird was already looking like he had no idea what had happened to him, but to be fair, he'd looked a lot like that when I'd first picked him up. I stayed with him long enough, I hoped, for the bad pigeon to forget about trying to kill him and not to come back looking to finish him off.

My mind was uneasy as I walked to the inland camp. I've spent three decades as a farm kid and a farmer, and another two working with fish and wildlife. So I know animals and understand their behaviors, their natures. Most of God's creatures live in ways that further their kind with remarkable cooperation and kindness. But nearly every species is infected with the trait for murder and have individuals that kill.

As a biologist, I was taught that a trait need not benefit the target or even the individual expressing it. Still, to persist through generations, it must offer some value to the broader population. Survival of the fittest and ensuring the strongest endure in most species, presumably.

Maybe if pigeons had the capacity to build societies and a mechanism to punish individuals who commit murder, they could rid themselves of the infection. Then again, maybe not. We haven't.

What the murder trait offers our specie is perplexing, but it seems we confer value onto it and glorify the idea in subtle and pervasive ways. We lionize a basketball player who sinks three-pointers by calling him a "stone-cold killer," or attribute a salesperson's ability to close deals to her "killer instinct." We may finalize a decision by putting the "last nail in the coffin," or we may "slay the audience" with our wit. And those turns of phrase are nothing compared to what we see in video games or war movies. Our society punishes individual murderers, while at the same time feeding and glorifying the murder trait that goads them to act. Doubtless, our murder infection will live on.

It was a strange thing to obsess about, those pigeons and all, I know. But you allow yourself to dwell on puzzles like that on a long hike, especially when you're alone for most of it and getting rained on.

When I got to camp, I decided not to write about the pigeons in my journal that night, and fully expected the episode would be another thing about my time on the path that I would forget. But it was so weirdly unsettling that I never have.

***

It didn't rain that night, but my tent was soaked again anyway from the heavy dew. I put the tent body and its fly into separate stuff sacks and strapped them to either side of my backpack, which kept my rear end drier in the morning but made walking more entertaining on account of the pack being imbalanced.

It seemed also that I'd either been losing weight or my pack's waist strap had gotten stretched from being worn through five weeks of rain or drizzle. It was tightened as far as it could go but kept sliding down my hips anyway. It would catch on my pants' waistband, curling it over to dig into my skin. I had some ideas about how to fix it, but in addition to my sewing patch kit, it would take a hair dryer and some kitchen utensils to do the job. Likely, Emma would be warning me to get a room again soon, and I'd work on it then. In the meantime, I stuck duct tape to the skin on my hips to fight the abrasion.

Sure enough, Emma soon came through with another weather warning text, and I booked another two nights off the path in an Airbnb studio in Tywardreath, pronounced TEAR-ed-death. It had everything I needed to fix my backpack, which I did. Also on the kitchen counter was an assortment of dry biscuits and the ubiquitous Tetley tea. Tetley had been waiting for me in every English room I stayed in since leaving the Travelodge.

I brewed and tried drinking it a couple of times, but had given up the concoction as manifestly poisonous. But that evening, as my socks were drying and wafting their signature funk through the room I wondered, why not combine the two hazardous elements? I emptied the entire box of Tetley's and brewed up an industrial-strength batch of the stuff in a soup pot, then steeped my socks in it with a wooden spoon. The results were miraculous. For the remainder of my time in Britain, I used up all the Tetley I got my hands on. The discovery is a twin triumph, being the only known process that neutralizes bio-hazardous footwear while also making Tetley tea potentially drinkable. Worthy indeed of the Nobel Prize in Chemistry.

Walking Wet

From Tywardreath, I made a good day to Polperro, then through the delightfully named village of Crumplehorn on my way to camp. Crumplehorn was more 'touristy' than Tywardreath had been, but like most of Cornwall's coastal villages, not ruined by it. What the villages do, is to find someplace nearby to build a parking lot without knocking down any centuries-old buildings. Holidayers leave their cars in them when they come to visit and go about on foot. It's nice, and something we could do a bit more with in the States, I'd think.

Emma texted that night, advising to make the most of the next day. So I made a hard push to Plymouth, leaving the path for a more inland route. As a consequence, I missed the stubby peninsula of Rame Head. Since even before the Mayflower left in 1620, Plymouth was England's major seaport for voyagers crossing the Atlantic or beyond, and the promontory of Rame Head was the last bit of home those sailors or whalers would see as they left, and the first home soil to come into view as they returned. There are ancient buildings there as well, dating back to before the eleventh-century Norman invasion, and I regret missing all of them.

I did, though, finally see a working dairy farm that looked well-maintained and prosperous. The inland route took me past the tide flats off the River Tamar. There were stranded boats along the shores, but they didn't appear to have anyone living in them like the ones near Barnstaple. I'd accidentally walked through an old-money estate already and the village of Anderton as well, and the area struck me as being more affluent. I wondered if the derelict boats were unoccupied and decaying because there was no one about who needed to live in them, or if the neighbors were acting somehow to keep them empty.

I did see people on dilapidated boats just across a narrow neck of the bay, and I doubted that the weather came in any rougher on the Alderton side that would make living in a stranded boat on its shore any less tenable.

The passenger ferry at Cremyll is on an old estate, where Mount Edgcumbe House was built in the 1500s. There is still an Earl of Mount Edgcumbe today, but he somehow shares ownership of the estate jointly with the Cornwall and Plymouth City Councils. Most of the estate is open to the public year-round. Its grounds have a collection of gardens, each about the size of a par-three golf fairway, and each of a different theme. There's an English garden, of course, and the Earl's Garden, an American garden, a New Zealand garden, a Jubilee garden, a French garden, and an Italian garden.

In the Italian garden is the Orangery, a sumptuous structure with pane-glassed views of the garden on one side, and a view across the bay to Plymouth on the other. It was built in 1755, is about a hundred feet long by thirty wide, and is single-storied but tall, with cathedral-height windows and ceilings. It must have been built for summer. I doubt they could have heated it in the eighteenth century, and they probably don't very often today.

But it was perfect when I was there, as it was uncharacteristically sunny and warm outside. There's a restaurant inside, with a vibe more relaxed and casual than I'd thought it would be. It's often rented out for wedding receptions. There wasn't one going on at the time, but I felt like I was in one. I got a pastry and some gelato, went outside with it, and shared an ornate wrought-iron picnic table with a kind family. We'd never met before, of course, but it felt like we were distantly related in some way, and that we should put our heads together to figure out how.

For the short ferry ride across the harbor to Plymouth, I sat in the open bow of the Edgcumbe Belle. Coming in to the landing, we passed a centuries-old wharf fronting immense and imposing buildings of limestone. I asked a fellow passenger what they were. She didn't know but thought they were old Navy barracks. A crew member overheard us and settled the matter.

"It's the old Royal Navy victualling depot," he said, "for their ships, right?"

I had no idea what that meant, but the location and the layout made perfect sense when I looked it up later. What the woman took for barracks were in fact a warehouse, a bakery, and a butchery, where farm animals would be processed into hardtack on site. 'Victualling' was the act of supplying 'victuals' for a ship's crew; food, drink, and provisions needed for long sea voyages. I'd been unfamiliar with the term and had always thought that 'vittles,' the backwoods Americanized version of 'victuals,' was original.

The ferry landed in an old and somewhat gritty neighborhood. There were some ice cream and curio shops just up the street from the landing, but the business they were doing wasn't brisk. They had probably seen more action back in their heyday while they were still taverns and brothels.

Plymouth is a sizeable city of nearly a quarter million, by far the largest city I'd see on the path until I reached Poole. Again. The section of Plymouth I found myself in was urban and industrial, and OS Maps showed a relative dearth of public rights of way cutting through it.

I searched Google Maps for 'campsite near me,' and it gave me a route through town to one seven miles out in the country. Halfway there, I ran out of sidewalk. By then, I'd walked into rush hour traffic on a main highway. And the highways in England don't have shoulders because the British call them verges, which is irrelevant anyway because none of their highways seem to have those either. I didn't expect the sidewalks to continue out of the city and into the countryside, but I had hoped that in a city at least, Google would look out for me. But I was mistaken. Google was making another attempt to kill me.

Walking Wet

I backtracked, then cut cross-country on a pathway unknown to Google. It wasn't shown on OS Maps either, but it looked like maybe it was going in generally the right direction. It led to a potato field. I was walking between bermed rows of potatoes when a furious ball of pheasant shot up from between my legs and stopped my heart, almost killing me again. I worked my way back to the highway just before the campsite at Brixton, where there was still no shoulder, or verge either, for that matter. I wriggled over a hedge regularly trimmed by truck mirrors, dropped into someone's backyard, then cut across lawns and driveways to the campsite I'd gotten reservations for. The campsite wasn't great, but it had a nice pub nearby.

***

I wasn't about to repeat walking that route the next day, so I caught a bus back to Plymouth. My plan was to get back onto the Coast Path near the ferry terminal, but I overshot and rode the bus all the way back to the city center station instead. A kid who couldn't have been more than eighteen was looking out from a tent he'd pitched on the grass opposite, and when I waved, he waved back. It was a high-quality tent and appeared mostly unused, as if he'd taken it from the garage as he'd left home, hopped a bus, and pitched it right there after stepping off.

The waterproofing on the fly was still robustly resistant to the morning dew and had globules and droplets beaded up on it, unlike the damp and saturated tent I'd squished into the pack on my back.

I used OS maps this time to get across town, through residential apartment blocks, a commercial and retail zone, then posh vacation hotels at the harbor's edge, finally regaining the Coast Path at a grand promenade. The promenade petered out into a marine industrial area, then the path went across another bridge. It looked familiar, and I realized I'd unknowingly walked some of the path the day before. There ahead was the McDonald's and the roundabout again.

Dang, the sidewalks will be ending soon, I thought. And it started drizzling again. I stopped and put my pack's rain cover on.

The Coast Path turned right at McDonald's where Google had kept me straight the day before, and then through another hour of suburbs. They were nice enough. I chatted with a lady weeding her flower garden on the edge of town, just before the path went rural again. The OS map showed a couple more miles to the next village and then a couple more to the next.

Things I don't see much as an American are defensive military installations. We have them, sure, but they're mostly on bases where service members can train more or less out of view. At home, they're not built right on city outskirts to protect a quarter-million peopled city.

The path had climbed to clifftops again, and I walked past lots of old structures that had guarded the harbor entrance below. A huge trench had been blasted and excavated into the granite below one of the concrete pillboxes so it could have a clear shot to the water's edge. It was in line with the harbor breakwater, a concrete dam built across the harbor's mouth so ships coming or going would have to pass near one shore or the other. Doubtless there was, or had been, a matching pillbox guarding the harbor from the Cremyll side.

At Wembury Beach, I stopped for coffee and a pastry at the Old Mill, a centuries-old stone building along the path that had been repurposed to sugarize and caffeinate tourists in need. And I was in need, as it had progressed substantially past drizzling.

Just upslope, the path continued towards the ferry at the Yealm River (or the River Yealm, if you're following the British convention) another two and a half miles further on. The ferry workers had posted a sign at Wembury with their regular operating hours, along with a disclaimer about how strictly the schedule may be adhered to. A phone number was hand-painted onto the sign to call for ferry times in "poor weather."

I'd thought the definition for "poor weather" was universal before I came to England and began talking to Cornish folk about it. So I shivered and dialed the number, wondering if this qualified as "poor" to whoever might answer on the other end. But the call wouldn't go through, as there was no cell service. Why would someone hand-paint a sign advising people to call his phone number, and then post it in a zone dead to cell service? It would seem a poor practice, even for a Cornishman, surely.

What to do? From looking at bus routes the night before, I knew that if I could get to the village on the other side of the river, I could catch a bus out and back to Plymouth, and from there back to my last night's camp. Or somewhere. So over the hill I went, following the path.

It was raining in earnest by the time I got to the ferry landing, where another hand-painted sign had been hung stating that the ferry was closed for the day. The bus stop was barely two hundred yards away, but across the river. My raincoat had done what it could, but I was soaked through and through. Its shoulders, where the backpack had been riding, had lost their waterproofing a couple hundred miles back. Now though, even the hood of my rain jacket had given up, and a rivulet of cold water ran down my forehead, around my nose and chin to an Adam's apple delta that emptied down the front of my chest.

This, apparently, passes as 'poor weather' to Cornishmen, I thought.

I found another footpath that led straight up to the top of Wembury Hill, where I could get cell service. I found a hotel and a bus route to it with Google Maps and was able to book a room for myself after the second try. Raindrops had almost booked me into a hotel with the same name, The Exeter, in New Hampshire. Google Maps told me I was ninety minutes from the nearest bus stop but wouldn't tell me how to get there. OS Maps didn't show any public

Walking Wet

footpaths heading towards it either, so I tried to follow my phone to it using Google's direction of travel beacon.

If you hold your phone flat, the little blue dot representing your location on the map will display a shaded semicircle showing the direction the top of your phone is pointing. I put the phone back in its baggie and the side pouch after I'd sighted a landmark to walk to. But my phone's internal orientation was messed up or something because when I got there and checked my phone again, it showed the bus stop even further away.

I backtracked, cut across a sheep pasture, and through another old-money estate. In the lane just beyond, an older lady in a hi-vis rain slicker was walking two fancy-pants dogs, similarly attired. The last time I'd met dogs wearing clothing in disagreeable weather, their human was disagreeably grouchy. She wasn't their owner, she had told me, just someone hired to walk the dogs when it rained hard enough.

So I was going to pass without offering a greeting, but as I did, the woman said, "Are you alright?"

Here was my chance. I stopped to deliver my line, but botched it. "No," I said. I'm not alright. I can rain a knicker of wring water from my bucket right now, can't you?" Then I stood there dumbly, wishing I could unsay it and try over again.

The woman addressed her dogs. "Aren't we the eloquent one?" Then to me, "Your shoes squeak. Where did you steal them?"

Wet countryside eventually gave way to wet pavement and, finally, residential neighborhoods. There, cell service and Google worked again. I followed Google's directions to the nearest bus stop, which turned out to be on the edge of town, just in front of the house with the flower garden and the lady I'd chatted with earlier as she was weeding it.

The bus took me back to the McDonald's at the roundabout, where I had to make a transfer. When I got onto the second bus, the driver asked what town I was going to.

"I dunno," I told him. "The phone says to stay on about thirty minutes, I think."

When Google told me to, I got up to get off the bus. The driver let me out in Modbury, in front of the post office, and into the pouring rain.

Aren't We the Eloquent One?

Walking Wet

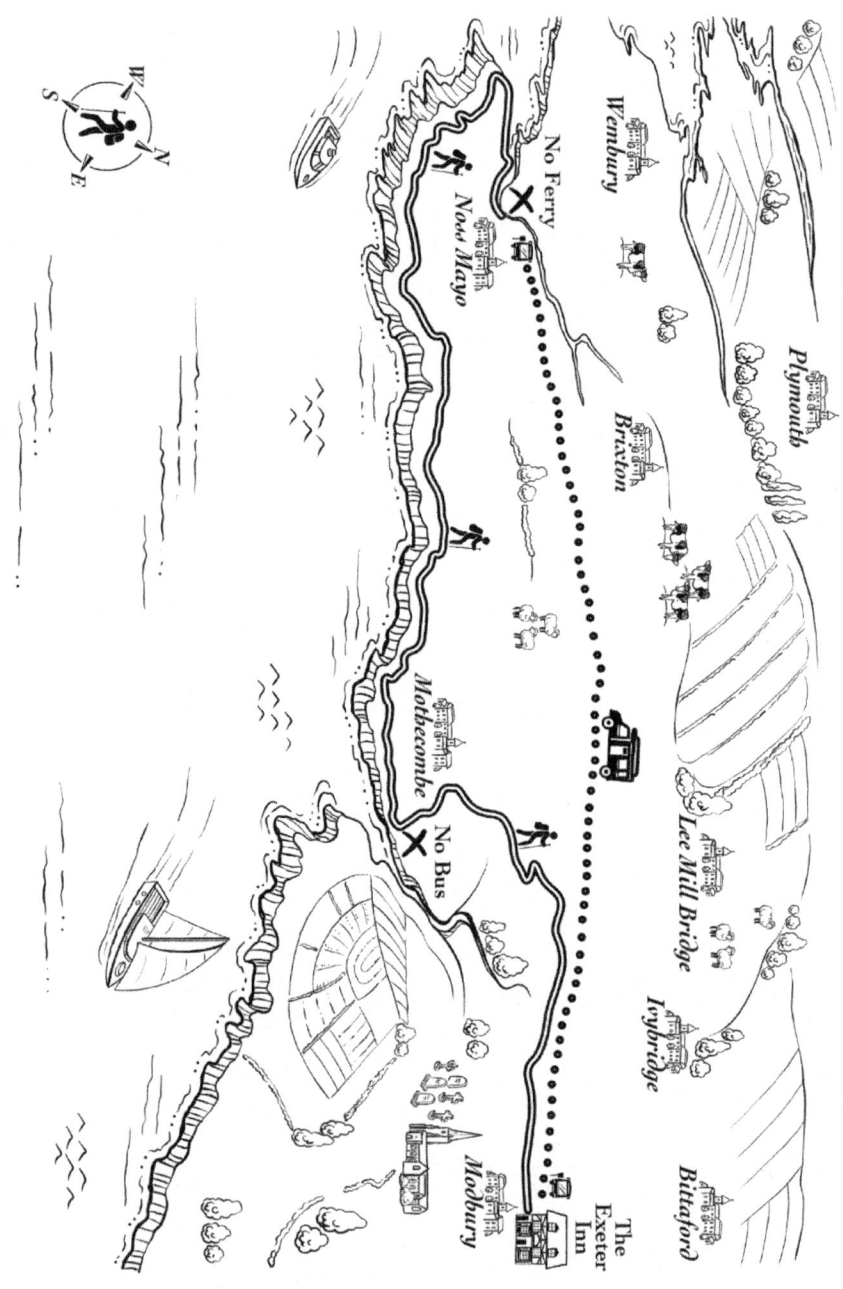

Isotopes in the Soil

38 ⋯ DAYS WALKING
399 ⋯ PATH MILES WALKED
525 ⋯ TOTAL MILES WALKED
https://www.southwestcoastpath.org.uk/walksdb/171/

The Exeter Inn's doors were locked and would be for another hour or so until the pub opened. On the door, a number was posted for early-arriving guests to call, but it went to voicemail. I left a message and wandered around town pretending to window shop, but actually looking for someplace to warm myself. It was only late afternoon on a Thursday, but most of the shops were closed. The ones that weren't, like a bakery across the street from the inn or an art gallery up the block, weren't heated well enough to get me warmed up. I went up the street to the grocery store, with the desperate idea that I could find a warm draft coming out from underneath a produce section's display case. I was wrong.

I took off my pack there in front of the carrots and cheese and rummaged for extra clothes. Nothing I had was dry. I was putting everything on anyway when I noticed that someone had tried calling me. I hadn't realized I'd turned my phone's ringer off.

When I called the number back, the inn keeper from The Exeter answered. She told me to hoof it down the street as she was waiting for me.

I hurried back out into the weather, and from a block away, I thought I saw my sister holding a door open for me. I ducked, and when I looked up again with the rain blinked from my eyes, it was the innkeeper. She welcomed me through a passage and then a side door to the inn.

The Exeter had been built in the fourteenth century as a coachmen's inn, and for the most part retains the same layout that it had been constructed with. I'd caught a glimpse of the beer garden out back, surrounded as it was by outbuildings that must have been stables originally.

The room Nikki the innkeeper had led me into was where she would serve her guests breakfast in the morning. I imagined it would have been the tack room, or maybe part of the servants' area in times of old. What interested me

Walking Wet

the most were the hearths. There were two of them, one in the breakfast room in back and the other in the main part of the inn, up front next to the bar. There was a small table just in front of that one.

I know where I'll be tonight, I thought.

My room for the night was through the breakfast room and upstairs. It was old but modernized enough to be perfectly comfortable. It had a shower, and the water ran hot. I stayed under it until well after I quit shivering. I hung my clothes up around the room to dry. Getting cold again, I stood for another shift under the showerhead. I wrapped myself in bed covers and determined to stay there till my clothes dried enough to put on again.

I heard singing and a mandolin below me shortly, so I put clothes back on early, still clammy and clingy, and went below. The breakfast room had filled with pensioners, graying rakes and artists by the looks of them, the sort that values wit and harmony more than hair dye.

They had set out the chairs, not in a concert arrangement, but in an arc facing the hearth, as if meeting for a book club. When the song was finished, the musician, a slight man with a long gray beard, handed the mandolin to the woman beside him and reached under his chair for his pint. He drank with both hands. One hand held his whiskers back while the other tilted the glass. The woman beside him began playing the mandolin, a quicker, lighter tune than he'd played that also required some string plucking and heel stomping.

The hearth in the main dining area was lit and I was able to claim the table closest to it. I asked for an Irish coffee, and when a young and flirty barmaid brought it to me with a "Here you are, Sweet Pea," I felt truly warm for the first time in a long while.

After a shepherd's pie, I went to the bar so Nikki's husband, Phil, could arrange for me to stay another night at the inn. He entered my info in a ledger behind the bar. Then, as I was already 'sat there', he drew me a pint.

I turned in early that night, feeling warm and tingly while the Silvery Gray Band down below sang me to sleep.

***

The next night, I was again back at the inn at the table next to the hearth opposite the bar. I was pleasantly over-warm and had an Irish coffee to nurse. I unfolded and put on my travel glasses, and situated my phone beside my coffee to compose an email to send home:

From: Me   ########@#####.com
To: The Tasteful One   ########@#####.com
Subject: Isotopes in the Soil
July 27, 2023, 07:45 PM

Dear Monica-

I hope you have a good drive to your sister's. You probably will have your music cranked loud and the dog up front with you, so you can sing to her.

Last night, I'd told Nikki, the innkeeper, that I would be off hiking early this morning. She made breakfast sandwiches and set them out for me with a note. That was so thoughtful of her and appreciated.

I rode a bus around for a couple hours for no good reason this morning. I'd used Google Maps to get bus directions back to the ferry landing opposite the one where the boat stood me up yesterday, and had set the departure time on the app for 5:30 am. I walked to the bus stop and got on the bus that it told me to, and it took me all the way back to the main bus terminal in Plymouth. The green tent with the homeless kid was still there across the street, zipped up. I went to the indicated platform, and after a longish wait, boarded that bus. It took me back out of town, retracing the journey I've made multiple times now, past the roundabout McDonald's and into the countryside. And at 8:15, it stopped in Modbury, at the very same bus stop that I'd started from in front of The Exeter! Why does Google do that? I could have had breakfast with the other guests! Instead, I inconvenienced Nikki because of my slapdash stupidity.

Once in Noss Mayo, the village with the ferry landing, the terrain was easier, and the path surface was better to walk on. I was able to stretch my legs and make about 3.75 mph. Weather came in again when the path took me out to the coast, and I could hear waves crashing at the base of the cliffs far below. But again, I saw only whatever came inside the five-meter bubble that I carry about with me through the fog and drizzle. Wet trail, wet grass, some bushes, and occasionally sheep, who would dart off into the fog in a blind panic, even though they had to have heard me coming, with my wet shoes squeaking as loudly as ever.

When I got to the next river, the River Erme, there was no ferry there either because there isn't one. You're supposed to wade across the river when the tide is out, which is a whole lot easier to do, I'd imagine, if one were to actually show up at low tide.

But no matter. I'd made good time and would walk to the next village inland and from there, hop a bus back to The Exeter Inn. I got to the bus stop and was waiting when a local guy told me I'd missed the last one. I turned my phone off, then back on, and checked again. The screen did the spinny donut dance, then told me to wait overnight where I was for the next bus.

So I plotted a walking route back to Modbury with OS, and it wasn't a bad walk. One of the public paths back was steep mud mixed with a sticky clay that I hadn't yet been treated to over here, as it's usually stoney or pebbly, and on the downhill I slipped and went splat, which made me think of you. "Out chasing hogs again, dear?" you would have asked. The route continued across an equestrian farm with a polo field and past spirited-looking horses in stables looking out into the courtyard over Dutch double doors. They were especially intrigued by my raspberry-colored backpack cover.

After the polo ponies was the ancient-looking big money estate castle featured in today's POD, and the track went down to parallel the main highway leading to Plymouth. The river that I couldn't ford because I'd been there at high tide was a small creek here. But it was flowing through a broad, swampy wetland and would still bring no joy to cross. To continue, I had to get onto the main highway's bridge. Of course, it had no shoulders or sidewalks and was but a single lane between dented guardrails. A driver waiting for oncoming cars for his turn to cross the bridge saw me and waved me over. When it was our turn, I ran ahead of him while he followed with his flashers on.

Just over, I scrambled up an ivy-covered 15-foot embankment. I'd passed the darned thing several times on my bus rides to Plymouth and had noted it was level up there. I had wondered if it was another old railroad grade, which I've found to be so nice to walk on over here. But this one wasn't nice; it was brushy. When it knifed out to an end without offering an easily sloped option to get off, I let myself down some vines into someone's backyard garden.

I was trespassing for sure, but the people I've met here so far have been patient and understanding for the most part and even the dogs have seemed friendly enough. Nobody was home, people or dogs, and I let myself out of their backyard through a side gate.

I walked into Modbury past their church, St George's, which they are renovating. It's sizeable and beautifully built of stonework and old, older even than the eight-hundred-year-old inn I'm sitting in

Walking Wet

and writing you from right now. It's on a hill above town, centered inside its own cemetery. I don't know which came first, the graveyard or the church. One of the barmaids here (the sincere one, not the one who calls me 'Sweet Pea') gave me a church newsletter to read, and apparently, people and a church were here already and listed in the Domesday Book before Modbury came together. The cemetery is a little lilypad pond of headstones, close together. The people must be buried head to toe and shoulder to shoulder in there under the sod. Then again, 800 years ago parishioners' bodies may have been shorter and smaller, and their graves correspondingly more economical. The cemetery all around is higher than the church's old stone footings, as the ground has been built up from all the folk buried in there.

I wonder what's in the soil surrounding St George's. I remember reading that some river valley soils back home are infused with ocean minerals carried there in the bones of salmon who came back to spawn and die in their rivers of birth. Those ocean minerals can be found even today by sampling for their isotopes.

Forty-odd generations of Modbury folk must have likewise absorbed into their bones those elements that had permeated their lives. They had been christened, married, and buried there at that same church, and had lived their lives near around it. Their isotopes must be radiating out even now into the soil they're buried in around that church, and the chemistry must be detectable.

I fancy I did feel something there: love, kindness, quiet wisdom. A sense of belonging. If I had any doubt about it after leaving the churchyard, those feelings have been reconfirmed this evening spent here at the inn, conversing with the people from Modbury whose bones are still in use. There may be a lot of good stuff in that cemetery dirt now, but I'll tell you, there's more to come.

Emma texted and said the forecast for the next two days is suitable to get back out and walk before the next big rainstorm comes in. Ha! What she doesn't know yet is that I've been out walking and making miles all through this last storm.

I'm still enjoying myself here in England, especially right here, in this moment. My Irish coffee is gone, and I'm 'sat' next to the fire now with a pint on a coaster in front of me. The path continues to be wonderfully informative, and this journey is a lot like fun, only different. I could do with a bit less misery and annoyance, but I will do with whatever I get just as well. Time spent here is well worth it.

Know that I love you, and that you are always here bustling around in my head all along the way ... -R

Walking Wet

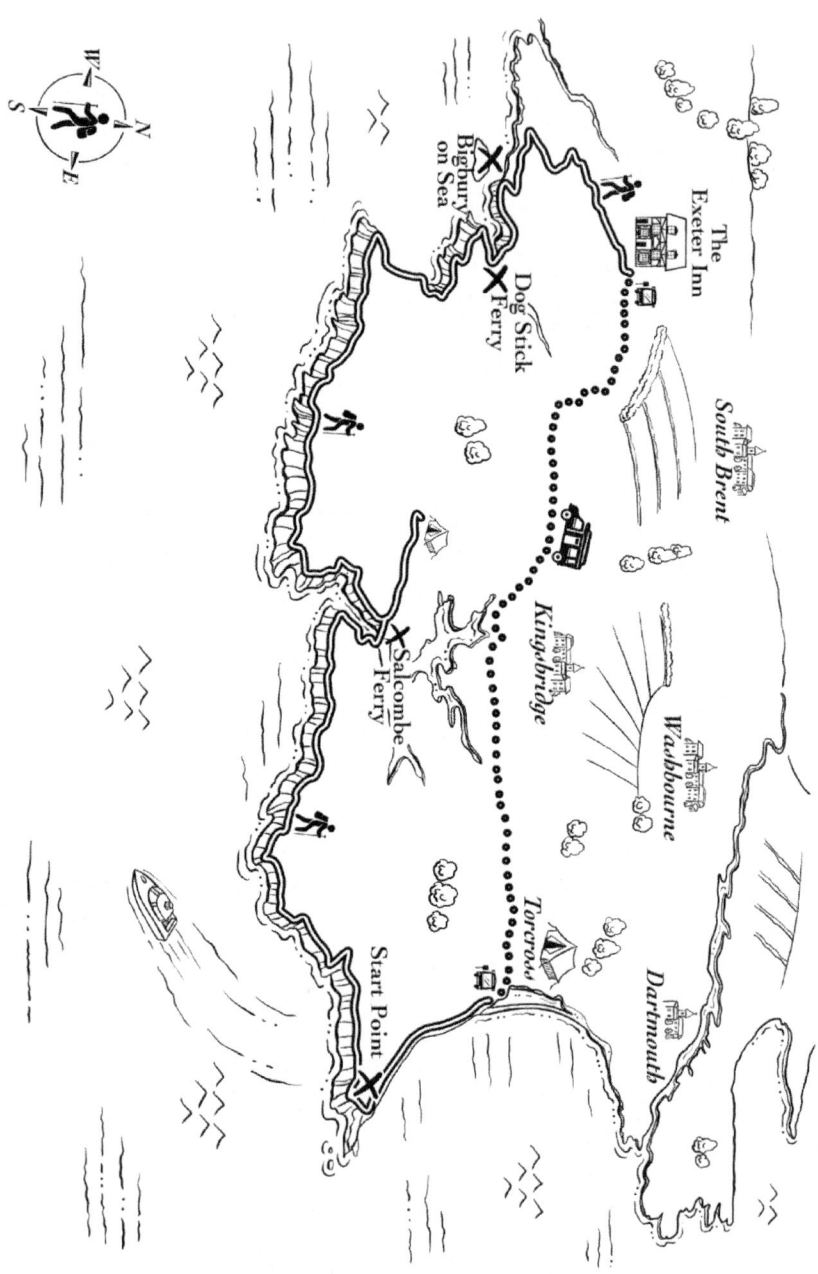

Every Night Booked

40 ⋯ DAYS WALKING
427 ⋯ PATH MILES WALKED
561 ⋯ TOTAL MILES WALKED
https://www.southwestcoastpath.org.uk/walksdb/173/

My walk 'home' the day before to The Exeter was so pleasant that I decided to forgo bussing and to strike out on foot to regain the Southwest Coast Path at Wyscombe Beach. Nikki had set breakfast sandwiches out for me again, and I was glad that, this time at least, I hadn't forgotten to make my goodbyes the night before. I quietly let myself out the side gate, walked the two blocks to the Post Office, and turned south. I was a couple miles out of town before the early bus to Plymouth would roll by The Exeter.

OS Maps hadn't found many public footpaths for me to follow back to the coast, so most of the morning would be spent walking on roads. But they were old countryside roads, and that makes all the difference. It's the new roads, the lettered highways in England, that are apt to kill you. Sure, the older and narrow single-lane, countryside roads offered up blind corners, but the vehicles on them are fewer and more polite.

The earth had birthed an early morning fog, and I wondered what personality this one had. Would it lift up and offer itself to the rising sun, or would it thicken, hew close, and drizzle? Maybe it would flee before a driving wind and heavy rain. But so long as I was in a lane, it didn't matter.

With old English country lanes, you walk through them rather than on them. They have cozy hedges on either side to protect you and keep you from wandering astray. At home, I live in a broad and fertile valley, and there's almost no bottom to our topsoil. If our pioneers needed a road somewhere, they'd start by digging a ditch. They would spread the spoils beside the ditch to make the road grade, and these roads were topped later with gravel or asphalt. The roads were thus elevated, and you walk or drive up on top of them.

Walking Wet

In England, especially in Cornwall and Devon, the topsoil is only a foot or so deep over bedrock. To make roads, their farmers of old would simply use the same tracks, over and over. Rain, hooves, and wheels conspired to churn the lane's surface to mud. If the track was steep enough, as most of them seem to be in Cornwall, the mud batter would eventually be churned viscous enough to be sluiced away. If not, it would be scraped to the sides.

Before long, the topsoil was removed, and the lanes cut down to the clean bedrock. They are paved or cobbled today, but their running surfaces are still a foot or two below the fields and pastures on either side. Add stone fencing or hedgerow vegetation to the roadside berms, and you have a walled lane to walk through.

This one ushered me through the villages of Great Tor and Kingston before reaching the coast and regaining the path at Wyscombe Beach. A breeze pushed the fog back from the sea, revealing a softer and sandier coastline than I'd had for the last several days. Perfect for making some miles.

It had taken five miles of country lanes and two miles of Coastal Path to meet my first human of the day, at Bigbury-on-Sea. He was carrying a bundle of slate up a ladder to the portico roof fronting a sea cottage. It turned out that he had walked the entire Southwest Coastal Path himself several years before, and it had given him "the bugs" he said. After that, he walked the Camino de Santiago in France and Spain, then flew to the United States to hike the Pacific Crest Trail. I asked which was his favorite.

He took a few steps down through the little garden gate to stand next to me.

"This one," he said. "This one right here where's we is stood."

"You don't mind walking wet, then?" I asked.

"It's walking wet what's makes it special," he said. "No matter how many times you walks this path, it's a different experience every time."

"Let's see," I said. "You've got your heavy fogs here to make you wet, or your dew, the drizzle, sea spray, or sprinkles. You might have rain showers, rain squalls, or cloudbursts."

"Or times you gets steady rain, or occasional rain, or driving rain," he laughed. "Or maybe it come in sheets, or torrents, or in buckets. But it's always different, innit?"

"Well, it's dry here at the moment," I said. There was a grand hotel across the bay on Burgh Island, backgrounded by a seascape of roiling grays. It was a moment's work to frame it as the day's POD.

"You know, I'm conflicted when it's like this," I said. "Should we be looking forward to the next rain, or should we be satisfied that it just has?"

"No worries." He laughed. "If it naught be raining this moment, we's do both."

He went back to his bundles of slate, and I carried on another mile or two to the River Avon crossing. Beside the path was another hand-painted sign with a number to call for a ferryman.

Right, why bother? I thought. The tide flats a quarter-mile upstream of me were exposed, and I saw that I could walk to within ten yards of the marina on the opposite shore, where two dogs were training their human to toss sticks in the water. When I got there, it looked to me like he was doing a fine job of it, but the dogs kept bringing the sticks back and demanding he try again.

"Looks to me like you're doing a fine job," I observed.

"You was supposed to call," he said defensively. He waved to my right. "Goes back to that point and wait. I'll gets someone to picks you up whens I'm done here."

I stood on my shore and watched him toss the sticks towards me a couple more times, disappointed that I'd been misunderstood.

"I meant that you toss the sticks just fine," I said.

With narrowed eyes, he looked at me again, and with the stick held aloft, shook it twice towards the point. "Go. There," he said with each shake. The dogs, I noticed, were watching the stick even more intently than I was.

"Oh. Kay," I answered, and squelched my way back across the tide flats.

Apparently, the dogs had decided their grouchy human needed a lot more stick tossing practice that day because it was another hour and forty minutes before he sent a boy in an aluminum skiff motoring over to the point. By then, I'd been joined by a hiking couple.

The man was middle-aged, tall and thin, had dark and gray-streaked mad-scientist hair, an unruly beard, and was excessively shy or possibly amnesiac. When I talked to him, he'd look at me for a second as if he needed to reidentify the speaker and then duck and turn his head so the rest of my remarks would be directed at his ear. Then he would look at me briefly again to answer, then close his eyes and nod towards his shoes, like an actor trying to deliver poorly memorized lines. He must have been carrying overnight gear, as his backpack was at least as large as mine.

The woman with him was also middle-aged but with strikingly blonde shoulder-length hair. She was pretty and petite, confident, and not shy at all. She had a smaller, day-trip-sized backpack that looked as though it had been carried for a long time.

Halfway across, the young ferryman noticed a snail hitching a ride across on my backpack. "That's yer lunch, is it?" he asked, pointing.

I hadn't seen it. It must have crawled onto my pack while I'd been sitting on it, waiting for the boat. The snail was sizeable. "Think I'll boil him up for soup. Want some?" I teased.

"Snail soup? No, but I'd be in for escargot."

Walking Wet

I didn't like the slime trail Mr. Snail was leaving on my backpack. I'd read about snails and schistosomiasis and sheep feces and various other intestinal insults before coming to England, and thinking about all that made me hesitate to pluck the little bugger off.

My new mad-scientist acquaintance shot his hand out and snatched it up. I looked over at him, with my eyebrows raised.

"I'll just keep him safe from you and give him a new home on the other side," he said.

"Good on ya, mate," said the kid steering the boat, laughing.

When we got off the boat, the man ignored several trail markers and turned left without a word, with my snail still clutched firmly in hand. The blonde lady continued walking, following the signs for the Coastal Path. I waited fifteen minutes for the snail whisperer to return to the trail, but he never did.

Up until then, I had thought he and the woman were traveling together. About a half-mile up the path, I caught up with her near the car park for Bantham Beach. At the far edge of the lot was a signpost with the Southwest Coast Path's acorn symbol, pointing up the hill. A light rain began falling, and we togged up in rain gear, then started up together.

Her name was Ellen, and like me, she was there to walk the entire trail. Unlike me, though, she had planned her trip meticulously and had booked overnight stays for herself all along the way. She'd no need to carry a tent, stove, or overnight gear. All she needed was a smallish daypack for a change of clothes and a leather waist wallet, slung around to the front to hold her phone and credit cards.

"This is my thirty-eighth day on the path," she said, "and I will finish the path in two weeks exactly, on my fiftieth birthday. My daughter will meet me there."

"You know the exact day you will finish a six-hundred-and-thirty-mile trail?"

"Yes. I know exactly what hotel I will stay in when I get there, just as I have known where I would sleep every night on the path since I've started," she said.

"That's impressive," I said. "Since Minehead, I haven't had advance reservations for anywhere. I don't even know where I'll sleep tonight."

"You're winding me up."

"I am doing what?"

"Winding me up, talking shite."

"Well, I'm not lying. I've got camping gear in here, right?" I turned my backpack towards her and bounced it on my hips.

"You are wild camping, then."

"I only wild camped one night, on a local's recommendation. I've rented tent pitches each night or got a room. It's worked out okay. But I'm kind of envious looking at your daypack. Getting tired of hauling this beast around."

"You walked every day since you started, then?" she asked.

"No, I've stayed put a couple of times to wait out the worst of the rainstorms. Even went to the Cotswolds for a couple of days and came back."

"Then I'm envious of your rucksack, big as it is," she said. "I booked myself one-night stays, fifty-two of them consecutive, and I can't reschedule. Whatever the weather is when morning comes, I'm out of my room and walking in it to my next."

"So, you've walked your legs every day, no matter what?"

"No matter what."

"Wow. You're a tough cookie."

"Sorry?"

"Tough cookie. A hard biscuit, you might say. Means you are very resilient."

"Yes, well, I've looked forward to this for a long time. I started planning for it years ago. I'm on this path to change my life… and to find a man," she added.

"Ambitious," I said. "How's it going so far?"

"Well," she said. "I have two weeks left."

"I'm not sure a hike works that way, changing your life," I said. "I hiked the Pacific Crest Trail back home and met some folks out there hoping it would change their lives. But most of the time, it didn't. Whatever it is that you find on a trail is difficult to hold on to when you leave it. Those things are often situational and ethereal, and they slip through your fingers when you get back home."

"Maybe I'll just concentrate on finding a man then, eh?"

Ellen turned out to be great company, chatty and personable. She was surprisingly interested in my stints as a firefighter and climbing guide. I'm more accustomed to listening to other people's stories, and only sharing snippets of my own as prompts to hear more of theirs. But with Ellen, I was getting a taste of my own medicine. When she mentioned her job in Wales as a university research assistant, I said, "Your job has got to be incredibly interesting. You learn about cutting-edge discoveries and mysteries before almost anyone else on the planet. Tell me something that only you and a handful of researchers know."

"My job is not as exciting as you think," she said. "It's a lot of reference library searching and making sure all the related previous research is cited. I write and format a lot of citations. It pays bills, is all. How do you camp on the ice? Have you ever been in an avalanche?"

Walking Wet

The path branched out and then disappeared into a maze of sheep trails, each winding up and around shoulder-high bushes and boulders. It was impossible to know which was the true path.

"Which one?" Ellen asked.

"I don't think it matters so long as we go up there," I said, pointing to higher ground. "This bluff we've been winding around is getting steeper, like it's setting us up for a fall. It's making me itchy. We'd be better off getting on top of it and looking over a precipice than bumbling on here and finding ourselves somewhere halfway down its face."

"Well, go on up then," she said. "And I will follow."

I reached the top ahead of her, far enough that my panting had almost subsided by the time she reached me. "Right," she said. "You still have a mountain climber's legs."

Ha. Looks like I've still got it, I thought to myself, knowing that in fact, I hadn't. But the attention was nice, nevertheless.

The morning passed pleasantly, and the rain tapered off as we neared Hope Cove, a middle-class holiday resort village. It was around lunchtime, so we went inside a small restaurant. It was dark and nearly empty inside, so there was plenty of room for our backpacks on the floor next to our booth.

We slid into the booth, and I ordered an Irish coffee, my drink of choice to warm up with. Ellen verified with the waitress that the Chardonnay was vegan, then ordered a glass.

"Isn't all wine vegan?" I asked.

"Not at all."

"You're winding me up?"

"Most wine is filtered through fish bladders. You've got to check if it's vegan." She got her phone out of her kit pouch pack and started to take it off, then paused.

"What do Americans call this?" she asked.

"A fanny pack," I said.

"Here, we call them bum bags. In the UK, 'fanny' means something very different. Do you know what?"

"I'm sure I don't."

"This," she said, displaying her hands in a V-shape below her navel, "is my fanny. And while I have this pouch spun around to front, this bag truly is, as you call it, a fanny pack."

I had no response.

"Ka-bloom," she said, and made a head-exploding gesture with her hands. "I have just blown your mind."

I attended to my Irish coffee.

Ellen sipped her vegan wine and said, "I wasn't hoping to meet an American on this trip, but I'm happy I did. You should put my number in your phone contacts."

I'd forgotten to pack my glasses in their usual spot that morning, and the dim light made finding anything on my phone impossibly blurry.

"You'll have to do it," I said. I unlocked my phone and handed it to her.

"Who's that?" She was looking at the photo of my wife smiling out from the home screen.

"That's my wife Monica," I said.

"So, you're married then?"

"Uh-huh."

"Why don't you wear a ring?"

"Hurts my finger," I said. "On account of my fingers being so fat."

"Huh," she said, squinting at the photo again. "You married a younger woman, obviously."

I wondered if that was a compliment or an insult. "No," I said, "we're born barely a month apart."

She glanced down at my phone, then back to me again. "You are having me on."

"Not at all," I said. "Should've seen her when she was your age."

She looked back at me without a response.

"Ka-bloom," I said and mimed a head explosion gesture.

"Hmph." She looked at my wife's picture again, then handed my phone back without typing in her number. "Where is she?"

"She's home. And enjoying perfect weather."

"Any particular reason she is there while you are here alone?"

"Not really. Long trips tenting it just isn't her thing. I thought maybe she would like walking inn to inn like you are, but after talking to you, not so much."

Our sandwiches arrived, and we tucked in and ate in silence for a while. Ellen didn't look like she was enjoying her sandwich, but having lunched with vegans before, I didn't think much of it.

"All British men are married, gay, or on the dole," Ellen declared.

"So, you have options, then," I said.

Ellen snorted. "And for a while, I had hope that American men might be different."

We hiked the rest of the day together, and with the recalibration, our conversations were more genuine and interesting. We talked about the hopes we had for our children and what we did to encourage them. Surprisingly, we both considered our careers rather mundane and hoped our kids would attempt more fulfilling things. I thought it was odd, our transference of greener grass

Walking Wet

wistfulness onto the next generation. She countered that it was universal, another facet of parents wanting better for their kids.

"I had a baby young, before university, and have been a single mom since I was twenty-two."

"What happened to Dad?" I asked.

"Skipped out. And never paid what he should. He works mostly off the books."

"Off the books?"

"When there's a divorce here in the UK, your child support payments are determined by income. Some guys work off the books then, do handyman and such work, and get paid in cash to avoid paying child support."

"Well, that's not fair," I said.

"He says it's fair because I have a posh academic job and make more money than he does. My daughter won't be doing what I did, having a child so young."

"My wife and I spent the first half of our lives chasing dreams and careers," I said. "I hope our son doesn't do what we did and end up having a child so old."

"I don't think that's so bad," she said. "Besides, it's only one of you who looks old."

And so, we carried on towards Salcombe, where she'd booked her next room. We came back into cell service a mile out, and it was easy enough for me to rent a tent pitch for the night, barely two miles north of town. We talked about meeting up for dinner later, but I didn't want to walk another round trip between the inn and the camping farm. We discussed walking together the next day, but she was unwilling to leave her inn before breakfast was served, and I couldn't stand to waste so many hours of early daylight.

So our two paths diverged in Salcombe old town, my way towards the camp and hers to the inn. We stopped and stood there awkwardly until Ellen clucked her tongue.

"Give us a cwtch, then," she said, and hugged me.[i]

There were sidewalks and footpaths and cell service all the way to my night's tent pitch. I called Monica and told her all about my day with Ellen. I hadn't expected her to be as amused as I was, but her reaction surprised and humbled me nonetheless.

"I trust you weren't unkind to her," she said.

It rained again that night, and although the squalls that rode through were no worse than usual, it was miserable. My tent had lost all its rainproofing. Slimy tapeworms of seam sealant glue peeled off and hung dripping from the tent ceiling, and the Velcro and tie-back loops fell off the fly. The tent sagged

---

[i] 'cwtch'- rhymes with a cross between 'hutch' and 'hooch' and is Welsh for 'warm embrace'

and billowed like a flaccid clingy sack, while groundwater percolated up through the floor. I put raingear on over myself and the sleeping bag as best I could and mopped up the water pooling on the floor with my socks, wringing them out the fly every ten minutes or so throughout the six and a half hours of that night's rainfall.

I'd never been inside a tent that had died so suddenly and completely before and wondered if I'd been the one who killed it. All my gear had been soaked through when I'd gone to The Exeter. I'd dried everything there in shifts, first by drip drying them in the shower, and then finishing them off under a hair dryer before stuffing them back into their sacks. Maybe tents can't survive that kind of treatment.

***

I was back down the hill in the morning and was the only passenger on the first ferry across Salcombe Harbor. The ferryman and then a croissant and pasty vendor later, became the only people I talked to that day. It was nice, resting my brain's speech generation and comprehension centers. I rounded the bottom of the South Hams peninsula alone, turned north at Start Point, and continued past beaches and through lazy cow pastures. Just before reaching the curio and ice cream shops at the long beach at Torcross, Emma's text came through:

[Please enjoy a right drenching these next two days.]

I thought about all the enjoyment I'd gotten inside my tent's carcass the night before. That was courtesy of only a normal drenching. A 'right' drenching would bring unbearable pleasure.

I thought of Ellen, somewhere behind me, sticking to schedule and walking every predetermined mile of her path, and wondered how she'd enjoy the next few days. She'd mentioned that with walking every day for over a month and a week, she'd never really gotten her footwear dry and that some strain of bacteria had taken up residence between her toes.

"Oy, my feet," she'd said, "they're all pruney and smell like bad cheese."

I told her of my breakthrough discovery involving Tetley's, but it was too late to do her any good. The topic hadn't come up while she had still supposed I was single, and everything I told her after that was met with a healthier dose of skepticism.

I called Nikki at The Exeter, and thirty minutes later, I was on a bus back to Modbury. Rain started falling again before I got there.

Walking Wet

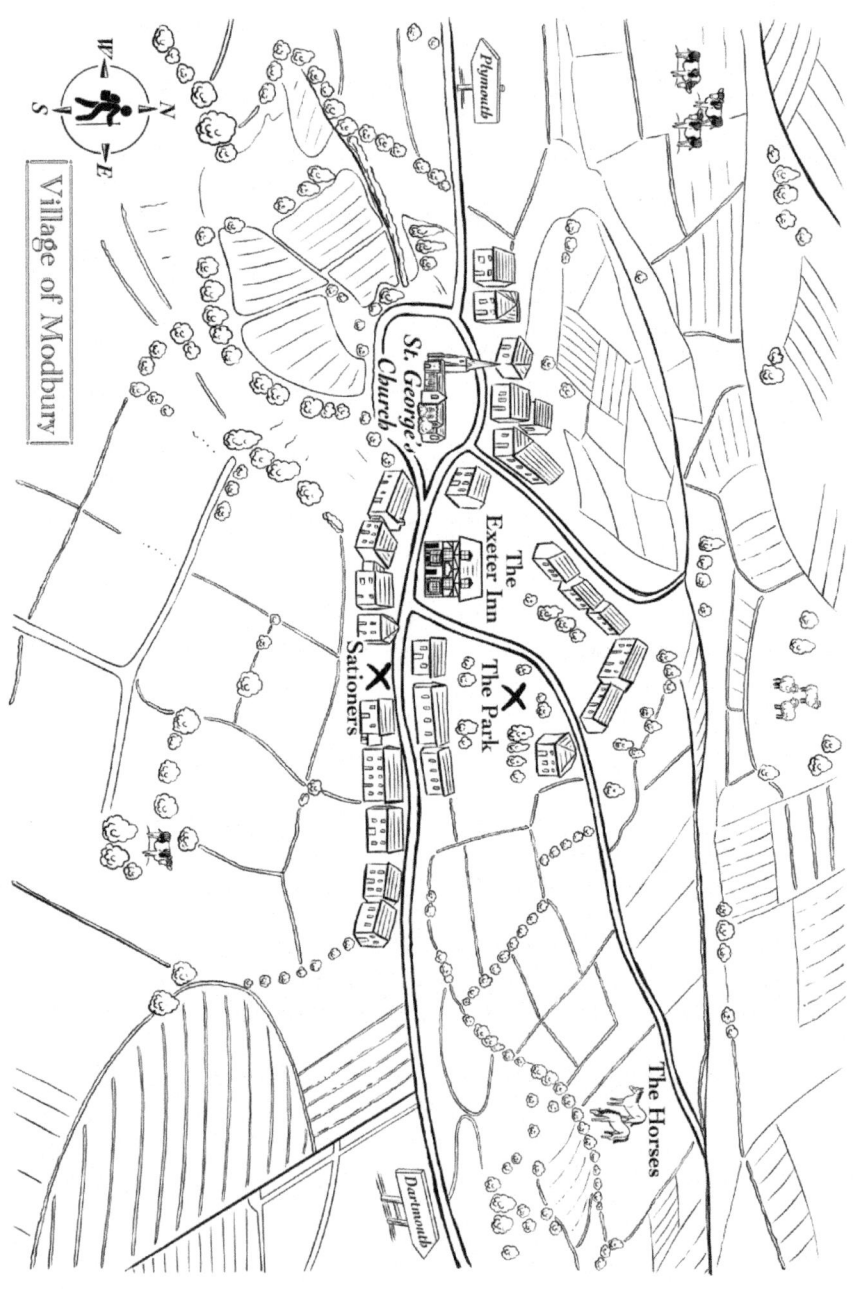

Feels Like Enough

```
41 ⋯ DAYS WALKING
427 ⋯ PATH MILES WALKED
565 ⋯ TOTAL MILES WALKED
```
https://www.modburytic.org.uk/

Nikki was genuinely happy to see me again. My old room had already been let out to other guests, so she led me to a different one, an odd half-story above my old room. Nikki had told me that the breakfast room below had once been stables and coach tack rooms, and I wondered if this room was an addition, built atop the original sloped stable roof. If so, it had been done long ago. The stuccoed walls looked ancient.

The new room was just as comfortable but lacked a small thing I hadn't realized I'd miss. The window in my first room opened above the rain gutter, just where the rainwater whirlpooled down into the downspout opening. At first I took it personally, that constant runnelling sound outside my window mocking my lack of progress on the path. But as I let go and allowed my anxiety to drain away, the sound became comforting.

When I cracked my new window open, I listened for the little spinning gurgle, and when it wasn't there, I realized that it had become an acoustic touchstone, joining things like the buzz of my grandfather's refrigerator on the back stoop of his lake cabin, or the thunk-shudder from my old hay baler when the knotters tripped.

I'm thankful that those touchstones, those soundbites from life that your mind deems unforgettable, don't all come from traumatic or weighty experiences. Because sometimes it's nice just to recall something nice.

I busied myself getting the wet things out of the pack and stringing them up in the shower, steeped my socks in Tetley's with my cookpot, then headed downstairs for an Irish coffee to make a plan next to the hearth.

Sitting this rainstorm out would make it difficult to finish the path before my flight home. Would I regret coming back to Modbury and not pushing through? Ellen was still out there sticking to her plan, and physically, she was less able than I was. Surely, if she could do it, shouldn't I be doing it? No insurmountable barrier had forced me off the path, only Emma's one-line text forecasting a little more discomfort.

On the other hand, the fire in the eight-hundred-year-old hearth was especially kind and warm, I thought, *and Evie made a delectable Irish coffee.* I took a sip and let it help ascertain the severity of guilt I should feel about my inconstancy and fondness for comfort. I called home to Monica.

"Spend the rest of your time over there sightseeing and doing touristy things," she said. "Hit the highlights. Go to London, see Trafalgar Square, Buckingham Palace, and the changing of the guards. Take a ride on the London Eye."

"I don't know," I said. "I came over here to hike the Salt Path."

"Most of the PODs you send me feature cows and wet sheep. It's like getting travel photos from a border collie. Just quit walking the path."

"If I were to quit, it would feel like quitting."

"Yes, that's called cognitive alignment."

"But I don't like feeling like a quitter."

"Is this another West Butterfish situation? Because that was dumb."

"West buttress, Fisher Peak."

"Still dumb, all three times. But you do you. At least you won't kill yourself walking over there."

"Well, it's a lot cheaper to keep walking than playing tourist in London," I said defensively.

"I can support you there one hundred percent," Monica said. "Anyway, Matthew will be home next week. It will be good to have at least one of my boys back home and being sensible. I've been worried."

"There's no need to worry."

"Really? Your nephew took Matthew shooting. With handguns."

"Target practice, with pistols," I said.

"Same, same. Matt sent me pictures."

"That chowderhead. I told him not to."

"Yes, that's what he told me you said."

After cutting the connection and finishing my coffee, I called Emma.

Time to rile up another one! a voice in my head crowed. *For Pete's sake*, I thought, and made the call.

I let her know I'd gone back to Modbury and asked her advice on which sections ahead were must-see and which I could possibly skip over. To my surprise, she had quit the path for good herself. The incessant weather had wrecked her schedule, and she had a trek to guide in Ecuador coming up. She had decided to spend the time she had left in England visiting family in Beaminster.

Emma suggested I skip over the next ninety miles and rejoin the trail near Lyme Regis. It was the home of the eighteenth-century naturalist Mary

Anning, who had discovered fossils of the pterosaur (a smallish pterodactyl) and the plesiosaur (a Loch Ness monster with alligator teeth) falling out of the cliffsides there.

"You may see something yourself," Emma said. "The Jurassic Coast along there is a world heritage site because of the fossils."

I imagined scanning the beach and cliffs and zeroing in on a suspicious lump. "I could find a dinosaur then," I said.

"Ammonites, more likely."

"You still have Puritans here in England?"

"What? No. Look for rocks that are sweet-roll-shaped. It might be a fossil snail."

"Boring. I'd want to find something with teeth, you know."

"Right, then. Try biting them," she said, and hung up.

***

Sunday would be my last with The Exeter. For a change, I'd hung around long enough that morning to have breakfast downstairs with the other guests. It was good. Early, hot and crisp, and just a little salty; everything a day's greeting should aspire to be. It was something I'd been missing this whole time by giving in to my itchy feet and anxiety.

I walked up to Saint George's again, and even though it was Sunday morning, I had the place to myself. Because the parish was having repairs and upgrades done to the old stonework cathedral, they had moved services temporarily. I looked inside and saw scaffolding spattered with plaster and stucco where the congregation and pews should be. I pictured myself as a local plasterer, spending five days of my week inside the church and another one with its congregants, and wondered what I'd have been doing yesterday. Did I spend it here in town? I wandered on.

It may seem strange to spend a day off from walking the path by walking around a town, but the intentions are different. On the path, it was about spooling out the miles. It was about pushing whatever was behind me farther back, and pulling whatever may be lying ahead closer. But I wasn't leaving anything behind me walking through town this day, nor looking for anything up ahead. It's a difference that makes all the difference. This day, I was just wandering.

I crossed Modbury's main drag and climbed into the steep neighborhoods above, where I ran into Evie, the barmaid from The Exeter. Her dog, Churchill, had just pulled her through a park, and they were coming out as I was heading in. Churchill was a brindle-coated mass of muscle and intimidation, who turned out to be as sweet and honest as the woman he towed behind him.

Slobberier, though, for sure. I thought he just wanted to inspect my hands for treats, but he went all in for a jowl rub instead. I'm sure he wouldn't have minded if I wiped my hands on him afterward, but I didn't want to insult Evie. Still, I didn't want dog saliva on my clothes either, since I'd just laundered them in my room's sink the night before. So, I stood there dumbly while Evie told me about the renovations planned for Saint George's, wondering if my hands would air dry before I found something leafy in the park to wipe them on. They didn't.

There were a few things to get in town before Emma's afternoon rain was due to arrive, so I meandered back to find Visqueen or painter's plastic. For my remaining nights on the path, I thought I might be drier if I draped plastic underneath and around my tent's corpse before crawling into it.

I bought kitchen trash bags as they were the closest thing to plastic sheeting I could find. The roll of trash bags was heavier than painters' plastic would've been, but if it did the job, I'd be happy to schlep it along.

My old reading glasses had been squashed and irretrievably bent in the process of wriggling the bottom half of my sleeping bag into my backpack and pulling raingear over it during that last night in the tent. I bought folding reader glasses in the stationery store in town. Practical and compact, and going flat into a tiny plastic case, perfect for slipping into a pocket.

Brits must be avid readers, I thought, *to have such a convenient little item available on Sunday afternoons.* Rain began to fall as I left the shop, so I went back to The Exeter to put them on and get some journaling done.

When I let myself in the side door, Nikki and Phil were readying the pub to open and discussing some horses he had just bought. Heavy rain was coming soon, and Phil thought it would be good to see how they would get on in it. I finagled an invitation for myself to tag along when the time came, then headed up the stairs to my room.

Presently, the weather turned sour outside, and Nikki rapped on my door to tell me that Phil was getting set to leave. It was blowing a good rain now, and it drove through my jacket before we even made it to his truck.

We nosed out of the back alley and turned steeply uphill. The wiper blades enjoyed long pauses between leisurely sweeps while Phil narrowly serpentined his truck between double rows of parked vehicles. Wavy sheets of rainwater conceded only an obscured and distorted view through the windshield, so I peered out my door window to see how close we were to sideswiping the cars parked on my side. I saw, and wondered what the best position was, within the confines of the truck cab, to get my body into before the airbags blew.

I asked Phil, "How long have you and Nikki owned The Exeter?"

"We don't own it," he said. "Nikki's its manager."

"How did that come about?"

He glanced at me briefly before returning his focus to the marginally translucent windscreen. "For centuries, these old pubs were family-run and passed down from one generation to the next. If you were born into it, it gave you a steady living. You'd never get rich, but it was respectable and steady." He paused. Then added, "Too steady, maybe."

"How so?"

"Innkeepers are themselves kept, in a way, by the inns they keep," he said. "There's always so much to do. You're catering to travelers all the time, but you can't much travel yourself."

That sounded like experience speaking. "So, how did Nikki come to run The Exeter?" I asked, "if she didn't inherit it?"

"She'd worked as a barmaid at The Exeter when she was a girl and came to love the place. Then maybe in the last decade or so, investors started coming through and offering real money for these centuries-old inns. For their owners, it was more money than they had ever put away in all their years of owning, and enough to leave behind, too, for their kids. A lot of them sold."

I nodded and relaxed. We'd made it out of town, and there were blurry soft hedgerows running past my side window now.

"So, when The Exeter sold and they advertised for a manager, Nikki jumped at the chance," he said.

What Phil had said explained a few things. I'd been in a number of old pubs since I came here, and though they were similar in how they were built and situated, there were differences in style. And some seemed, to me anyway, a bit kitschy or inauthentic. There was a pub in Penzance, for example, with walls overly festooned with seafaring trinkets, a jumble of odds and ends seemingly scavenged from swap meets.

Another pub's tables appeared ready to accommodate a dozen seances at once. In another, TV screens had been mounted illogically near a dartboard target. I'd gotten up to inspect it, and though the target itself was liberally punctured from dart tips, the wood-paneled wall behind it was not. I tried to imagine tossing darts over variously inebriated patrons shouting at a football match and sticking nothing other than the target. I couldn't, and decided it must have been a decoration.

I'd chalked up those oddities as natural consequences of the sensibilities you'd expect from a country that puts unremarkable people on the telly so they can look at them naked. But now, it made more sense. Those pubs' affectations hadn't evolved through generations of heritage. They were the newcomer managers' attempts to differentiate themselves, to stand out. They were throwing things at walls to see what stuck.

When we arrived at the pasture beyond town, the horses were huddled at the far end, heads bowed against the rain. They wouldn't be coaxed over, and I couldn't blame them. They looked miserable.

"Looks like they're settling in fine," Phil observed.

On the ride back, I told Phil that when I'd bought a dairy farm back home, I'd expected to have property and a vocation to pass on to my offspring if they chose to take it up. "But it didn't work out that way," I said.

"You think your son would be a good farmer, then?" he asked.

"Ha! He's on a ranch, giving it a try right now. But I'm afraid sometimes that video games will keep him from moving on to a future career."

"You are not alone with that worry."

"You know, back home," I said, "it seems harder for boys now than it was when we were their age."

"Same here. School seems easier for girls than boys now, and that gets them into careers more easily. Or they could be stay-at-home moms, or almost anything else, and still be respected. Boys don't get that same leeway."

"I know, right? And where boys do have advantages, like in physically demanding jobs, there's not much respect and even less money."

"So, when you were dairy farming, you made a lot of money and garnered lots of respect?" Phil asked.

"Money, no. But respect, yes. So, how did you do when you were training horses?"

"Same, and same," Phil said.

***

The pub doors closed behind the last patron, and the last of the meals were brought out of the kitchen for the five of us still inside. Phil opened the big bottles of 'French' wine while Nikki opened the door to the back, letting his four hunting dogs fly in to look for their master. She came back with her dog, Maisie, who may have possessed less breeding and intelligence than her four mates, but made up for it in loyalty and sweetness. When Nikki sat at the bar, Masie jumped up onto a barstool and sat there casually between us.

"My dog loves the nose-boop game," I said, and raised my finger up in front of her, then slowly dropped it down to her snout while whistling a descending bomb-drop sound. "Boop!" I said, as I booped her nose. She loved it.

Evie had arrived to join us, even though it was her night off, with Churchill in tow. The two other humans inside were Tom and Jane, both of whom were also products of Modbury. Jane was a no-nonsense, blunt-speaking gardener who'd spent most of her married life in a city, but had come home when that was over and her son grown. Tom had left Modbury long ago and was now the chef at a four-star restaurant he owned in Australia. His father had recently died, and he was back in town to settle the estate.

As the wine flowed, the conversation turned lively. At some point, I boasted to Tom about the school I went to. Although I'd gone there for an environmental degree, my alma mater was regionally renowned for culinary arts. "You may have heard about us?" I asked.

"No, but it sounds like another nightmare," he said.

His response surprised me, but Nikki and Phil were nodding. Obviously, they knew what third rail I'd tripped over. "How's that?" I asked.

Tom set his glass on the table, shaking his head. "Look, I don't have a problem with your school in particular," he said, "just culinary arts schools in general. There are too many of them, and I think we'd all be better off if there weren't."

"Then how would we get chefs like you? How would they learn the craft?"

"By watching and listening. By starting at the bottom and working their way up. Whenever I hire someone with a culinary arts degree, they don't want to start at the bottom. They've paid good money to get their degree, and they've been told that having that degree makes them ready to walk in and run a restaurant. And that's what they expect to do, even though I'm hiring them to keep the bins emptied and make sure the dumpster lids are locked down."

I said, "Someone's got to do it, I suppose."

"Someone's got to do it, absolutely," Tom said. "And not only that, but a thousand other unglamorous but essential tasks need to be done, and done well, to make a restaurant run. No matter how good your preparers are, you've got to have good people satisfied and willing to work their way up the ladder, like the rest of us have.

"But the fresh grads, they want to shop and source ingredients at the markets, plan and devise the menus. That's my job." He took a sip from his wineglass and tilted it towards Phil before settling it back onto the table. "This is a good Bordeaux," he said.

Then to me, "That's the part I enjoy anyway. Lately, I'm spending too much time on personnel issues. We have a lot more turnover now, and it's because of those culinary programs like the one at your school."

"Interesting," I said. "I thought it would boost students' value in the marketplace, already knowing what they'd learned. Like auto repair shops hiring graduates who already know how to rebuild an engine."

"Yes, that could be true if restaurants were anything like mechanic shops. But they're not."

To change the subject, Jane brought us into a discussion about personal grooming. The general consensus that emerged from around the table was that we were roundly tied in third place behind Tom, taking first prize, with Phil's dogs taking second. A debate about which local music venues were worth driving to followed among other conversations, some light and some deeply personal.

I recalled my discussion with Charles back in Barnstaple, and thought, *If a Mayberry could ever exist today, it's out there just through the front doors of this pub.*

Walking Wet

It occurred to me that the group at the table drinking wine with me represented a cross section of natives and that they could shed light on a mystery that the wine and I had somehow decided was bothering me.

"Hey," I said, addressing them. "I've noticed while walking that cement work done here is usually finished carelessly. Why's that?"

They looked at me as if I'd just dropped in from Mars.

"I mean, instead of brushing it out or trowelling it smooth, it's left lumpy and rough here, and more often than not, marred with footprints. Is it because you have so much world-class stonework around? Maybe concrete isn't seen here as a legitimate building material?"

Jane was laughing, but the rest of them didn't know what to do with the question. I tried again. "I mean, there's some like that just outside the side door. There's even paw prints left in it. Do all the skilled tradesmen work with stone, and the cement is just mixed up and laid by whoever is left?"

Jane laughed harder.

"It was us who patched that concrete out there," Nikki said, "and right glad I am that Jack put his prints in it. He was well the best cat I ever had. He came to me just after I took over The Exeter, and he was in here every day. Some people loved him, and some people he took a disliking to, and that was okay because Jack was a good judge of character. If you were a kind person, you could do anything with him. You could pick him up and put him over your shoulder, or set him in your lap and scratch his head. But if he thought you weren't, you'd best keep your distance.

"Jack was with us for a good ten years, and this was his favorite spot right here. When people at this table complained about having to eat dinner with a cat, I'd tell them there were other pubs in town because Jack wasn't about to be moving anywhere.

"I never knew where Jack went before the pub was open, but he was here every night till close. And the dogs didn't bother him." She scratched Maisie behind her ears and continued.

"Until one morning at the end, when he didn't want out in the morning, but curled up next to the hearth and died right here. Cats know. They can feel when death is coming and usually go out and lose themselves in the woods somewhere to die alone. But I think Jack knew how much that would hurt me, not knowing what had happened to him. And that was his final gift to me to die right here next to the hearth where he was loved."

"To Jack," Phil said, raising his glass.

We all did the same, solemnly.

I'd asked a dumb question about cement, and had been answered with a story about a cat. It struck me then, hearing that story of love, what wonderous people are those with such capacity for it, and how fortunate one is to be sat in their midst.

Nothing gives you a sense of belonging like sharing wine in a circle of kind souls and their dogs in a building that's housed countless similar scenes, re-enacted by generations through the eight centuries of its existence.

It felt like home, like a place to curl up in. It felt like it should. It felt like enough.

Walking Wet

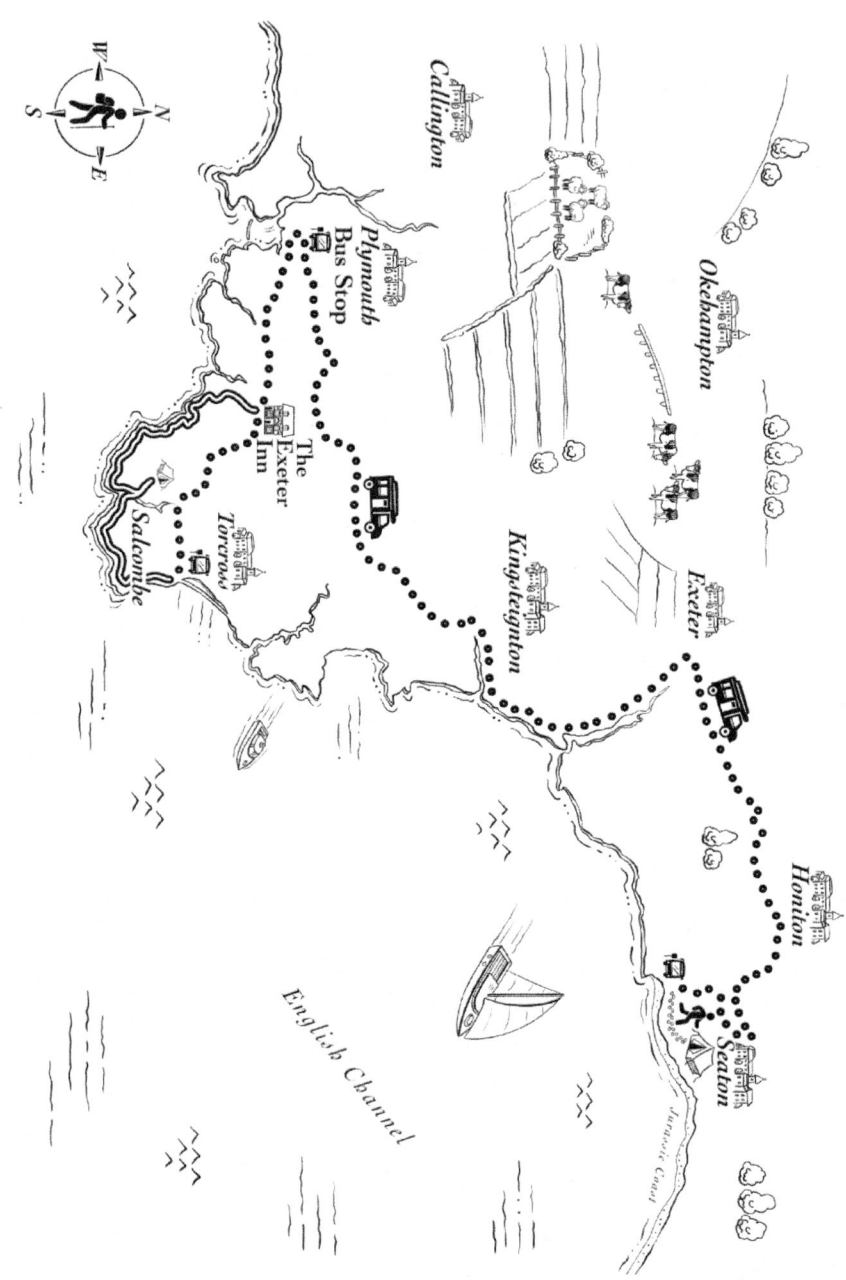

Four Ways to Say Widow

46 ⋯ DAYS WALKING
491 ⋯ PATH MILES WALKED
641 ⋯ TOTAL MILES WALKED
https://www.southwestcoastpath.org.uk/walksdb/181/

I smiled at Jack's kitty prints in the cement patch outside the side door and eased it closed as quietly as I could. I'd catch the early bus to Plymouth like I'd done before, but this time, thankfully, there had been no sandwiches waiting for me on the sidebar downstairs. It was Nikki's day off, and she had earned it. All of them from the night before would be going to a garden show later with Jane.

And I'm heading out early and alone again, I thought, and wondered why.

Usually, leaving early to reach the next place feels like progress, like the continuation of momentum. But this felt like a mistake, like moving on after having just discovered where I belong. The bus taking me away from Modbury reinforced that feeling, rolling past now-familiar landmarks, cradling a community I feared I'd never see again. A tumbling wave of homesickness rolled over me. I wanted so much to stay home, and just as much to go home.

When the bus arrived at the main station in Plymouth, I glanced across the way and the tent and the homeless kid who sheltered in it on the lawn were gone. I wondered if he'd been pushed along by the police, or if maybe someone had been out looking for him and took him back home. If so, I hoped he'd feel at peace when he got there.

I had a coworker once who had become a space cadet and kept forgetting what needed doing from one moment to the next. He was late getting me the survey points I needed and wasn't answering messages I'd left him one day, so I walked over to his office. When I got there, his laptop was closed with his forehead on top of it.

"Too bad they don't pay us to sleep here," I said, "because it looks like this is the only place some of us can."

"Uh, right," Todd answered. My voice had snapped him upright, but his eyes were bloodshot and the HP logo was embossed into his forehead.

"What's going on?" I asked, concerned.

His son, who was only a few years older than mine, was missing. He'd been labeled a deviant online by a couple of classmates, and even though the rumors were thoughtless and demonstrably false, they were amplified and repeated. At first he stayed home from school, and with both parents working, spent his days alone. He found new friends online who understood and commiserated with him, and after taking some camping gear from the garage on his way out, he left to meet up with them. His new friends accepted him with open arms and then introduced him to fentanyl.

Todd had been driving around the city nights after work, searching for his son. He'd learned where all the homeless encampments were in town and went through each of them several times a night. In the dark and cold, he wouldn't recognize his boy without being right on top of him.

It was a month before he found his son and brought him home. They got him enrolled in a drug treatment program and an alternative high school, but two weeks later he disappeared again. Todd was out nights looking again, but couldn't find him. He suspected his son had taken a bus out of town.

I looked for the homeless kid's tent up and down the street.

Damned buses, I thought, remembering.

I boarded a motor coach out of Plymouth and had a smooth, quiet, and partially hungover ride to Exeter. There I had to transfer again, this time to a more commonly uncomfortable smaller bus that would take me back out to the coast.

It dropped me off in Seaton, right on top of the Southwest Coast Path. The path led me across a bridge, then up a steep driveway to a golf course. From there, it followed the cart path uphill beside a couple of fairways before continuing onward into the brush.

I was just stepping back onto the path when a woman passed me. She was thin and wiry, and moving with a businesslike efficiency. I'd had a slow start and been dawdling that morning, I admitted to myself. Maybe what I needed was a pace rabbit to get me going.

"Morning!" I said. "Mind if I try keeping up?"

She answered, "Not at all, not one to discourage, me."

I fell behind and stepped up my pace. We introduced ourselves, sharing abbreviated bios in short bursts to accommodate breathing at our strenuous clip. She shouted so I could hear her from behind, and I gasped at her daypack. Her name was Louise. She had no kids and was married. Her husband was older and retired. She lived a couple of hours away, outside of Exeter. Curious, I asked why she was in such a hurry.

"Have's a biopsy appointment I can't miss. For the lump they's found."

"There's a health clinic up ahead, then?"

"No. We went on holiday after the lump. Was told we'd have a long wait. Got a call this morning. Biopsy was just scheduled for today. You know how it is."

"So where are we going?"

"Back to our campervan. I'm going to put things away. Gets it ready to drive."

"Your husband is not going?"

"He's going. I don't drive. We were in Seaton when we got the call. And no bus back to the caravan park until later. Hiking back to get things ready, save time. When the bus brings him up, we'll go."

"Why isn't he hiking back with you?"

"That wouldn't save time. Doesn't like to hike this fast."

"No surprise there," I muttered.

"Say again?" she asked.

"Let's get you there," I said louder.

It was an admirable plan, the execution of which would dissipate Louise's nervous energy while at the same time getting her to the clinic on time. But it made me wonder: are our HMOs back home more compassionate than the Brits' National Health Service? I'd had no cause to admire the compassion of our health administrators before, but here were people completely at the mercy of their provider, and accepting it as normal.

The path came to a road, and the acorn-symbolled trail marker told us to follow it to the left. Louise stopped.

"Our campervan is just the other side of that private estate there," she said. "About fifteen minutes if we go through."

"Let's go, then," I said.

"But it's not a public pathway."

"How long would it take us to follow the road?"

"Forty-five minutes, an hour maybe," she said.

I headed across. "Follow me," I said, and she did.

I wanted to be sure I didn't slow her down now that I was in front of her, so I kept the pace brisk, jogging almost, so I hadn't air enough left to talk with.

I wondered if Louise, had she been on her own this morning, would have taken the longer route. Maybe she would then miss her appointment and that would have forced a delay for her biopsy. And what would that mean for her health, for her family?

Walking Wet

It was silly speculation, I knew and admonished myself for it. Denying that coincidences can be random can be an unhealthy mysticism. Still, miracles do happen, and holding one of your eyes open so you can see them can't be worse than keeping both of them closed so you can ignore them.

If Louise did need a mini-miracle, Providence had sent her the right guy. Since coming to England, I'd already traipsed through Clarkson's backyard and several others besides without a compelling reason to be in any of them. She was jogging now behind a repeat offender.

We came up on the estate house, a grand and intimidating brick and stone heap of a building with a circular driveway fronting an imposing entrance. It embodied power and privilege, and from the upper floors of the glowering behemoth, mullioned windows looked down on us through ancient ivy.

I felt a pang of unease and thought, *There's a POD no border collie would take*, as we hurried past. But it didn't seem prudent to stop for a couple of reasons.

We didn't see anyone until we were almost off the estate, approaching the gatehouse at the far end of the long driveway near the road. A car came around the gatehouse, heading toward us. I expected a Bentley or a Rolls, but it was nothing remarkable. I waved at the driver as he passed us, and he waved back. He wasn't brooding and didn't look scary at all.

By the time we reached Louise's campervan, the weather was getting snotty again. She invited me to stop by later for wine and dinner, promising they'd be back that evening. She'd pointed out a camping farm that welcomed tents and walkers near the estate we'd passed through, and suggested I go there to get settled and come by later. I thanked her and wished her luck. She was already busy folding and stowing lawn chairs.

Heading towards the camping farm, I walked slower and breathed easier than I had all day, which allowed slower thoughts to mosey into my head and mull around more leisurely in there.

It may seem odd to connect with a stranger so quickly, but I've found it's often the nature of encounters like these. People facing predicaments that cut through everyday concerns don't have time for idle pleasantries. When they need help, they recognize it when they see it, and they'll accept it without vetting. I suspect their intuition is sharpened, and they rely upon it instinctively. I know that when I stepped across the road to trespass, it wasn't a well-calculated decision. It was an intuitive compulsion.

The woman at my campsite assigned me a pitch near their putt-putt golf course, and I found a little shed nearby with a power outlet. I took advantage of it, passing the afternoon inside reading and charging my phone while keeping all my belongings inside, thinking to delay the setup of my tent in the rain. I wasn't at all confident about my garbage bag solution holding up.

As dinner time approached, I left the campsite and walked to a nearby coffee shop that also sold pastries and artisan bread. I doubted Louise and her husband had much time to prepare anything other than spaghetti maybe, so I bought bread and a bottle of olive oil to go with it before heading to their site.

When I arrived at the camper van park, their van was still gone. I rapped on the door of their friend, an older man in his seventies, in the camper van next door. He invited me in and told me that after undergoing the biopsy, they had decided to stay at the clinic to get the results in person. "Who knows when they'd hear back from the lab if they don't stay on site," he said. "You know how they can be."

Maybe I don't, I thought for the second time that day.

He expected them to return late that night or possibly in the morning. I asked him to pass along a message. "Let Louise know it was great to meet her. And I'll be thinking of her, and hoping for all the best."

"I'll do that," he said. As I got up to leave, he grasped my hand. "No, no, take your bread and oil. I've got a meal for them here already if they make it back."

That night, I peeled several kitchen trash bags off the roll, laid them out to pitch my tent on, and then draped several more over the dome netting before attaching the fly. It still got wet inside that night, but it worked better than I'd hoped. In the morning, I packed up and went back to the caravan park and saw that their spot was still empty. I turned and headed back to the path. I never had the chance to meet Louise's husband, and I never saw or talked to Louise again.

***

It was a few miles along roads and hedgerowed lanes back to the coast at Lyme Regis, Mary Anning's town of origin. I was feeling a bit odd, unsteady and lightheaded, and wondered if it was from eating artisan bread and olive oil for both dinner and breakfast. Maybe I was experiencing a blood sugar drop from the lack of protein or fats or something. Before last night, I had been eating rather well after all.

When I walked through Lyme Regis, I was surprised to see fossil ammonites casually displayed in a crate outside a curio shop. The crate itself was a wooden half-yard forklift container, the kind you would see filled with bricks or landscaping pebbles at a nursery or lumberyard. It was full of rocks, each about the size of a blackboard eraser, and all of them holding fossils. It looked as though the shop could sell out this bin and simply forklift in another from behind the store.

There was a detour as the path left town and went uphill, on account of a section of it sliding recently into the ocean. This got my attention, prompting me to take note of the change in terrain. Up until the ninety-mile stretch of the path I'd bussed around, the coastline I had walked along had been composed

Walking Wet

mainly of solid rock. The soil underfoot now was a compacted light golden-brown, chalky, and brittle. The cliff faces were of the same material all the way to the beach, likely extending even below sea level. Waves had been

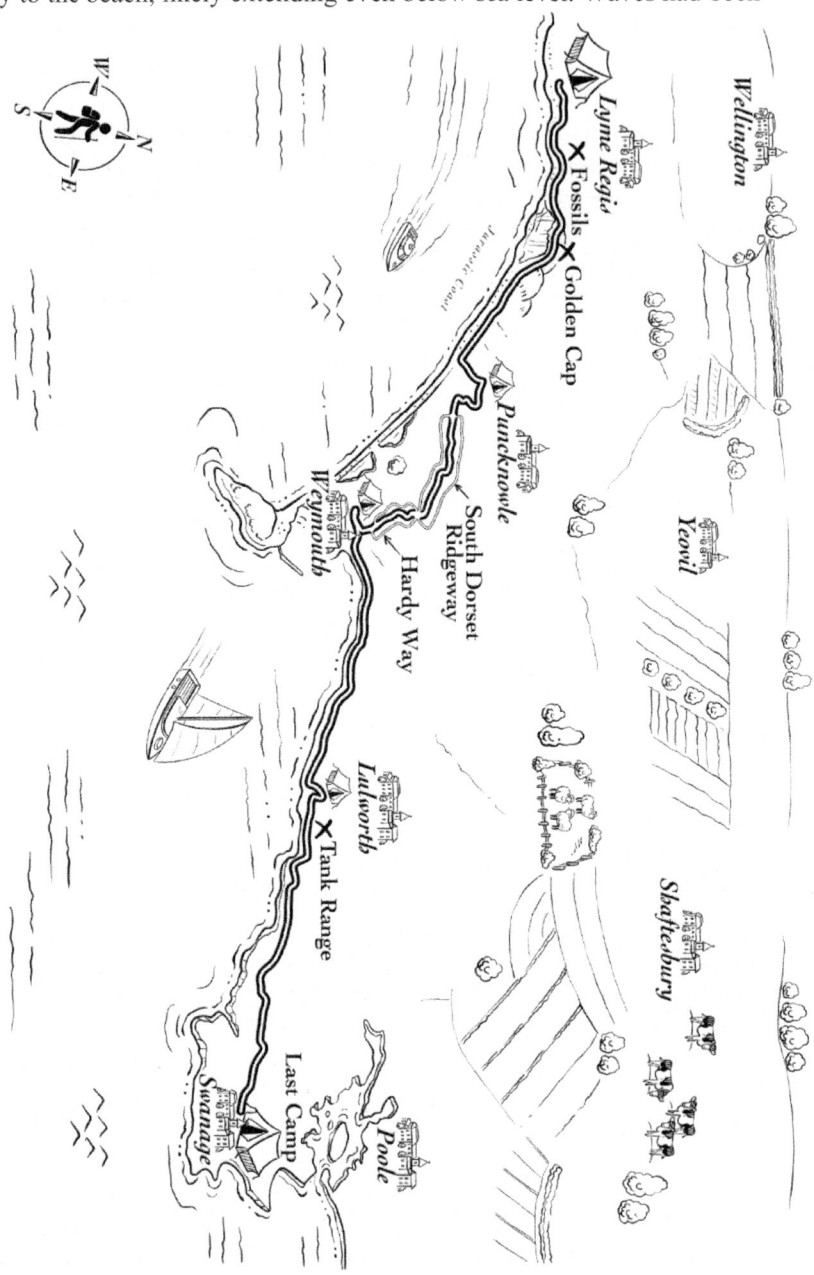

washing at the base of the cliff ahead, undermining it until it gave way and tumbled over.

After the detour, I made my way back down to Charmouth Beach and crossed the creek-sized River Char, stepping carefully over rock bowling balls in a bed of rock blackboard erasers. Most of the erasers held ammonite fossils. There were fossils here by the truckload.

The books I'd read had painted the English naturalists who pioneered paleontology as remarkably keen observers, toiling untold hours towards insight and genius deductions. But standing among these truckloads of fossils, it seemed obvious.

Maybe what set those early scientists apart wasn't so much their brilliance, I thought, *but their social class.* I wondered if all it took to spawn a new science was a couple of comfortably unemployed people who had the time to sketch and document what was lying about in plain sight.

Rats, I thought. I'd been eager to make my own little discovery and send Monica a POD, captioned that we were the only two humans ever to have seen it. I sifted through for a particularly photogenic specimen and did just that, but the same caption could almost have applied to any of the grains of sand I'd stepped on.

The path led up to Golden Cap, and as I climbed, the unsteadiness I'd felt earlier that morning returned, and my head grew swimmy. I stopped and slipped my wrists out of the straps on my hiking sticks. In case I lost my footing, I wanted my hands free to slide down the shafts. The last thing I needed near the edge of a precipice was to dislocate a shoulder or involuntarily pole-vault myself in an unfortunate direction.

As I walked, I tried self-diagnostics by testing my cognitive function. *Name four words that mean 'dizzy'*, I asked myself, then answered, *Swimmy. Vertiginous. Unsteady.*

I wondered if a word test actually proved I was still mentally with it. I looked ahead and behind, noting that no one else was in sight in case I stroked out or something, then realized I hadn't yet thought of a fourth word. *Featherbrained*, popped to mind, though it didn't help me relax.

The path went through two more cycles of climbing and descending hills before dropping into Seatown and returning me safely to a beach that carried me along the shoreline until it was time to turn inland to my next campsite at Punknowle.

***

I was rewarded with another episode of dizziness when I started moving the next morning, so I made the prudent choice to stay inland for the day's walk. Whatever was going on with me didn't appear to be life-threatening, as it wasn't affecting my breathing or heart, or, as far as could tell, my mental faculties. It simply made me unsteady, and that's only hazardous if you place your body near the edges of clifftops or subway platforms, and I had already seen plenty of clifftops and coastline. Some more inland scenery wouldn't hurt.

OS Maps plotted a path that took me through rolling farmland to the South Dorset Ridgeway. Gaining the ridge required climbing higher than the cliffs along the Southwest Coast Path, and as I exerted myself the dizziness intensified. I administered another self-diagnostic: *Name four words that mean 'unwise'*, and stopped to catch my breath and think.

Foolhardy. Injudicious. Ill-advised. Hmm, I thought. *Being a doo-doo headed numb-nuts. Right, then.*

I put in an earbud and played the soundtrack from *The Good, the Bad, and the Ugly*, letting the distinctive 'Wah-wah-wah' of the title track slow me down and follow a more manageable pace for gaining the ridge.

From the top, not only could I see better inland, but I also had a broader view of the ocean. And from here, the landscape made more sense. When you're travelling along the coastline, you tend to fixate on the opposition between land and sea. But from the inland ridge, I could see how they shape and influence each other, details that are missed at the fault line itself.

The route linked to a section of the Hardy Way, named for the nineteenth-century author and poet Thomas Hardy. I'm not proud to admit it, but I get impatient with writers from the Victorian era.

"Yes, we've established how clever you are," I want to tell them, "now get to the point."

But that was the style back then. The trail commemorating Thomas Hardy starts at his birthplace in Dorchester and ends at the church barely a mile and a half away where his heart is buried. But to get there, it winds through some two hundred miles of English countryside. An apt tribute for a Victorian writer, I'd say.

We'd had the usual heavy dew that morning, so my shoes and I were squeaking as loudly as ever with each step, something we'd enjoyed doing together since I'd bought them. I came upon a man tending his garden just off the trail, and when he heard the noise, he looked up.

He unbent himself, rubbed his back, and asked, "Hey, where did you steal those shoes?" Apparently, it's a common joke in England about squeaky shoes being stolen. I'd heard it a dozen times already since I'd put them on.

I laughed politely and told him, "They just like to be noisy."

He looked me over and said, "I've a good pair of hiking boots you can have for the Way. They're set right there on my back step. What size are you?"

"These are a fourteen American," I said. "I think that's a thirteen in the UK here?"

"Can't help you, then." He shrugged. "You'll have to keep to those stolen shoes, mate."

It turned out he'd assumed I was walking the entire Hardy Way, understandable given my appearance. If I had been, I would have covered about a hundred and fifty miles to reach his garden, with another sixty or so still ahead. He had been willing to lend me his hikers for those last sixty miles, confident I'd bring them back when I finished. Right then, I decided to come back someday and walk the Hardy Way, meandery or not.

***

It rained hard that night, but it was letting up the next morning when I set out early, walking through Weymouth before the town had fully woken up. The older part of town was near the beach and had a faded, carnival-like feel, as if it had been a bustling holiday destination in its prime but hadn't seen many repairs or upgrades in the fifty years since. The only signs of life when I walked through were seagulls and a couple of delivery lorries preparing for the day ahead.

I followed the beach for miles, passing erosion-control weirs made of pilings driven into the sand. Most were weathered and rotting but still doing their jobs, holding the sand in place and slowing the erosion of the beach. Eventually I left the shore, climbing a steep track back to the official path.

The farther I walked, the more the cliffs turned to a lighter colored chalk, and the surf frothed milky white where it pounded against their bases. Seeing the sea actively undercutting them unnerved me, and I decided to move inland once more, following a sheep lane that took me away from the cliff edges. Interestingly, from there I could see crescent-shaped scarps and depressions seaward of me that marked past slumps and landslides, subtleties that hikers faithful to the path on the edge would never see.

I rented an Airbnb in West Lulworth unprompted by Emma and, unlike previous stops, never met my host. We communicated only by text, which suited me fine. At this point, I had only a couple days left on the trail, and I wasn't particularly interested in meeting any new people.

I left early enough the next morning to treat Monica to a session of heavy breathing via video chat. I told her about my vertigo condition as I climbed and panted up a sheep pasture to a ridgetop.

"And you've been walking what, three days like that?" she asked. "And it never occurred to you to quit walking or call and let me know?"

"Well, yeah, it occurred to me," I stammered and puffed.

"How do you know nothing is seriously wrong with you? How do you know you're not throwing a brain clot and killing yourself right now as we speak?"

"I've been checking myself every day."

Walking Wet

"With what?"

"With vocabulary questions. I'll think of a word and then try to come up with four synonyms for it. I've passed every time."

"Really? What does that prove? Give me four ways to say widow," she demanded.

"Lady in black. The bereaved. Um, uh-," I couldn't think of any more.

"Well, you're flunking this one," she said.

"That's no fair. You think of one for 'widow'."

"Former wife of a stubborn guy comes to mind."

"That's not... see, you can't think of one either."

"This is West Butterfish all over again."

"West buttress, Fish-"

"I know what it is," Monica said. "Look. How can I know that you'll come home to me? You're not as hard to kill now as you were when I married you, you know."

"I am acutely aware of that."

"Promise me you'll be careful and bring yourself home."

"I promise."

"Stop a minute and turn your phone around." She looked at my face, and I couldn't tell if she was trying to read it or memorize it. "I love you," she said.

"I love you, too. I won't let things get out of hand here."

"Okay, then. So I'll say goodnight and go to bed. Goodnight, husband."

"Goodnight, wife," I said.

"Surviving spouse!" she said, and disappeared from my phone screen.

The ridge ran into the Lulworth Tank Range. It would be a lively prospect walking through during live fire exercises. The public footpath passed near several targets, rusted tanks and heavy trucks liberally pockmarked with heavy machine gun rounds and punched through with armor-piercing shells. Some of the target tanks had their turrets blown off, and metal debris was scattered about.

Just after the artillery range, the coastline cut in to meet the footpath as it came off the ridge at an unavoidable steep section near a cliff's edge. Stairs had been cut into the chalky earth, but the dampness made them slick. And with my dizziness, every step down was an adventure.

When I'd land on a relatively wide stair, I'd stop to shake out the cramps in my forearms caused by the death grip I'd been holding my sticks with and remind myself to go slow. The ground wouldn't pitch me over the edge into the sea, I told myself, if I didn't do anything stupid to help it along by getting impatient.

Once down from that, I mapped a route securely inland back to the camp above Herston where Rhonda, Matt, and I had stayed during our earlier attempt to hike the Southwest Coast Path from the Poole end. *We'd been so innocent then*, I sighed to myself, *thinking we'd find better weather here*. I still had the camping farm's number in my phone, so I texted ahead to book my stay and began making my way there.

A long and uncharacteristically muggy day brought me to the campsite, and when my tent and trash liners were pitched, I walked down into Herston and returned to the pub we'd visited there before. It was still early, and I was their only customer. I ordered a beer and took it out to the beer garden, pulling out my phone to noodle around while I sipped. Not long after, three others, two young men and a woman, took one of the patio tables nearby to drink and smoke cigarettes. I eavesdropped on their conversation, and it became clear they were the pub's managers.

They talked a lot about the wild party they'd had in the pub the night before, laughing about how hungover they were and speculating on how crazy the night ahead was going to be. Listening to them, I remembered what Phil had told me about managing pubs and wondered if these three had inherited their roles, or if they'd been hired. Either way, it seemed they'd fallen victim to a pub's most dangerous occupational hazard. I hoped the youngsters would make clear of it, but Phil had told me how these usually end.

It was morning back home, so I sent Monica what I hoped would be a comforting message and a POD of a donkey doing his best to look cute, followed by a video of him trying to bite me when I wouldn't open the gate for him to aid his escape.

That night, as I lay in my tent, I got a text from Emma,

[I trust you are staying indoors tomorrow]

To heck with that, I thought. It had started raining again, and I wasn't about to spend another day or night in this dump of a campground, scrunched inside a floppy tent carcass wrapped in garbage bags, sitting around and getting dripped on.

The end of the path was only nine miles away. I was getting up in the morning early and going there.

Walking Wet

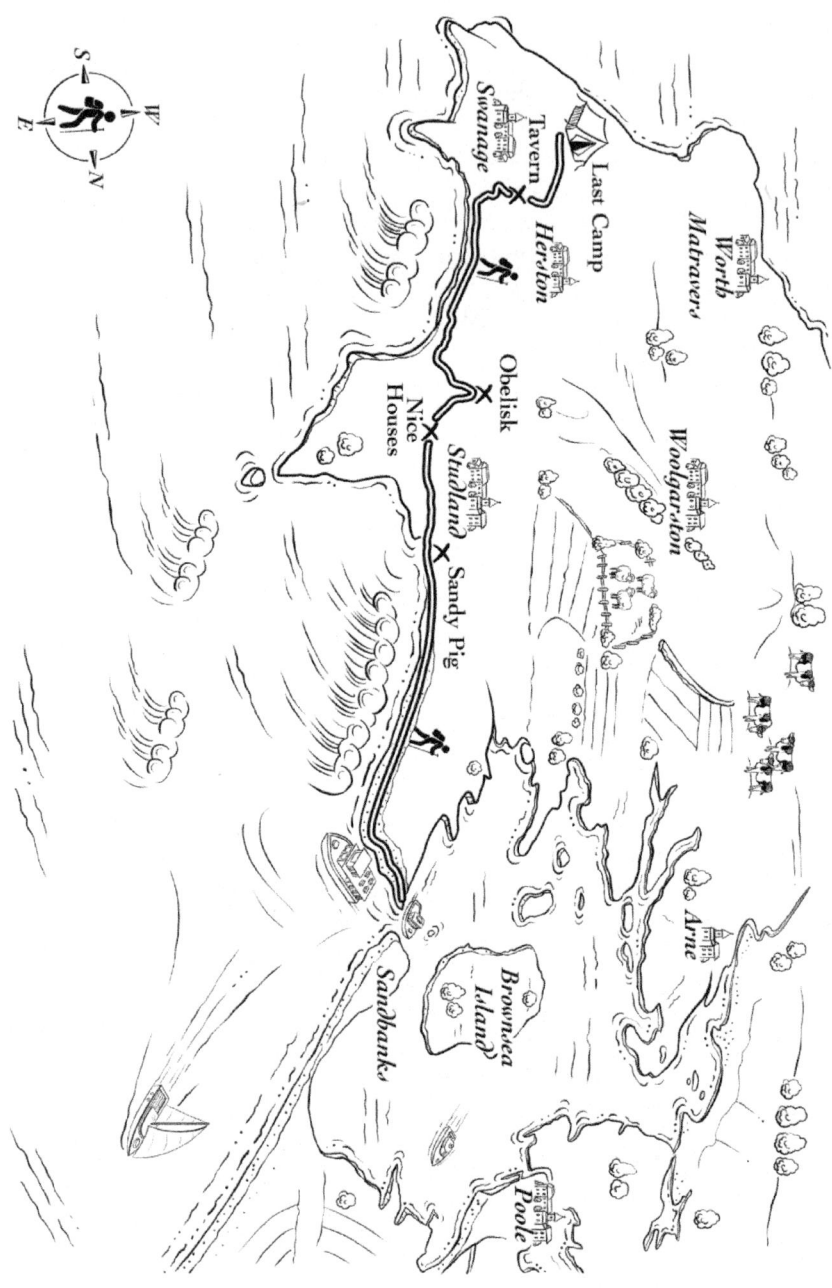

Never Die Stupid

```
47  ⋯  DAYS WALKING
498 ⋯  PATH MILES WALKED
651 ⋯  TOTAL MILES WALKED
```
https://www.southwestcoastpath.org.uk/walksdb/187/

The wind had picked up overnight, and the tent whipped and clawed at me as I packed it away. In the woodlands behind the quarry, leaves were tearing free from the trees like flocks of sparrows tumbling before a tempest.

Emma had told me to expect some unpleasantness. Her texts may have been terse, cryptic even, but they were never, I had learned, inaccurate. But the end of the path was so close, and my thoughts so focused on family and getting back to my home continent, that her overnight warning had done little more than irritate me. And so the ridiculous wind, the stripped leaves, and the tent fabric flogging my face only annoyed me. More. I was too impatient to feel anything else. I just wanted to get moving.

Let's finish this, I thought.

I walked down the hill through Herston, passing the pub I'd stopped at the afternoon before. It was closed, of course, and from the outside, there was no sign of damage. But if I'd heard right, surely some had been done inside overnight. I hoped the three youngsters managing the place had handled it okay.

They were probably in bed now, making another recovery, I thought, *before their next round.* I sent a short prayer out onto the wind for the three of them, that they'd find more recoveries within themselves than they'd welcome rounds up ahead.

A little farther on, I passed the grocery store where the bus had dropped the three of us, Rhonda, Matthew, and me off when we had all been here together. I hardly recognized the building, even though only a couple of months had passed since. This store, this pub; this whole town hadn't imprinted in my memory the way the landmarks in Modbury or Padstow had, or even many of the other towns I'd walked through. The details were already being stripped away and disappearing on the wind, like so many sparrows.

The path led to Swanage Beach and kept to the street that fronted it for a mile or so. From there, it went uphill through a mix of cheerful homes and holiday rentals, before leaving the asphalt behind to ascend another hill. There, the path yet again began skirting a raw edge where the sea had sheared the land away. Well before the path topped out, a side trail branched off, and to save the embarrassment of being blown over the last cliff face on the Southwest Coast Path, I turned onto it.

The side trail went up through a pasture towards the peninsula's spine instead of following its perimeter and at first, I was partially shielded from the wind. But once I reached the top, it came shrieking over the ridge and made me, literally, take a few steps back. I ducked back down the trail a bit the way I'd come, into the leeward side where the wind was still howling but not shrieking, and sat on the ground and tucked over, my back to the wind.

I'd had cell coverage the whole time since getting back onto the path at Seaton, so I pulled my phone from its hip belt pocket to check the British MET Office forecast for myself.

It was probably something I should have done sooner.

I could expect sustained winds of sixty miles an hour or so and gusts upwards of eighty according to the British MET Office, who had issued a 'Danger to Human Life' warning for Storm Antoni, the first named storm of the season. A spasm of fear buffeted me momentarily, before defaulting back to annoyance.

Emma, the Oracle of Understatement, I thought, and sent out my second prayer of the morning, of sorts, onto the wind.

The wind was relentless when I went back onto the ridge, and I did my best to follow the trail on its spine. Being dizzy didn't help. The gale began unleashing volleys of high-velocity rain pellets that drove ice water through my raingear and shrank visibility to a bubble.

With my senses limited by the wind screaming in my ears and the observable sphere constricted around me, my thoughts had less volume to drift through, and thus confined, I spent more time reflecting inside my own head.

These emotional responses of mine, irritation instead of fear, made me uneasy. I hoped my reaction wasn't just exasperation, but years and experience. I had aged well past faith in my own invincibility, but I had seen and been through enough dilemmas to stop reacting with panic. I might get hurt, but I knew keeping a level head wouldn't make it any worse.

With each violent gust, I had to drop to a knee and bow my head to the wind. Sometimes, I mused that's the best a person can do, kneel with bowed head until the winds relent, or you're given the strength to stand up and start moving again.

I became a parent in my late forties, and I think age and experience made me a better father then, more willing to bow my head and take a knee for a bit, less reactive and more measured. But now, finding myself a teenager's dad in my sixties, that tendency towards measure and annoyance isn't interpreted as wisdom, but something else. Curmudgeonliness. There was still some parenting to come on the path ahead, and I wondered sometimes if it would be better to scramble a bit more, pull a few more fire alarms? After all, a parent who never seems surprised never looks impressed either. I thought about Matthew and wished he knew that I was.

My lack of animation isn't a reflection of disapproval. It's from a chronic unease about his future in a world of constricting opportunities. He should be, and is, a joyful goofball at this stage of life, but instead of celebrating these moments with him, they often make me worry. Will the son I'm turning loose into the world have what it takes to get by? Because when I was his age, the world had been so much more welcoming to goofballs like me.

The wind howled, trying to make me change course, but I thought I knew where the end was, so I wouldn't.

It was a slow mile to the end of the ridge, marked by a tall concrete obelisk. The wind shrieked around it, unable to knock it over. I crouched low on the leeward side of its plinth and checked my phone again. The path split here, the two forks leading down either side of the ridge. The one leading into the storm would take me the direction I needed to go.

I did a quick self-assessment, consciously relaxing my shoulders, chest, and core to see if it would trigger shivering.

Think of four words meaning cold, I demanded. *Chilly, frigid, brisk, nippy*, I thought, without shivering. If I had started shivering, I'd have needed to retreat down the leeward side. But since I hadn't, I figured I was good for another mile or two into the wind, and by then, I should be dropped to an elevation low enough where the exposure would be more manageable, and less unhealthy. I left the obelisk squinting, with my head down, and plowed a furrow into the wind.

The trail dropped off the ridge and to a narrow lane with hedgerows broken by driveways that led through manicured lawns to detached bungalows.

The wind still snapped my backpack straps against my face, but it could no longer push me around or knock me over. The storm still raged, but where I stood in it now made moving through it easier. I was reminded again that how badly a storm hits you has less to do with the force of its winds than it does with where you stand when you're in it.

The upscale neighborhood wasn't extensive, and I passed through it quickly, returning to the narrow lane that had brought me there. Its hedgerows thrashed in the wind and gave me what protection they could as they ushered

Walking Wet

me onward to a cross, what an intersection is called in rural Britain, where I took a cobbled road that seemed to go in the right direction.

Before long, though, it dead-ended at a small stone church. Loath to turn back, I walked between the church and its rectory, unintentionally taking a shortcut through the cemetery.

Out the other side was a car park, empty of vehicles. At the far end of it stood a small, plank-sided concession stand with a sign reading "The Little Sandy Salt Pig". It was closed, its top-hinged hatches folded down and latched shut against the wind. So far, I was still the only person I'd seen all day.

I passed the Salt Pig and stepped through to the beach. The last leg of my walk would be on sand along the water's edge, with nothing between me and Antoni.

At least I'll have company, I thought.

I went through the wrack line and crossed the beach straight into the wind to reach the compacted sand near the surf line that was easier to walk on. When I reached the firmer sand and turned parallel to the surf, I noticed a curiosity of physics. While walking into the wind, the front of me had been soaked through to the skin from the raindrops that blasted against me. But now that my right side was taking the brunt of the storm, that side of me was being soaked through to the skin while the front of my clothes and my face were being quickly dried.

The physics of drying depends upon two things: heat and moving air. But if you move enough air, you get plenty of drying action without adding much heat. I smiled, remembering the night we tested the hypothesis at home after Monica had washed her hair. I stationed myself on one side of her with a hair dryer while Matthew took to her other side with the leaf blower. Preliminary indications were that his side was drying faster, but our subject ended the experiment early and, quite forcefully, banned all further testing to confirm our results.

I walked along the shore, watching the wind dry the top layer of compacted sand and setting the finest grains in motion. They streamed across the surface in shifting sheets like a roiling liquid. It looked unstable, and my eyes insisted I would fall through at any moment. My dizziness made it even more difficult to trust my footing, even though I could feel the solidity of the ground underfoot.

I experimented with walking blind, closing my eyes to the illusion of the shifting sand, and was surprised at how quickly faith returned. Relying on the feel of the wind and sensing its angle against me, I could walk a hundred yards or so unerringly between the violent gusts that shifted me off course.

Walking like that, literally with my eyes closed to the sands of illusion, I found it impossible not to dwell on the thoughts bubbling up inside my own head and to grasp for symbolism. And as usually happens when I start introspecting and analyzing too much, what surfaced was my chronic anxiety about tomorrow's world and how Matthew's generation will navigate themselves within it.

They're growing up in a world built on illusions. YouTube influencers, algorithm-driven shorts and reels, CGI, and AI deepfakes. They rarely read anything, and when they do, it's likely been churned out by a content-generating hackbot. And the information they're offered is almost always designed to manipulate them, skewed, fake, or outright fabricated. How do you navigate a world like that without getting lost? Without falling through the thin sheets of shifting sand?

When I talk to Matt and his friends about it, at least as seriously as you can talk to any group of gangly teenagers, I'm struck by how they've adapted. Their relationship to information is completely at odds with how I grew up and how I'd learned to process knowledge.

For them, all facts are suspect. Any fact they take in is set lightly on a mental shelf because, before it can even gather dust, it's likely to be pushed aside and replaced by a counterfact. And that new data will be placed just as lightly, ready to be cleared at a moment's notice when something more suitable or fashionable comes along.

My generation had it easier. When Walter Cronkite told us, "And that's the way it is," we'd know that that was the way it was. We learned to hold on to information, to keep it in place. But that's a poor strategy to navigate the world Matthew's generation is inheriting.

The problem is, I can't bring myself to accept their approach, this constant willingness to exchange one belief for another, as the best way forward. Because if you believe that everything you hear has equal value, you might also believe that anything you say would be no more consequential than any other thing you might have. I mean, why bother with integrity if no one else would recognize it as such anyway?

Roiling sand may obscure my feet, but I knew where I stood because the earth I was grounded in wasn't shifting beneath me. Or so I believed. It made me want to give Matthew and his friends an immutable canon, or something else solid to hold onto, something that won't move. An anchor, possibly. Or a dead gorilla, maybe, when I die.

Another gust of wind pushed me sideways, this one more heavily laden with rain. But when this gust subsided, the intensity of the rain didn't. And just like that, things were getting serious.

More water blasted through my rain gear and my wet right side turned icy, and as the additional rain forced its way through, the rest of my body was wetted all around. I got seriously cold, fast, and started shivering.

Walking Wet

My old climbing instructor had a mantra that I took to heart when I was a student decades ago, and later passed on to my students when I became a mountain guide myself: "Never die stupid."

"Dying stupid," he explained, "means getting yourself killed in a way that, when described in a newspaper obituary, would make a person wonder, 'What the heck was that guy thinking?'"

Regrettably, that's a question I can partially answer, having walked in a few margins myself. I remember exactly what I'd been thinking in those adventures, and I was thinking it again now.

This is stupid, I thought.

I took off my backpack, held it to the ground, and stuck my foot through one of the chest straps to keep the wind from stealing it. Then I pulled off my raincoat, stuffed it inside the pack, and rummaged for my down puffy. I yanked it from the kitchen trash bag I'd stuffed it in, then wrestled it on, pirouetting in the wind to get my arms into the sleeves while they whipped about like antenna flags on a freeway.

Once I had it on, I retrieved the trash bag, bit three holes into the bottom, then tore them wider so my head and arms could fit through. Facing back into the wind, I stretched my arms out like a diver on a board and let the storm yank the bag down over my head and shoulders, wrapping my torso in a restless film of plastic.

My puffy had soaked up plenty of water in the process, and it took on a little more as I dug my raincoat back out of the pack. Another spinning move against the wind, and it was on. Finally, I shrugged my backpack back into place. The whole operation had taken less than a minute. I was still wet, but my core was warming up, and I had stopped shivering.

I looked out across the water, facing the storm. "Not today," I told him.

The trick wouldn't last long, I knew. Rainwater was seeping through the trash bag's arm and neck holes, and the goose down in my puffy would eventually compact to mush and lose its insulating value. But it was working for now, and probably would for long enough.

I couldn't have been more than a mile or two from the end of the path and the ferry that would take me back to civilization and comfort. A massive cross-channel ferry came towards me from the opposite direction, from Poole harbor, fighting its way against the wind.

The tide was out, and it had left a wide stretch of exposed beach landward of me as I walked along the shoreline, which meant that the deep water was closer than usual. Still, the ship seemed dangerously near to shore, close to impending disaster, even. She came up fast and passed so close that I could have hit her with a bagel if the wind hadn't been so wild.

I got a close look at her, the first moving human artifact I'd seen all day, I realized. She was two or three hundred feet long, mostly white, and about four stories high. A vehicle exit door at the bow was up and battened shut, and all the windows on the upper levels were rectangular rather than rounded.

Her keel at the waterline was painted red, and she was riding deep enough that most of it was submerged. A car ramp about twenty feet wide was folded up into the stern, and the great white sides of her hull were striped with blue and red. Above the stripes, a vaguely flag-like and cheery logo stretched above fifteen-foot-high, forward-leaning black font that read: *Brittany Ferries*.

Aft of that, near the stern, smaller black lettering spelled out *Barfleur*, and just below that, *Cherbourg*. While most of the hull was a dazzling white, rust stains streaked down from scupper holes where water drained, as if the ship regularly purged from herself any sign of imminent corrosion.

And she looked confident and unshakable as she cut through the water. But surely, she had almost no margin for error. A strong gust at the wrong moment, a slight miscalculation at the wheel, and she would run aground right there beside me.

Antoni was slamming against her port side's vast sail area, a massive force trying to push her onto the beach, and she was moving through a medium that was chaotically fluid, just yards from a solid and unyielding sandbar. The ship had nothing chaining her true to course other than momentum and bravado.

I thought how foolish I must have looked to anyone watching from those rectangular windows, soaked through and walking alone through a hurricane, stumbling along in the wind. I, at least, had my hiking sticks, even if they couldn't see their tips pressing into the ground beneath the swirling sheets of wind-driven sand. My feet, too, may have been hidden, but they had firm ground underfoot.

I watched her for a couple long minutes, trying to understand how she didn't crash into the beach I'd been walking on. I turned back several times to check on her, but she never ran aground, and eventually I saw her turn out to sea.

That will be one heck of a crossing, I thought.

When the beach made a final bend, I could see the Sandbanks ferry landing at the path's end. The boat was already there, unloading cars. If I wanted to catch this next crossing, I'd have to run the last quarter-mile.

So that's what I did.

I ran right past the blue metal mesh monument marking the official end of the Salt Path. I had planned to take a selfie photo of the moment for Monica's POD, but there was no time.

A crewman was waving me in, and I jogged onto the ferry without pause or ceremony. Just frantic movement, panting, and relief.

I made my way between chocked cars and into the passenger cabin. It was small, with a long storage locker for life vests running along one side, beneath

Walking Wet

a cushioned bench for seating. I let my backpack slide off my shoulders into a puddle of its own making on the floor and looked out the side window.

The rain struck the glass, and frenzied rivulets streamed to the edges of the pane, barely a quarter-inch from my face. But I was sheltered, and well out of the storm and wind for the first time that day.

I closed my eyes and imagined being back home with Monica and Matthew and getting back on with life. Like most people, we don't really know what blessings or misfortunes lie ahead. Paths ahead rarely bring more certainties than uncertainties, but now, it seems, even the certainties are uncertain.

I had the cabin to myself, the other passengers electing to stay inside their cars. A crewman entered and went up the stairs marked "Authorized Only," and moments later, the boat shuddered and clanked into motion.

I moved to the end of the cabin where I could watch the machinery. The ferry was small enough that sea spray was blowing all the way over its top, pygmyish compared to the massive cross-channel ferry I had just encountered. But it had something the larger ship didn't, a haul chain.

Each link in that chain was a solid hundred pounds, and the ferry hauled us along it, pulling the links through the boat's driving cogs with resolve. Its haul chain was well anchored to the landings both ahead and behind, so its course was certain. No matter which way or how much the wind blew.

Epilogue. Stonehenge

53 ⋯ DAYS WALKING
498 ⋯ PATH MILES WALKED
699 ⋯ TOTAL MILES WALKED

I spent a couple of days drying out in Bournemouth. Storm Antoni had over-performed and set new British wind records for August. The gusts that knocked me sideways had felt like it.

After the storm, Emma told me, the weather would finally be pleasant. I briefly considered bussing back to the part of the path I'd skipped over, but decided against it. My journey on the Salt Path had been wet, mildewy, and often uncomfortable, and it felt as though Antoni had already given me a fitting send-off. Besides, there were cliffs back there. And cliffs and dizziness don't mix.

So, what should one do in England when feeling stoned and unsteady? I went to Stonehenge.

I bussed to Tilshead and camped a night, then walked to Stonehenge the back way, past old military grounds, polo farms, and finally, past illegally camped druid wannabes reeking of cannabis. Some were dancing, and some were chanting, but all of them seemed to be at least as dizzy as I was.

While taking pictures of the big rocks, I met a delivery driver there doing the same thing, and he offered me a lift to London.

In the city, I spent a day with Ken, a pen pal and lifetime Londoner. He walked me to exhaustion through the historic district around the Globe Theatre and Borough Market, the old haunts of "artists, actors, prostitutes, and wharf ruffians," as Ken put it. Some things don't change, I guess. Ken kept an office in the neighborhood. If you want a sample of the work he does in that office, look at this book's cover.

Walking Wet

I spent my last day watching the buskers in Camden and flew home with only a fiver left with me as a souvenir.

And that was that.

Except for one thing. My dizziness stubbornly remained even after I got home. I went to a local walk-in clinic to see why my body was failing me. The answer came relatively quickly. It was operator error.

The doctor asked what I'd been up to lately, glanced through my charts, and gave me a brief exam.

"Oh, there's your problem," she said, shining a small flashlight into my eyes again. "Yep, you have nystagmus."

"Nystagmus?" I repeated. "What's that?"

"Involuntary movement of your eyes," she said. "They're doing this." She held two fingers up to my face and waggled her hand. "Your eyes are moving like that when you try following my flashlight. You have BPPV, Benign Paroxysmal Positional Vertigo. That's why you're dizzy."

"From allergies?"

"I doubt it." She moused the exam room's computer and typed on the keyboard. The printer behind her started up, and she pulled the top page from the printer's tray to show me. "Your inner ear has these structures in it called the vestibular system that you need to keep your balance."

"It looks like a Christmas bow on a cinnamon roll," I said.

"If you say so. These," she said, "are your semicircular canals and vestibule. They're partially filled with fluid and lined with hair-like nerve endings. As you move, the fluid moves around inside the canals, and the hair-nerves send that information to your brain. If the fluid inside gets too viscous, like Jello, it doesn't move freely through the tubes. Those signals from the tube's nerves will conflict with the other information your brain is getting, like what it sees and where it feels your body is in space, so you feel vertigo. Nystagmus is the tell." She moved her penlight before my eyes in a cross shape again. "Yep, you've got it good. Here."

She pulled another sheet from the printer and showed me sketches of exercises called Epley maneuvers, a set of head and body movements done slowly enough to let the thickened fluid get back where it belongs. "Lie back on the table," she commanded. "Let's do this."

I lay down, moved my head as directed, turned over, repeated the moves on my other side. She sat me up slowly.

"Stand up," she told me. "How do you feel?"

The dizziness was gone.

She flashlighted my eyes again. "There you go. You'll need to do these exercises a couple times a day for a while. Take these with you," she said, handing me the printed handouts. "And drink plenty of fluids."

Epilogue. Stonehenge

"Do you think not drinking enough water after a night of wine drinking caused this?" I asked, thinking of my last night at The Exeter.

"That certainly wouldn't help. But the fluid you use for balance doesn't thicken from hangovers or short bouts of dehydration. You would need to be dehydrated chronically for a couple weeks or so. Were you?"

"I think maybe I was."

"Then you need to change your habits," she said. "Drink your fluids. Come back in two weeks if you're still having trouble."

Then she was gone.

***

If you've read about my earlier trip hiking the Pacific Crest Trail, you might remember that most of the water I drank on that journey was untreated. I'm not especially reckless or indifferent to my health. It's just that most of the Pacific Crest Trail is at high elevations, near the headwaters of watersheds and far above pollution sources. The water was usually crystal-clear and purer than what you can buy in a bottle or get from your tap. And most of the time, the air was dry enough or thin enough to bring on thirst. Having enough water and getting the cues to drink it was rarely a problem.

But in England, the Salt Path stays at the low end of watersheds, meaning everything that can pollute the water is upstream of you. I was especially paranoid about the sheep I constantly saw in the fields landward of me, and I didn't trust the water in any of the streams I crossed. I carried water treatment chemicals with me, but was too afraid to drink the water even after treating it.

So, I only filled my water bottles in towns and often ran dry between refills. And because I was always near sea level where the air was thick, and because it rained almost every day, I rarely felt thirsty. Between a lack of feeling thirst and the long gaps between safe water sources, I had been for quite some time tiptoeing along the edge of dehydration. When I spent a night drinking wine in Modbury followed by a day of jogging, I was pushed over.

All the trouble and worry those bouts of vertigo had caused my wife and me. And how easily avoidable they were!

Thank you so much for your kindness and patience, staying with me here to the end of this book. It means a lot to me. If you like walking and can get yourself to England and onto the Salt Path, I think you should. But it would be wrong to head over, as I did, expecting easy miles. I've got some stats about the Salt Path that could be instructive for you in the appendix.

And if you don't like walking, or walking no longer likes you, it's still worth a journey through the heart of Cornwall and the Southwest of England. The Salt Path, after all, just goes around it.

Goodbye to you for now, and God bless.   - Rick Rogers, March 2025

Walking Wet

Epilogue. Stonehenge

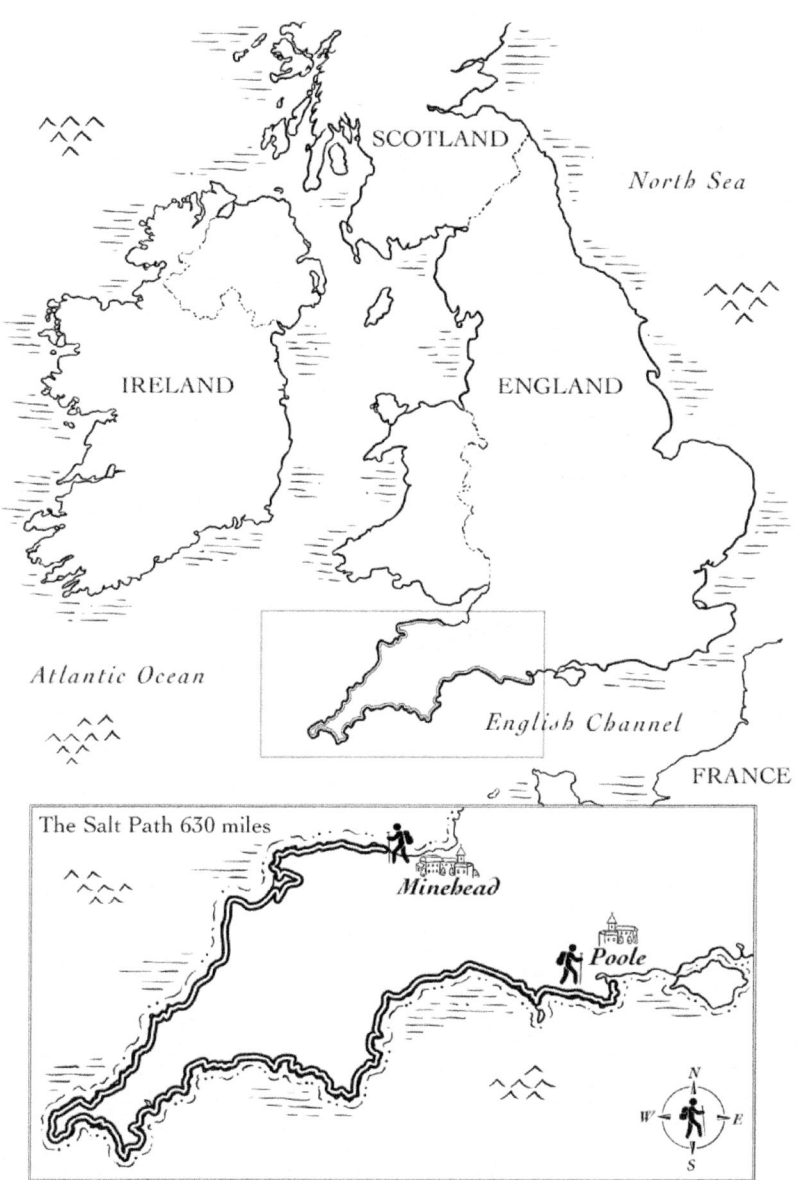

Appendix

Which challenges on the Salt Path had come from the silly things I had done and which were inherently a part of the Salt Path? Clearly, I had underestimated it. It's true that almost every day you can get pasties, ice cream, fish and chips, Irish coffee, or beer. You can almost always find a bus or rent a room. All these are things you can't do most of your time on the Pacific Crest Trail. Even so, the English trip felt plenty tough. The Pacific Crest Trail had given me semi-regular beatings, but the Salt Path offered more persistent punishment.

Consider the following Statistics:

Weather...
Here's the weather I had on the Southwest Coast Path...

Total Days in England	55
Days shuttling or touring	7
Days sitting out rain	7
Days hiking	39
Days rained on while hiking	38

The one day I had of walking under clear skies on the Salt Path in England was from Falmouth to my only wild camping night at Nare Point. In contrast, I'd spent 150 days on the Pacific Crest Trail and had been rained on for only 17 of them.

Appendix

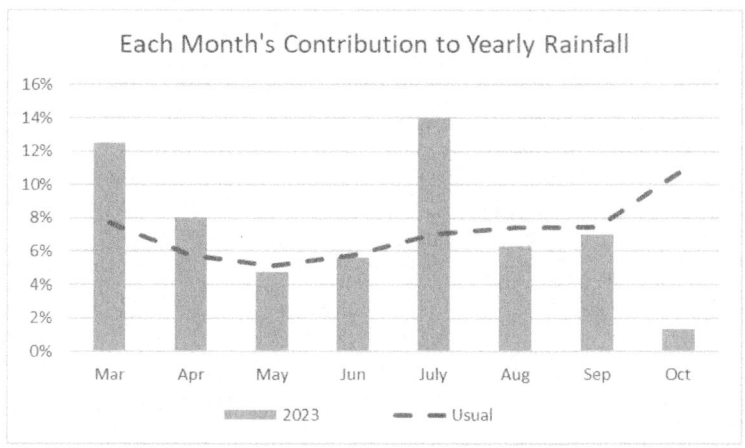

Cornwall gets about 36 inches of rain each year, on average. The graph above shows how much of that total falls in each month of the hiking season. The dashed line shows what you can reasonably expect (the 15-year average), and the gray columns show what happened the year I walked the Salt Path. You guessed it, I walked through the month of July. When I go back, I'll walk earlier, in May. The Salt Path expects to get only 5% of its rain in that month.

Walking Wet

Trail Companionship...

The Southwest Coast Path reportedly plays host to nearly nine million walkers every year. It's possible I suppose, but I certainly didn't see that many. My personal social experience on the Path is laid out below.

People I met on the Salt Path:

Total	Hundreds
Intending to hike a section	Dozens
Intending to hike the entire Salt Path	9 {I am in this group}
That did hike the entire Trail	3 {I am not in this group}

When I hiked the Pacific Crest Trail, it was a very social experience. I almost always had a hiking partner, and rarely did I hike or camp completely alone. After Matthew and Rhonda left me on the Salt Path, I never camped with anyone twice and almost always camped and walked alone. Emma was the closest I had to a walking partner, and almost all of our communication was via text messages. One of the three people I met who walked the entire path was Justin, and he was travelling in the opposite direction from me. The other two were going the same way but had walking paces too unlike my own, Ellen a bit slower, and a forklift driver on holiday from his job in Poland, much faster.

Appendix

Mileage...

One nice thing about modern technology is that it's relatively easy to track yourself and collect statistics.

Distances in:	Miles
Length of Salt Path	630
Salt Path portions I walked	498
Inland Alternatives I walked	87
Walking to/from campsites	78
Other Paths I walked	36
Total Miles I walked in England	699

The 'Other Paths' were those around Diddly Squat, on the way to Stonehenge, and walks in London.

The actual elevation gains and losses were also recorded on my person.

Elevation Stats, hills on Southwest Coast Path climbed in feet:

Salt Path, on or near	108,985
Other Paths	5,325
Total	114,310

Walking Wet

Difficulty…

Except for the time commitment, the Pacific Crest Trail subjectively seemed easier to do than the Salt Path. My shoes survived twice as many miles on the PCT trip, and I didn't get dizzy, for instance. So I looked up my Pacific Crest Trail stats. A comparison is below.

	Pacific Crest Trail	Southwest Coast Path
Miles hiked	2,580	498
Highest Point	13,100 feet	1,043 feet
Days Hiking	123	39
Hills climbed, all	305,200 feet	108,985 feet
Body weight lost	28 lbs	9 lbs.

In the table above, it looks like the Pacific Crest Trail was tougher. It was longer, it went higher and farther than the Southwest Coast Path, and I lost three times as much weight doing it. It's pretty nice in England, having pubs with fish and chips and pints of beer each night before turning in. But the Salt Path sure as heck ain't flat. To illustrate, take a look at these stats below:

Daily Averages	Boston Marathon	Pacific Crest Trail	Southwest Coast Path
Miles	26.2	20.9	12.8
Feet climbed	891	2,481	2,794
Feet up/mile	34	119	219

I included the Boston Marathon above for comparison's sake. I haven't done it, but if anyone ever let me onto the course, I'd try to get it done in a day.

Now, let's make an index for trail ruggedness and use the Pacific Crest Trail's 119 feet/mile as the standard. The Southwest Coast Path's 219 feet/mile is 1.84 times the PCT's 119 feet/mile, and the Boston Marathon's 34 feet/mile is 0.29 times as much as the PCT's. Let's see how a typical day on each path compares, once adjusted using their respective 'ruggedness factors.'

Daily Averages	Boston Marathon	Pacific Crest Trail	Southwest Coast Path
Miles per day	26.2	20.9	12.8
Feet climbed	891	2,481	2,794
Feet up/ mile	34	119	219
Ruggedness Index	0.29	1.00	1.84
Daily miles X Ruggedness Index	7.6 miles	20.9 miles	23.6 miles

I know there are a lot of marathoners who will bristle when their accomplishments are compared this way. And I wouldn't argue that a crude treatment of some selected stats accurately describes how much stress a person puts on their body doing any of these treks. I'm no marathoner, just a long-distance hiker. And only an average one at that.

On the other hand, though, an average marathoner takes about four hours to get their day's work done, well before dinnertime. And they get to travel fast and light, and don't usually wear smelly clothes or carry a thirty-pound backpack along with them as they do it. And they wouldn't have to do it again daily for the next month or six. Unless they wanted to, of course. So yeah, I'd argue a little that it's a fair enough comparison.

If you've thought about walking the Southwest Coast Path, I think you should. But I'd also advise you to spend some effort training and preparing yourself for it. Would you show up to run a marathon cold, with no training or preparation? Probably not. Look at the table above again and ask yourself if you should maybe exercise a bit before taking on the Salt Path. And also, if it applies to you, ask if you should drag a heart patient along to do it with you.

I loved the Salt Path's beauty, setting, and the people and characters I met on the journey. Besides a little training, there are only a few things I will do

Walking Wet

differently when I go back. I'll go a little earlier, in May, and try to do more of it in nice weather. I'll carry more water with me for sure and rehydrate myself less often in ice cream shops or taverns, maybe.

So go out and walk the Salt Path, and take a friend. Allow yourselves enough time to take your time, sit out a rainstorm or two. Give yourselves some grace, and enjoy the journey.

Appendix

About the Author-

Rick started life as a bratty kid in southern California before moving with his family to Washington State near the mouth of the Columbia River. There, he became a farm boy in timber country before getting onto his own dairy farm amongst the tulip fields of Washington's Skagit Valley. After spending most of the first half of his life getting milk out of cows, he sold his herd, started climbing mountains, and returned to college. Post-farming, he taught Backcountry Travel, Mountain Climbing, and Cartography at the junior college level, and worked outdoors spawning fish and tracking elk for another twenty years until he was fired under puzzling circumstances. He then built and remodeled a few houses before leaving to hike the Pacific Crest Trail. Writing a book about the adventure, *Walking Home - Common Sense and Other Misadventures*, was so satisfying and rewarding that he made writing his newest full-time job. Let's see how long he keeps this one.

Rick lives in Conway, Washington, with his wife Monica and son Matthew. *Walking Home - Common Sense and Other Misadventures* is available on the Amazon Books or Kindle websites.

Printed in Dunstable, United Kingdom